P9-DWO-355

You Can't Print
THAT!

You Can't Print THAT!

Memoirs of a Political Voyeur

Charles Lynch

Hurtig Publishers
Edmonton

To my children
Andrew Burchill (named for two grandfathers
who are in this book); Blake, for the Blakes of
Galway, described herein; Susan, the Brazilian
Cariocazinha; Danny, who mourned his older
brothers' departure from home saying, "I'd rather
be bashed than bored"; and Cindy, born in
Teaneck, New Jersey, who had the best of it.

Copyright © 1983 by Charles Lynch

No part of this book may be reproduced or
transmitted in any form by any means, electronic
or mechanical, including photocopying and
recording, or by any information storage or
retrieval system, without written permission
from the publisher, except for brief passages
quoted by a reviewer in a newspaper or
magazine.

Hurtig Publishers Ltd.
10560 - 105 Street
Edmonton, Alberta

Canadian Cataloguing in Publication Data

Lynch, Charles, 1919-
  You can't print THAT!

  ISBN 0-88830-245-2

  1. Lynch, Charles, 1919-   2.
Journalists — Canada — Biography.   I. Title.
PN4913.L95A3   070'.92'4   C83-091230-4

Printed and bound in Canada

Contents

By Way of Introduction

Humbling are the forces of celebrity. Riding up in a crowded elevator in our building, I get off at the fifth floor and a mellifluous female voice comes from behind me, "Charlie!" I turn, smiling, to acknowledge the greeting, and as the doors start to close the voice says, "Your stuff stinks!" The crowd roars, the doors slam, and the elevator goes up, leaving me pounding the chrome wall like a tom-tom.

In the lobby of that same building, a fluttery woman approaches with cries of delight, saying she has always hoped for us to meet and that she must tell her sister and isn't this wonderful, and she wants me to know that *The National Dream* and *The Last Spike* are the best things I have ever written.

In a downtown Ottawa store where I've gone to buy some tobacco, the cashier exults, "Wait till I tell everybody Douglas Fisher was here!" In a country store, the proprietor greets my arrival with total calm until his wife rushes up and says to him, "Don't you know who you're talking to?" Blank silence. "You read his column every day in the paper," she prompts. His face brightens: "Fotheringham!" And when I give the usual half-friendly, half-wary street corner greeting to a stranger who says hello, being on my way to a bank that is closing in five minutes, he looks at me with scorn and says, "You damn fool, I'm your dentist!"

Mike Duffy once asked Harry Reasoner, the American TV newsman, how he handled the business of being instantly recognizable to everybody; and Reasoner said the only thing to do was relax and enjoy, there being no way out — as he discovered after joining CBS.

"Walter Cronkite!" strangers would exclaim.

"No," he would say. "Harry Reasoner."

He became increasingly annoyed and, finally, when one woman

pranced up and tittered, "Aren't you Walter Cronkite?" he replied, "Yes, I am. Now bugger off." Reasoner pulled it a few more times until he got a call from Cronkite, pleading, "Harry, give a guy a break, will you?" Cronkite being who he was, Reasoner did.

This book, then, is about the joys and otherwise of being a journalist and about the people I have known, with a few prime ministers thrown in. Prime ministers aren't people, nor do I claim to have known them very well. People stop being people when they become prime minister; they turn into something else, just as they begin to look like the caricatures the cartoonists do of them. And nobody gets to know them after they become prime minister. You may have known them before, but once they get the royal jelly into them, forget it — though they themselves may want to keep some old relationships alive on the theory that high places are lonely places; or, as John F. Kennedy once said, that "the presidency is a poor place for making new friends, so I'd like to keep a few of the ones I had."

Over the years, I have covered seven prime ministers and written millions of words about them, without ever really knowing them. Two — John Diefenbaker and Lester Pearson — were treasured and admired friends before they became party leaders. We called them "John" and "Mike," but all that ended when they reached the summit, and both of them wound up their political careers damning my name.

Besides the prime ministers, this book is about many more ordinary folk, whom I hope the reader will find as extraordinary as I did. And what it's chiefly about is me. After all these years, it's hard to break the habit, even by the dodge of pretending to write about others.

There's a lot of journalism here too, and quite a few journalists. We used to say it was fun being in the newspaper business, because you met such interesting people and they were all in the newspaper business. That was true in the days before celebrity became the prime goal of reporters, corrupting the standards of the business and the people in it. Of course, there still are celebrated reporters who retain a degree of perspective, but many are caught up in the syndrome pioneered by old friend and colleague Lionel Shapiro, who once said, "I've talked about myself long enough. Now you talk about me."

Some of the newspaper people in this book were people in the full sense, though they may have suffered from the great failing of the

8

business, which is that we don't know our subjects all that personally, and we don't get to know anybody else very well either. But we do get to exchange banter with the greats . . . .

Henry Kissinger says he never wants to see me again after I have described him as stupid for bringing the sick Shah of Iran to New York for medical treatment.

Sir Peter Hayman, the British high commissioner, tries to strangle me with his bare hands after I've told Prime Minister Harold Wilson that relations between Canada and Britain have ceased to exist.

Pierre Trudeau wonders indignantly why I stoop so low as to ask him about the prospect of a separation agreement between him and Margaret. Six days later the agreement is made public.

Robert Stanfield pleads with me, when his chances for the prime ministership look brightest, not to praise him in print or he is doomed.

Joe Clark, when I ask how he expects to win with a name like Joe and hasn't he another name, says, "Sure. It's Charlie. But you wouldn't expect me to run on that, would you?"

On CBC's "As It Happens" I say that Clark will fight off his foes "because he's got an ace up his hole," and in the shocked silence that ensues I add, "Sure. That's why he walks that way." And Flora MacDonald, hearing this on her car radio, swerves into the ditch.

W. A. C. Bennett tells me Social Credit leader Réal Caouette is the greatest French Canadian since Sir Wilfrid Laurier.

René Lévesque calls me "Chuck" — and I fume, and he knows it.

Claude Ryan tells me to get serious, but his mother sends the message, "Keep 'em laughing."

Eugene Forsey says the word for English-speakers who try to be more Québécois than French-speakers is "mugs."

Joey Smallwood says his opponent Billy Browne "has a face like a robber's horse" — and he makes it sound like "arse."

West Coast lumber king H. R. MacMillan laments the political failure of his tycoon friend Wallace McCutcheon, calling him the most brilliant mind in Canada and adding, "Such a little thing to do such big harm. Rye whisky."

Che Guevara, representing Cuba at the founding conference of President Kennedy's Alliance for Progress, jumps to his feet and rushes from the room during a speech by U. S. Treasury Secretary Douglas Dillon. And I, presuming a walkout, join the press corps flocking at Guevara's heels. He clomps down the corridor in his heavy military boots, turns in the door to the men's room, rips open his fly, turns to us with a look of immense pleasure and, shaking his free fist, shouts "Liberdad!"

Margaret Thatcher blinks when I ask her how come, if she's a grocer's daughter, she speaks the same la-di-da English as the Queen.

And Prince Philip greets me with a baleful "Not you again!" Later, in the Camp Borden officers' mess, he remarks that the Queen's principal interests are in things that eat oats and fart.

PART ONE

The Best Place to Be From

1/Saint John

Being a New Brunswicker has advantages, since it is the only place in Canada you can be from without somebody being sore at you, though Prince Edward Islanders tend to regard New Brunswick with suspicion, having to pass through it to get anywhere. The native industry of New Brunswick is poverty, genteel and otherwise, and it continues to evoke sympathy in other parts of the country, as long as people in those other parts don't find out how good life is in the land of the herring-chokers. Not being a born New Brunswicker, I have to tread softly, as the natives are jealous of their credentials, and a family that moved into the province from Montreal in 1795 is still referred to as "those people who moved down from Montreal."

My mother was in Cambridge, Massachusetts, when I was born. This is just the first of many tricks she played on me. She was a New Brunswicker all right, born in Fredericton, right on the spot where the Lord Beaverbrook Hotel stands today on the banks of the beautiful St.John River. Her father, Charlie Burchill, was the town druggist and a man of strong will, who once warned a piper who was practising on the sidewalk that if he didn't stop he was going to put a bullet through him. The piper played on, and grandfather got out the rifle he kept handy, and from his counter at the back of the store drew a moving bead on the piper, who was marching up and down. And just when the man was opposite the door, grandpa fired. The bullet went the length of the store, through the door and across the road, scoring a clean hit on the bag of pipes, which collapsed forthwith, the dying moan giving grandfather great satisfaction. The piper went away and was not heard again, but I've often wondered what would have happened if a customer had come through the door just as the bullet was on its way out.

Father was from Saint John, the son of a famous builder of wooden ships, David Lynch, who launched forty-six hulls and sent

12

them into the world to trade, investing his money in them. Thus it is that the family fortune rests with the bones of those ships on reefs and shorelines around the world. When grandfather died and grandmother wrote to the shipping companies to see what his estate consisted of, they sent back a memo saying that every vessel was rotten, leaking, or sunk, and that she owed them $185.40, which was a lot of money back in 1905.

In those times, it was fashionable for Maritimers to seek their fortunes in the Boston States, and you could get there twice a day from Saint John on the S.S.*Calvin Austin* or the *Governor Dingley*. Mother went there to study nursing, and father went to practise engineering with the Boston and Maine Railroad, and they were married in Providence, Rhode Island; following which, father got drafted into the United States army, which delayed my birth until 1919, when I appeared in the very shadow of Harvard University.

Mother always said she wanted me to be born in the United States so that I could be president — something the parents of Franklin D. Roosevelt Jr. ignored when they had him on Campobello Island, which by some oversight of the old treaty makers belonged to New Brunswick, whereas usually the U.S. got all the good places. People were careless about boundaries in those days, and when the family trekked back to the Maritimes carrying me, two weeks old, in a bureau drawer, no record was kept of our ever crossing the border. As a result, both the Canadian and American governments have always regarded my credentials with suspicion, and at one time both washed their hands of the whole thing, leaving me minus citizenship of any kind, which is a long way from becoming president.

Growing up in Saint John was an advantage, since when you moved away the competition was so much less. (There is a legend out West that the smart ones all come from Saint John, and the smarter they are the quicker they come.) You had to be on your toes just to stay alive, and having a smart mother made it even tougher. She smoked cigars and studied painting and French, and taught me to play the harmonica; and she once blew the rent money to take me for a flight in an old First War biplane — the two of us huddled together in the open cockpit in leather coats, helmets, and goggles, and mother laughing with the joy of looking down and seeing the reversing falls. She said after that, that when she died she wanted her ashes thrown out of an airplane over the city, but later she changed it to wanting them thrown into the Bay of Fundy off the back of the Digby boat, and when it happened we couldn't bring ourselves to do either and she got buried in Fredericton. She never did get the red petticoat she craved, but she did get to see the Grand Canyon.

When I was three years old, mother sent me to the store to get an ice cream cone for her and one for me, and when I dropped one on the way home and told her I had dropped hers, she countered with the view that I had dropped mine, and she proceeded to eat the surviving cone. It was also when I was three that I wandered into the forbidden High Woods near our house, came home late and gave mother a breathless tale about being pursued by a fierce finnan haddie that had chased me into the woods; the pursuit ended only when I turned and gave combat, finally subduing the finnan haddie and tying it to a tree. Mother's response was to grab her hat and sweater, and insist that I take her through the darkness of the night to the spot so that she could see the captured finnan haddie and either let it loose or give it something to eat. Off we went into the woods, but we couldn't find the thing and I said it must have escaped. There wasn't even any sign of the rope. So she washed out my mouth with soap.

Thus did mother equip me for life, which has continued pretty much in that same vein ever since.

Father sold Ford cars during the twenties, returning to Boston one summer to run an A & P store and sending us wonderful drawings of his big coffee-grinding machine — but evidently not caring very much for the work because he came home to sell insurance. When the Depression hit, he took a 75-per-cent pay cut, but President Herbert Hoover was paying out a bonus to U.S. war veterans, and as father had served in the United States army during the First World War, he was due for $300.

When the money arrived early in 1931, mother took it and bought me a steamship ticket to England and back. I was eleven at the time and was to accompany an old friend of hers who was going over to pick up some illegal Irish Sweepstake tickets for the North American market.

Crossing the ocean meant getting on one of the big CPR liners that came and went in Saint John Harbour every week without anybody in Saint John ever thinking of getting on one. You got on the Digby boat and the Boston boat, but nobody you knew ever got on the Mont boats or the Duchesses with their big black hulls and their yellow funnels higher than church steeples. Sometimes you heard about local people going aboard for tea, but that was all. Friends weren't just envious of me, they were awed, and they filled the little four-bunk stateroom on the *Montrose* with flowers (which were scarce in those days) and fudge (which was plentiful). The band played when we sailed, and I remember mother laughing and waving from the dock as she consigned her only son to the ocean deep in the hands of an Irish roustabout named Jimmy Archdeacon.

Jimmy didn't have much money, but I think he may have had syndicate backing on the caper with the sweepstake tickets. He had wealthy relatives in London, his sister having married a surgeon named Brian Quinlan, and I was dumped at their big South Kensington house on Old Brompton Road while Jimmy went off to Ireland to line up the sweepstake scam. He was gone for three months, and the Quinlans found that the best way to deal with the barbarian boy from the colonies was to give him the bus fare and turn him loose to discover London. This started a love affair with the city that has lasted me all my life.

Surgeon Quinlan was Irish to his fingertips, and some Sundays he would take me along to Hyde Park Corner, where he would mount his soapbox and make speeches advocating the overthrow of the British government, or at least that portion of it that had to do with Ireland. This sort of stuff gave my mind a permanent anglophile warp (the Irish part didn't take).

The family also took me along to Brighton for a month, in the course of which I discovered that the British changed into their bathing suits right there on the pebbles, in full view, and I got an early introduction into the mysteries of the female form, heightened by the strange conduct of couples writhing together on the beach and on the benches along the promenade. I have never understood where the British got their reputation for being inhibited or proper, let alone both.

While in Brighton, I wrote to mother that I didn't want to come home, ever, and that I wished to be enrolled in an English public school so that I could share the adventures I read about in the *Magnet* every week, involving the Famous Five of Greyfriars and companions like Billy Bunter. But soon after we were back in London,

Jimmy returned from Ireland with his suitcase filled and announced that it was time for us to be going home and no, I couldn't go to a public school. So I helped him smuggle the sweepstake tickets into Canada. It subsequently turned out that they were counterfeit — half the countryside was after his hide — but he escaped and nobody thought of coming after me.

On the way home, I had a shipboard romance with a young lady from Saskatoon named Ruby Parks, whose father had just spent five years in the Soviet Union building a power dam at a place called Stalingrad. He talked with admiration of the things that were being accomplished there, but I had eyes and ears only for Ruby. When we started that voyage my hair was straight, and when we landed at Quebec City it was wavy — and it has stayed that way ever since. I pretended it was because of the salt sea air, but secretly I've always believed it was Ruby.

Besides hearing about the wonders of Russia from Ruby's father, I'd heard a lot about Germany during my months in England. There was a family called Smartt who were related in some way to Jimmy Archdeacon, and one of their sons had just returned from Germany where he had got involved with an organization called the Hitler Youth. He was full of the idea that this was the wave of the future. With the Depression well settled in, the only ideas that seemed to hold any excitement for young people were the ones coming out of Germany.

These touches of European politics were not things we heard much of in Saint John, whether we were young or old. Yet less than a decade later my own generation, having engaged in very tentative and very private discussions about how we would never ever go to war, went off in great numbers. As for the Irish question, my only insight was that some of us in Saint John (the good green guys) celebrated on 17 March, while others (the bad oranges) marched on 12 July. I once wore a green sweater on the twelfth, with a felt shamrock sewn on the front, and left it with my clothes to go for a swim at the Bay Shore beach. When I returned, I found it slashed to ribbons.

The Depression hit as hard in the Maritimes as anywhere, but it didn't make radicals of us or our parents. When the socialist CCF sent people down from Upper Canada, we called them Communists and wished they would go away. We grew up with the impression that hard times were normal, an attitude that persists in the Maritimes to this day — and I suspect always will, sustaining the sanity and longevity that has always marked the people of the region, to the despair of their supposedly more enlightened brethren elsewhere.

I grew up with one sister, Virginia, who was the smart one in the family, though she had to make her own way. Being younger and a girl, she didn't get the attention I did. I was an altar boy and she was not; I was a glutton and she was not. And I once sold her half a large Easter rabbit that she already owned.

At school, I always got good marks until Grade 8, at which point mother, having seen to it that I went to the public (Protestant) high school rather than the Catholic one, lost interest in my education. Consequently, my marks fell disastrously, capped by getting four out of a hundred in French in my final year in high school. But I was saved by getting decent marks in what was known as "English composition," though heaven knows how that happened because our whole class made a mockery of Willie Denham, our English teacher, parroting his speech defect and calling him "plucker" and squirting ink on the back of his jacket and pinning garters to his coattails.

My own contribution to the chaos was to put out a publication called the *Hourly Gazette* which Willie (having confiscated a copy) found more interesting than anything else the class put into his hands. For him, the thing seemed to represent a glimmer of light amid the encroaching literary gloom, and he said to keep it up, which I have through the years.

Going to college in 1935 was out of the question, there being no money for it, and my marks indicating a distinct lack of capacity for higher studies. As a result, I spent a year in the Saint John Vocational School and learned to type, the most useful thing anybody ever taught me. My passage out of vocational school coincided with the starting up of a new newspaper in town. In those days, starting a new paper wasn't the big deal it is now. Anybody with an axe to grind could start one, and at one point in mid-Depression, Saint John had four dailies.

Largely on the strength of my typing skills, I got a job as a cub reporter on the *Saint John Citizen* at $7 a week. My first assignment was to cover the opening of a new city waterworks plant out at

17

Spruce Lake and take pictures of the event with a Speed Graphic camera, which I had to learn to operate before leaving the office. On my return, I was thrust into the darkroom by the city editor, who locked the door from the outside and said I could come out when I had developed and printed the pictures, the techniques for which were pinned up on the wall. All the chemicals and trays were clearly labelled — provided I could read them in the dark. Three hours later I emerged triumphant and with a distaste for photography that has remained with me to this day.

That same flinty editor — whose name was Robert C. Hanson, alias Simon Legree — next assigned me to do an exposé on slum housing, the only thing our city had more of than any other centre in North America. We had so many slums that we grew up not noticing them, and it was with no sense of shock that, armed with notepad and camera, I explored the warrens of the city, interviewing the residents amid scenes of squalor and debris. None of them seemed sure what I was after, but they were happy to have their pictures taken, and the paper kicked off the series with a big spread of filth, decay, and hardship, headlining the quote of one toothless and tattered lady who had kept screaming, "I am Stella Dallas!" She didn't know who Stella Dallas was and neither did I, but it looked good in black type.

The paper came out at 2 P.M., and within an hour a crowd of people had arrived outside the office carrying a noose and shouting my name. I suggested to Hanson that he go out and face them, since the series had been his idea. But he said that as I was the writer, I should go out and explain my stuff, which I did. Whereupon the crowd announced its intent of stringing me up to the handiest lamppost for casting aspersions on their happy homes.

It's true that nothing so concentrates the mind as the prospect of being hanged — not the next morning, but in the next ten minutes. I told the mob that if they would return to their homes, I would go there that evening and we would reason together, and another article would ensue putting things in a better light. They dispersed, taking the noose with them. But when I returned inside, the word from Hanson was that I was on my own from there and that he wouldn't promise to run any piece inspired by fear or cowardice.

The *Citizen* owned only one vehicle, a Ford V-8 delivery van. I talked the driver into taking me to the dreaded neighbourhood that evening, against his better judgement and despite the fears of the management that its entire fleet might be wiped out. When we arrived, the natives were assembled, rope and all, and they seized the van and started to shake it; and the driver gunned the engine, and we shot out of there amid flying bodies and kept on going, with our hides — if not our dignity — intact.

Hanson's orders were to continue the series. Consequently, we alienated not only all the slum landlords in town (whose identities we never did reveal) but all the slum dwellers as well, though the paper's circulation went up and people wanted to know who the smartass kid was who was giving the city a bad name.

Hanson was nineteen at the time, which made him three years older than me, so I had many lessons to learn from him, as well as from the editor, Alexander Thorne, whom we all called Sandy (though he was encrusted with age, being all of forty-five at the time). Sandy Thorne was a long-suffering man with a faint air of mystery about him because we all knew he was Something High in the Masonic Order. Although we knew quite a lot about the Orange Order and the Knights of Columbus, and didn't think much about the Pythians or Foresters or Elks, we didn't know anything about the Masons and weren't supposed to. It was rumoured that they had a secret handshake and that strange deeds were done within their hall, especially in the upstairs rooms, but we never dared ask and Sandy never said.

He seemed harmless enough, and it was suspected that he even knew who owned the paper, a fact that it took the rest of us two years to discover. The owner was Kenneth C. Irving, already well along in his empire building with a string of service stations and auto supply stores and car dealerships. He had started the *Citizen* to give him a safe outlet for news about the bus franchises he was developing — and also to give him a place to suppress stuff he didn't like, such as accidents involving his trucks. Eventually, he was to own just about everything that mattered in New Brunswick, including all its newspapers, but at the time all we knew was that the *Citizen* had a list of sacred cows as long as the ash on Sandy Thorne's drooping cigarette.

It was Sandy Thorne who told me that going into newspapering was like joining the priesthood, in terms of its effect on one's personal life. He also gave me another very sound piece of advice. I had come back from filching a photograph from a family whose beautiful daughter had just been killed in a traffic accident, and I felt guilty about stealing the photograph. I wanted to get it reproduced quickly so that I could return it to the family; and, having scooped the opposition paper, I wanted to write a story that would truly convey the tragedy of the whole thing — the impact on the girl's family and friends, and all the sort of stuff that newspaper stories never catch. I made several runs at it, each worse than the one before, until finally Sandy came and leaned over the typewriter and read the copy, splattering it with cigarette ash and blinking his eyes in the cloud of smoke he carried with him. He clucked his tongue and snorted, "Why don't you just try writing what happened?" So that was the way it came out in the paper, a bare report about a traffic fatality, alongside that lovely photo. The real story didn't get written, as it hardly ever does. But the job got done, and I never shed tears again over any event encountered on the job. And that's how it comes that I've always got my copy out so fast. And so cleanly typed.

To this day, I think Sandy was wrong, though his was the only practical approach to the business of reporting. What he was saying was that you shouldn't get involved, and he held the same view about joining clubs and organizations, saying that newspapermen should stay aloof so that they could report without fear or favour. It's a rule I've always tried to follow, though Sandy might have added that you wind up with very few friends. And he never did explain that business of his about the Masons. We got the feeling that it was bigger than all of us, and we looked on Sandy as our friend and confessor until the day when, as matter-of-factly as if he was lighting another cigarette, he came into the newsroom to tell us that the paper had been sold and was closing up, right then and there — not even a chance to say good-bye.

When the paper folded a lot of stuff disappeared, and it was suspected that a certain John Fisher (later to become Mr. Canada) got the Speed Graphic camera, though when I asked him about it years later he said he couldn't remember. Fisher had been sent to us from the Halifax *Herald* in the *Citizen's* last year — a hotshot editorial writer to jazz things up, though he didn't write many editorials for us. But he made a lot of speeches about the co-operative movement, which was the closest thing to radicalism to come out of the Maritimes in the Depression. Some of the other equipment went far afield: the Duplex tubular press, which had been brought in to replace the original flatbed, went to Timmins, Ontario, the paper there having been bought by some guy named Roy Thomson.

The end of the *Citizen* seemed like the end of the world, and at the age of nineteen I was out of work. Although a job opened up across the street at the *Telegraph-Journal* in a couple of weeks, the experience of being on a paper that folded left a mark that endures to this day — a sinking feeling that one shares with all whose papers have folded on them, a compound of rage, frustration, and hopelessness. And nowadays, there isn't any paper across the street to offer the prospect of a job. But although I had a job, I found it wasn't as much fun working for old money, in the person of Howard Robinson, as it had been working for new money, in the hidden person of K. C. Irving. Everybody at the paper was scared, and the managing editor was so put upon that he wound up throwing his typewriter out of his office window, following which he ran to the railway station, got on a train, and kept going as far as Regina, Saskatchewan, where he did well and became a sage.

But that sort of excitement didn't happen often. For the most part, things were quiet, and the paper didn't even put out an extra for the outbreak of the Second World War. So when the Halifax *Herald* (which I'd always looked up to) offered me a job at $15 a week, away I went.

2/Halifax

In the late 1930s the Halifax *Herald* was a far better paper than it is now, but it was still one of the worst places in the country to work, though we didn't know it at the time. The problem was the managing editor, Robert J. Rankin, who pioneered the idea that news could be weighed by the pound, a theory that has since been perfected by the Thomson newspapers. The *Herald* was a morning paper, so you came in at one o'clock in the afternoon and worked until two in the morning. And your workday began with a note in your box, saying "See me. RJR."

When you went to see Rankin, he would have a pile of clippings in front of him, representing your output for the previous day and night, and he would ask if you thought this was a fair return to the paper for having you on its payroll, and how could you hold your head up among your colleagues and in the community having turned in a mere ten or twelve items? The interview would gradually turn into a pep talk, with Rankin urging you to go out there and bring in fifteen or twenty stories — or else — and he would thump the desk with his fist.

This brought on a hatred for Rankin that burned the soul, but it had the desired effect and we worked our butts off — a staff of three reporters turning in more news per capita than I have ever seen achieved since. It was later a source of wonderment to me, after Rankin became head of the National Harbours Board in Ottawa, that he turned out to be the most human, humane, and good-humoured public servant in the country. We became fast friends, and he once said he had no recollection of ever writing those "See me" notes, and if he did, surely we knew he was kidding. We knew nothing of the kind.

One of the three reporters was a fellow named Bob Steck who, like many reporters in those days, was known to have a drink in him from time to time. That's the way we used to describe it, "having a drink in you," and in Steck's case it sometimes meant that he was late for work, though it often put him in a rollicking mood for his summons to Rankin's office. It was reported that Steck once crumpled up one of Rankin's summonses right in front of Rankin's face and set fire to it. But none of us really believed that.

What finally got Steck fired was an assignment to cover a speech being made by Premier Angus L. Macdonald at the auditorium of the School for the Blind. Steck got himself well primed before going to the auditorium, and the meeting was in progress when he arrived and took a seat at the back of the hall, not wanting to appear conspicuous. He strained to catch the premier's words, but although the famous voice carried clearly, Steck couldn't get the meaning of what was being said.

Spotting a vacant seat halfway towards the front, he moved forward and cocked his ear, but he still couldn't make sense of what he was hearing. Finally, he went right up to the front of the hall, mounted the steps leading to the platform, and leaned over the table to a man who was sitting beside the podium — where the premier, the flow of his oratory broken, stood silent, eyeing the intruder. In what Steck thought was a whisper, he hissed, "I'm from the *Herald*, and I can't understand a goddam word the premier is saying. What the hell is he talking about?"

What the assignment slip had neglected to tell Steck was that this was a meeting of the Gaelic Society of Nova Scotia and that Angus L. was speaking entirely in the ancient tongue. In the shocked silence that followed, the premier's aide looked around and saw that there was a doorway at the back of the stage. He grabbed Steck, frogmarched him to the door, opened it and thrust him inside, slamming the door behind him amid applause from the audience.

The aide then returned to his seat and the premier resumed his speech. What they didn't know was that the room into which Steck had been put contained the console for the mighty pipe organ that was the pride of the School for the Blind, and that Steck was an expert organist. Having bolted the door from the inside, he switched on the organ, opened up all stops, and lit into "God Save the King" with variations, rocking the hall to its foundations.

They tried to break down the door but nothing would prevail, and finally everyone had to leave, all holding their ears, including the premier, whose phone call was one of the first to get to the *Herald*. The switchboard virtually melted, and the owner, Senator William Dennis, was summoned to the office, where he chaired an emergency meeting of management to decide what to do with Steck in the event he ever came back. It was felt that sacking would be too lenient, and consideration was given to drawing and quartering, keel-hauling, flogging, and other Maritime procedures from the historic past, but eventually they settled for the sack, which was administered by Rankin after one of the most vivid "See me" notes in the history of the paper.

It is the nature of our business for reporters to profit from other people's misfortunes, since the worst news makes the biggest impact. And that's the way it was one morning when I was returning to my room at the YMCA, having worked all night and having had breakfast at Norman's, then the only place in Halifax where the food was fit to eat. I was passing the Queen Hotel when I heard a shout from an upper window. I was the only person in the street, and on looking up I saw other people at the hotel windows, with smoke behind them. They were yelling, and as I watched, a curtain of fire swept forward through the lobby of the old hotel and broke through the big plate-glass windows, shooting great tongues up the stairwell and bursting out of the roof six storeys above.

I was rooted to the ground and stayed that way while people threw knotted bedsheets out of the windows and while some started to jump, landing on the sidewalk in front of me and lying very still. The outside fire escapes were in flames, being made of wood, and were no use at all. Somebody must have rung in the alarm, because the firemen arrived and got out their nets and tried to catch people as they fell. But they couldn't get their ladders up because of the mass of wires on the lampposts, and they were crying with anguish. Sometimes they were able to catch a falling body in their nets, and sometimes they weren't.

Within forty-five minutes, the whole place caved in with a great crash, bringing down all the wires and filling the street with bricks and rubble and bodies. I ran back to the office, roused enough people to get out an extra, and sat down at the typewriter, where two columns of copy got written according to Sandy Thorne's dictum just to tell the story. What I didn't know was that the falling walls of the hotel had cut the power supply to the rival paper, the *Chronicle*, where Hanson, my old Saint John nemesis, was city editor. Consequently, we had him over a barrel and had the town to ourselves. By day's end, the number of dead in that fire was fifty-two, and when I got my "See me" memo from Rankin that night it had a $10 bill attached to it, the only bonus I ever had in forty-eight years of newspapering.

That became a world story, even though most of the world's newspapers were by then headlining the war news. The slight degree of fame it brought me led to an offer to join the local bureau of the Canadian Press, Canada's national news service, which Rankin cautioned was the biggest dead end in the business, a real swamp. (He later became its president.) But they were offering $17 a week, two more dollars than I was making, so I went and fell into the orbit of Andrew Merkel, as extraordinary a newspaperman, poet, gentleman, and roustabout as ever strode a Nova Scotia beach or quaffed a salty jug of bootleg rum.

I had heard of Andy Merkel, everybody in the news business had. It was said that he knew where every jug of rum was buried from Halifax to Yarmouth and that he practically invented the schooner *Bluenose*, along with the *Silver Dart*, the transatlantic cable, Marconi, Alcock and Brown, and the pony express that used to meet the ships off Halifax and gallop the news to Boston to get it there first.

Merkel was a big, hearty man with a splendid paunch and a fine, crooked nose and a shock of silver hair that hung down over his forehead. He had delicate hands and a big, rollicking voice, and he didn't give a damn for anybody unless they could write, or sing, or fish, or sail, or fly, or fuck. He was one of the few people in the news business who told the bosses to go to hell and got away with it. He did it with the publishers of the Maritime papers who were supposed to control his activities, and most of all he did it with the management of Canadian Press in Toronto, who kept insisting that the Maritimes were a subservient part of the news network, while Merkel insisted he was supreme.

Occasionally, he would send the bosses in Toronto jugs of black bootleg rum, which kept them quiet, and he had a secret weapon that he used against the general manager of Canadian Press, J. F. B. Livesay. Livesay had problems with his eyes, and the only thing that seemed to help was sea water taken from Peggy's Cove. Whenever

Livesay came down to see if he could sack Merkel, Merkel would take him to Peggy's Cove and Livesay would bathe his eyes and the soreness would go away; and Livesay would return to Toronto healed, with Merkel committed to sending bottles of the magic water throughout the year. He did too, though sometimes it was suspected he just went down to Halifax Harbour and filled the bottles there, sewage pollution and all.

Although inclined to be careless in his personal habits, Merkel kept his office files meticulously, on the not-unjustified suspicion that the bastards in Toronto were out to get him. He had a sixth sense about plotters above and below, and had mastered the dogma that the best defence is a good offence.

What really sustained him was the fact that the Atlantic provinces generated an endless flow of wonderful and dramatic news stories, and that he managed to attract, and hold, a number of reporters who could write. It was never clear whether Merkel was encouraging them to be poets or newspapermen, but whatever it was, "Merkel's men," as they were called, made the wires sing while making a series of marks on the national journalistic scene that remain unequalled. And two of them actually did win the Governor General's Award for poetry.

Drink was only part of the stimulus — some of us merely breathed the fumes exhaled by the imbibers. The atmosphere of Halifax in the first year of the war did the rest, and it didn't matter at all that the identity of the place was hidden in the dispatches as "an East Coast Canadian port." While that could also mean Saint John, N.B., or St. John's, Newfoundland, or Sydney or Shelburne or Lunenburg or Yarmouth, it was nearly always Halifax, and I doubt that the U-boat captains were fooled, for God knows they sunk enough ships right off the mouth of Halifax Harbour.

Merkel's most effective answer to censorship was to get the censor drunk, or at least get him to the point where his suspicions were lowered. Thus it was that he was able to get aboard the big British warships that came into port, including H.M.S. *Hood* and H.M.S. *Renown*, with their vast kegs of demerara rum, a liquid to which Merkel and his friend Bliss Carman had once written an ode. Such was Merkel's way with censors that late in 1939, with a censor watching out for the police, he concealed himself behind a tree and photographed the entire departure of the convoy carrying the First

26

Canadian Division overseas, using a movie camera he had acquired from Stefansson, the famed Arctic explorer, who was a pal of his. When he sent the film away to be developed, everybody told him he would be interned for the duration of the war. But nothing was ever said, and he delighted in showing the film to the great and humble alike.

Merkel and his wife always held open house. They were masters of the art of genteel poverty, known to seacoast people everywhere, the trick being to keep up appearances regardless of a shortage of ready cash and the awfulness of depleted capital. Merkel had long since exhausted what had been left to him by ancestors who had founded the Royal Bank ("They took that one away from us, never forget") and sent ships to trade along the sea lanes of the world, but he dispensed largesse and hospitality with such an open hand that in the end it was his undoing. When he finally opened a rural restaurant on the spot at Port Royal where Champlain had wintered in the early 1600s, he invited all his customers back to the house for tea and cakes. That meant he went broke and so was unable to carry to fruition his plans for a Shakespearean repertory company in a natural amphitheatre on the site where Champlain and Marc Lescarbot had staged the first North American revels 340 years before. But he did get the name of the place changed back to Port Royal, from Lower Granville.

One vivid memory of him goes back to a day when he decreed that the day's bag of lobsters, a whole gunnysack full of them bought for a couple of dollars, should be broiled rather than boiled, which meant slaying them by hand before putting them into the oven. These were three-pounders, fresh from the chilly depths of the Bay of Fundy, where lobsters get that extra kick from the tides that gives them a muscular tang achieved nowhere else. (That's also what makes Saint John Harbour salmon superior to any other on earth.) These lobsters were so spry we raced them on the kitchen floor before Merkel, carving knife in hand, approached them for the slaughter.

If you've ever seen a lobster under water, you will know they are not the sluggish creatures they seem to be on land. They are more like spiders, so nimbly do they move, and they get up on their hind quarters and wave their claws like boxers. I had never seen them do that out of water, but when they saw Mr. Merkel approaching they got the idea at once, forming a lobster line and rearing up with their claws waving.

Splitting a single hale and hearty lobster in these circumstances is a considerable feat, and dispatching six of them in a row can test a strong man to the outer limits of endurance, because the lobster has an armour-plated underbelly right where you want to slit him open. Mr. Merkel emerged the winner with only a few bruises and contusions, though he was so mentally and physically exhausted that when the lobsters finally reached the table he was unable even to mumble his usual criticisms of the cooks. Loyal and devoted though he was, it was not unusual for his family to get the worst of his temper.

We called him Grumpy, after the dwarf of the same name in *Snow White*, though he was a towering figure and one that moved with ponderous majesty. When he entered a room he didn't just arrive, he loomed. His wrath was something to behold — once, when a collection agent came to the house to arrange for a garnishee on the wages of a member of the CP staff, Mr. Merkel hurled him bodily from the premises.

He gloried in the excitements of wartime Halifax, and unlike many Haligonians he had soldiers and sailors and airmen around to the house, always making sure they violated the Official Secrets Act by telling him what was going on, along with their part in it. One of his greatest days was when the French battleship *Dunkerque*, which had gone missing after the fall of France, steamed into harbour and docked at one of the quays, her presence shrouded in official secrecy despite the fact that the streets suddenly teemed with oddly dressed matelots with pom-poms on their hats.

They too shared in Merkel's hospitality, though he didn't succeed in persuading them to join in the allied war effort. About the only people he didn't have around to the house were the hordes of whores who came down from Montreal to cash in on the lusts of the fighting men who poured through the port in greater numbers than the local talent could handle. The ladies from Montreal were readily identifiable because they spoke only French and they all wore white rubbers or overshoes on their feet — as a result of which, any Halifax lady with white footwear threw the items out in the garbage.

Mr. Merkel hated Catholics, blacks, and Liberals in roughly that order, though hard-drinking priests were often at the house, sometimes for weeks. If somebody had a talent he admired, he was willing to overlook their antecedents, and on one memorable occasion he had as his house guest James D. Gillis, the author of those great Cape Breton literary epics, "The Cape Breton Giant" and "The Great Election."

Gillis had come, on invitation, to take part in a tribute to Joseph Howe, the architect of self-government and the great dissenter of Canadian politics and Canadian newspapering. Mr. Merkel had arranged for a ceremony that involved placing showers of mayflowers on Howe's grave, and this meant waiting for the mayflowers to bloom in the countryside, at which time the native Indians would bring them into the Halifax market for sale. The mayflowers were late that year so Gillis stayed longer than usual in the Merkel household, which was fine, except that he insisted on practising on the bagpipes by day and by night, so that he would be in shape for the ceremony. A further complication was the fact that Gillis was not in the habit of bathing, and he developed a ripeness that threatened to render the entire house uninhabitable. Mr. Merkel insisted that genius had to be humoured, but in the end he sided with the majority, and the tub was filled and Gillis was informed that he should deposit himself therein. He did so, clothes and all, and found it so comfortable that he called for his pipes and sat there in the tub, wailing away like billy-ho.

James D. didn't smell much better after the event, but mercifully the mayflowers bloomed shortly thereafter and the ceremony duly took place at Joe Howe's grave. And when it was all over, they took Gillis to the train and sent him back to Cape Breton, despite his protests that he was quite prepared to stay a little longer, six weeks being hardly enough to get the feel of the place.

The Merkel house was also patronized through the years by such freeloaders as Bliss Carman, the demerara man, and Sir Charles G. D. Roberts. Roberts's physical strength and sexual drive, even in his eighties, were such that the women of the family had to be kept under lock and key, all except for Merkel's wife Florence, who was regarded by one and all as a saint, and hence inviolate. Towards the end of his life, Sir Charles married a woman fifty years his junior, who thus became Lady Roberts — much to the disgust of his long-time companion and loyal biographer, Elsie Pomeroy, a pillar of the teaching profession in Toronto as well as of the Canadian Authors' Association. Upon hearing the shocking and unexpected news of

Roberts's untimely wedding, Miss Pomeroy telephoned his abode to discuss with him the recovery of certain of her possessions, and the new bride answered the telephone with "Lady Roberts speaking."

"Lady Roberts," snorted Elsie, "my ass!"

Merkel often used to go off on seaborne excursions with his bohemian friends, bringing out occasional issues of a subterranean newspaper called the *Song Fisherman*, while his loyal staff in Halifax kept assuring the anxious CP bosses in Toronto that everything was in order and that Merkel was indeed on deck. And so he was, though the messages never said which deck he was on.

With Wilson MacDonald and Robert Norwood and Bliss Carman and Sir Charles G. D. Roberts he would sail, and he inspired Charles Bruce and Kenneth Leslie into writing some gorgeous lines about the native heath. It was in the *Song Fisherman* that Carman published his hymn of praise to demerara rum, as eloquent in some of its passages as the Rubaiyat. And it was in the *Song Fisherman* that his fellow writers paid tribute to Carman on his death, Kenneth Leslie's lines being the most haunting:

> Go lank rover get you home
> Where the red-streaked orchards roam!
> Dust-red road and sea and stone
> Call and claim you for their own
> Tempting you with honey-mist
> Apple-wine and amethyst!*

Merkel himself wrote bursts of lyric poetry, which everybody who read marvelled at but nobody bought. The most beautiful lines ever dedicated to the builders of wooden windships came from Andrew Merkel's pen, addressed to William J. Roué, the designer of the schooner *Bluenose*. These are the opening lines:

> Joy of the Master Architect is yours,
> Who saw the common things that lie at hand —
> The soughing spruces of our native land
> Giant hardwoods whence the Autumn glory pours,

* The poem was subsequently published in the volume *Windward Rock* by Kenneth Leslie (New York: Macmillan, 1934).

Spun splendour of the spindles' whirring hours —
And saw that they were good. And gave command
Until there left the builder's littered strand,
A ship that soars by, as the seagull soars.**

Merkel taught his reporters some of these eternal verities, along with some temporary ones, and was the delight of most who knew him and the despair of the rest, leaving a legacy that still bears dividends in newsrooms around the country.

When Andy Merkel died, we laid him beside his beloved and much-abused Florence in the country cemetery at Port Royal, and people from all walks of life came to the funeral, the most eloquent tributes coming not from the poets and not from the newspaper people, but from the fishermen who regarded Merkel as a kindred soul, perhaps because of the rum. I never crack a lobster or swig demerara or marvel at a poetic phrase without thinking of him.

The Merkels had a daughter named Mary-Elizabeth, of whom the poet Constance Davies Woodrow wrote some lovely lines:

Darling of my heart is the little maid, Mary,
All the moods of April in her lovely eyes of brown.

She was the sweetheart of the newspaper fraternity, and of poets and fishermen, and the mascot of Peggy's Cove when the access road was still a country trail with a gate on it.

We fell in love and married and were together forty years, sharing the births and growths of five very varied children, as well as most of the experiences recalled in these pages. Unhappily, there was something prescient in the closing lines of the poem:

Life, be very gentle with the little maid, Mary!
Let no cruel thorn surprise her little dancing feet!

For Mary-Elizabeth, the poet's wish held true for a long, mostly wonderful, time.

**From *Schooner Bluenose*, text by Andrew Merkel, photographs by
W. R. MacAskill (Toronto: Ryerson Press, 1948).

31

3/Vancouver

From wartime Halifax to wartime Vancouver was a big jump, heightened for me by the fact that I was leaving Canadian Press, the holy of holies in the news business, and joining the upstart opposition. My old benefactor and nemesis Bob Hanson was by this time in Montreal as news editor of British United Press — an offshoot of UP in the United States — and he had persuaded me to join BUP as Pacific Coast bureau manager, for $25 a week and all the scenery thrown in.

The only way to get to Vancouver was by train, and in those times newspapermen got around by conning passes from the railroads and promising to write articles for their company magazines. There was competition between the CPR and the CNR to hand out passes, and the railroads maintained departments of flacks whose sole job was the care, feeding, and watering of transient journalists, some with jobs and some without. You operated on the assumption that travel was something neither you nor your bosses ever had to pay for. Publishers, it was reported, had gold lifetime passes and never had to promise to write anything.

The trains were far more numerous then than they are now, and a lot faster too, but it seemed to take the better part of a week to get across the country, deciding through Ontario that the one thing Canada would never run out of was trees, but then crossing the prairies and encountering the tail end of the Dirty Thirties in the form of towering dust clouds that filled the horizon and blotted out the sun.

The towns and cities all had a temporary look about them, and so did Vancouver when the journey finally ended and I got off the train and there was nobody to meet me and I had never felt so lonely in my life. That first impression has stayed with me in all my return visits to Vancouver — the feeling that nobody gives a damn, which they don't in any city if you're a stranger. But Vancouver has a multiplier effect. It may be that a city without fear lacks warmth to strangers, and nobody in Vancouver was afraid, then or since. It was the reverse of the Maritime approach to life, and it was hard to accept the blithe indifference of Vancouverites to their own fate, or anybody else's.

I have never had this feeling in New York, the city that is supposed to be the most heartless of all. Some years later, when living among New Yorkers, I discovered that their callousness is less than skin deep, that if you scratch a New Yorker you find a caring person just beneath the surface — the surface being a protective coating against the sheer pressure of numbers, and the pace. New Yorkers are realistic enough to be afraid — not of one another, not of being killed on the street with nobody caring, but of life itself.

The most hospitable city I have ever known was wartime London, where everybody was scared to death and adjusted to the possibility that each day would be their last. And maybe the reason our far northerners are so hospitable is that deep down they are frightened and are genuinely relieved when a stranger comes among them (I refer to the white northerners, not the natives, who tend nowadays to be as indifferent to strangers as Vancouverites).

Perhaps in 1940 Vancouver the fault may have been with the new arrival, because my own feeling was that there was nothing linking me to civilization except the bands of steel snaking through the mountains, those same peaks that make British Columbians feel so splendidly isolated in their paradise. I tried to get my bearings by walking through the streets, which were lined with wooden buildings that didn't look anything like the wooden buildings we had at home. Here everything seemed slapped together, without frills and usually without paint, reflecting the general philosophy of the inhabitants. On the back streets some of the sidewalks were made of wood, and there seemed to be more beggars and drunks than we had at home. Hardly anybody said hello, nor did anybody seem to care when you told them where you were from and what you had come to do.

I had heard a lot about the camaraderie of newspapering and had experienced a good deal of it in Saint John and Halifax, but those first weeks in Vancouver taught me that everybody in the business there cared about only two things — Vancouver and British Columbia, in that order. The rest of Canada was a far-off place. And to the extent that there was a war, it was Britain's war, though they seemed glad to be in it at her side.

The city bred a kind of newspaperman unlike those in other places, a tradition that has carried on through the years in the form of columnists and hotline radio hosts and eccentrics of every stripe. Everyone who worked at (or owned) the *Sun* was crazy, and the *Sun* itself reflected it. The morning *News Herald* wasn't much different and was launching the likes of Pierre Berton and Jack Scott on their careers, developing the fine irreverence that marked their subsequent work. Nobody gave a damn.

The sane people, I was told, all worked at the big paper in town, the *Province*. But as I worked for BUP, I wasn't permitted even to pass through its hallowed portals — and when you bought a copy of the paper, you were supposed to read it in reverent silence, something you could never do with the raucous *Sun* or the half-baked *News Herald*.

Where Halifax had been all convoys and warships and troopships and departing soldiers and arriving whores, Vancouver was all enthusiasm and cheers for Winston Churchill, a neon portrait of whom stood in the middle of Victory Square, radiating confidence and inspiration. There weren't any U-boats offshore, and I don't recall that we had to use the dateline "a West Coast Canadian port," though we may have done so just to create atmosphere.

Since Vancouver wasn't a transit port for troops, it didn't come to be hated the way Halifax was. Anyway, who could hate a place with all that scenery? Though the city itself was ugly as sin. Its only redeeming features were the old Hotel Vancouver, quickly demolished, the new Hotel Vancouver, still there, the Marine Building, the new City Hall, and the incredible old Sun Tower, atop which the BUP offices were located — and atop which we responded to the distant directions of Robert W. Keyserlingk.

Keyserlingk was as different from Andrew Merkel as Vancouver was from Halifax. Known as "the Count," he was a refugee Baltic baron who hated Communists and the Soviet Union and who held sway over a news service that hacked out a living selling supplementary news to Canadian newspapers and main news to radio stations that couldn't afford anything else.

Keyserlingk had his headquarters in Montreal, but he was well connected in Vancouver, having come there initially as a representative of the Guinness interests of London and Dublin. He had a hand in the development of the British Properties on the mountainside across the harbour from Vancouver, and he had a lot to do with the building of the first Narrows Bridge that made those properties accessible by road. He carried an air of mystery about with him, something like Sandy Thorne's involvement with the Masons, except that where Sandy was a rough diamond, Keyserlingk was a polished one and people tended to be in awe of his tastes in things like food and wine and the proper way of doing things. He never did master the proper way of running a news service, but he did the best he could with what he had, including me. When all else failed, Keyserlingk would give a dinner for a critical client and the contract would be saved for another year. The problem was that the dinner often cost more than the contract was worth.

At BUP Vancouver, our main news wire came out of San Francisco on printers that could only handle thirty words a minute, because sixty was too expensive. So we had the only stuttering, hunt-and-peck teletypes in the world. It was a news wire on which exasperated editors would cut in with messages like "When in hell are we going to get some news on here?" When this happened, it irked the San Francisco management, headed at the time by Hugh Baillie, who subsequently became president of United Press. He insisted on knowing who was putting these hostile messages on his news wire, and when it emerged that the culprit was somewhere in Vancouver, suspicion fell upon our night editor, William A. Wilson — the same Bill Wilson who is now a distinguished Ottawa columnist. Bill went on to become the most fearless war correspondent ever to go into battle, and he didn't flinch in the face of Baillie's demand for his head. He just kept saying he didn't do it, and he was vindicated when the telegraph company traced the outrage to our local client paper.

Keyserlingk, with his European suave, had conned the only morning paper in town, the *News Herald*, into taking our service, since they couldn't afford Canadian Press. But the *News Herald* had a new editor, the terrible-tempered Robert T. Elson, and he wasn't going to let our lousy news service stand in his way of making the *News Herald* a great newspaper. He had called me in on my arrival in Vancouver to tell me that since Keyserlingk wouldn't let him break the contract for our news service, he was going to break me instead.

He didn't mean physically, though Elson could have managed that without trouble. He meant he was going to break my spirit, and Bill Wilson's, and anybody else's who got in his way of dumping BUP and taking CP.

From then on, he insisted that we match every item and filler on the big news wires, and he kept watch by reading the Seattle *Post-Intelligencer* and demanding that we duplicate every item therein. This project kept me busy scalping and stealing news from every possible source, with Keyserlingk urging me on from the safety of Montreal, until one day we got this hassle about somebody demanding "Let's have some news please!" on the wire and I went to Elson and asked him if he had done it.

He blushed for the only time in his life, and when I told him that both Bill Wilson and I were up for the sack, which normally wouldn't have bothered him at all, he laughed and said the devil had made him do it — he had come to hate that slow-speed wire so much he couldn't stand the sight or sound of the thing. He signed a confession, which we wired off to Baillie in San Francisco, but Elson said he would still be laying for us, and he did until the day we came up with an exclusive that softened him up.

In fact, there were two exclusives. The first came on a tip that Robert W. Service, the bard of the Yukon, who most people thought was dead, had turned up in Vancouver, having been chased out of his retirement in France by the advancing Germans. I found out where he was and went and did an interview, in the course of which he said he had spent the years between the wars living off his royalties and playing the concertina in a whorehouse. The interview got big play and gave the *News Herald* something the *Sun* and the *Province* didn't have. But the second exclusive was much yeastier, causing a small sensation that was felt around the world.

We had a young reporter on the staff by the name of Laurence Duffey, who went on to become the national news director of CBC TV. On the side, Duffey was a poet of promise and a music lover who used to sit on the window ledge with his feet hanging out over downtown Vancouver and pretend he was conducting symphony orchestras. He was assigned to meet a ship coming in from Australia carrying Sir Thomas Beecham, the noted British maestro. Beecham had left Australia shouting oaths over his shoulder about Australian concertgoers being barbarians and baboons, and the assignment was to get some more quotes from him along the same lines. But when

Duffey returned to the office, he said there was no story because Beecham wouldn't see anybody.

Had Duffey been able to find out why? Yes, he said he had. The reason was that a brigade of young Australians on board had taken umbrage at Beecham's views of Australian culture, and one night they had crept upon him in his stateroom, pulled him from his bunk, lathered him up, and shaved off his chin whiskers, which were his trademark in the music world. Beecham refused to be seen in public, much less give interviews, until the whiskers had grown back in. So, said Duffey, we would have to wait. Wait! We threw him down at a typewriter and instructed him to write, which he did. The story got world play and the *News Herald* got another scoop. Elson was ecstatic, and even Hugh Baillie sent a wire of congratulations. That took some of the heat off, though not all.

One of our wartime problems was Keyserlingk himself, whose hatred of the Communists kept getting the better of him when the Soviets became our allies after they were attacked by the Germans. Hating the Hun was the prevailing mood, and we in the news business were supposed to be part of the propaganda effort. Or, to put it more politely, we were not supposed to do anything to impede the war effort. Meanwhile, heroes and heroines of the Red Army came over to help with our Victory Bond drives, and we had a big love affair going with Moscow. But in our shop you had to be careful about it, and to this day I'm not sure whether we helped the war effort or impeded it. Keyserlingk certainly did not share in the general gloom at the string of Soviet defeats, and he gave the rest of us the impression that if we knew what he knew about the way the Russian reds had acted towards the Baltic States and his own people, we wouldn't be cheering them on or helping them in any way.

At all events, none of us got arrested. And eventually I made my escape into wider pastures, having learned more from Keyserlingk about fine wines and stately dinner parties than I ever did about news. Though I did learn the tricks of the trade; I learned them so well and could type so fast that I won promotion from Vancouver to BUP's head office bureau in Montreal, and thence to Toronto as bureau manager. One of my biggest jobs there was an assignment to report on the Quebec Conference of 1943, when Winston Churchill and Franklin D. Roosevelt met with their senior staffs in Quebec City to plot the liberation of Europe and the closing stages of the war. At last I was going to have a personal contact with Great Events.

PART TWO

Great Events

1/How Quebec Was Won

The prevailing impression today about wartime Quebec is one of conscription riots and sullenness and general rejection of the English war, but that wasn't the way it seemed at all. The crowds in the city streets seemed as enthusiastic about the war as crowds anywhere, and it was the most natural thing in the world that Quebec City should have been chosen for the most significant meeting of wartime leaders held in this century.

It is hard to portray the degree of idolatry that Canadians had come to attach to Churchill and Roosevelt. It came from a combination of factors — from the qualities of the men themselves, from propaganda, and the lack of homegrown idols, either politicians or warriors. Our own leader, William Lyon Mackenzie King, was the least inspirational head of government in any country, friend or foe. Besides, Canadian newspapers hadn't developed the art of ballyhoo the way the British and Americans had. We leaned towards borrowed celebrity and adopted foreign heroes as our own, the way British and American history and culture have been made part of Canadian life from the nation's beginnings.

In the war-torn world of 1943, Canada was a mainline country in a sense that she had never been before and has never been since. She was fancied for the first time to be the hinge between Britain and the United States, and the Quebec Conference seemed to put the seal on her importance.

It was taken for granted by Canadians at large, and I believe by most Quebeckers too, that Quebec was a full-fledged part of Canada, sharing in the war effort not only in terms of the fighting regiments she put into the field overseas but in the contributions her people were making to the war effort in the manufacture of what we called the "sinews of war." This was the source of Quebec's urbanization, the beginning of what came much later to be known as the Quiet Revolution.

Montreal had greater financial and industrial importance than Toronto, and in addition had the distinction of being Canada's only cosmopolitan city (Toronto being known as an overgrown collection of villages). In Toronto, as in all the cities of English Canada, the liquor laws were just a step removed from prohibition. Montreal was wide open — fun and sin uptown on a scale that brought New Yorkers flocking for a fling, and all business down along St. James Street. The legends of Montreal newspapering rivalled those of Chicago, but amid all the hubbub the *Montreal Star* was the nation's most respected newspaper, and the *Standard* vied with the *Toronto Star Weekly* for national circulation.

If Montreal was the most macho city in Canada, Quebec City was the counterpoint, ancient beyond any New World measurement, a place of charm and beauty living up to its slogan of "hospitality spoken here." This was before the re-awakening of the Quebec independence spirit, but nobody who knew the Quebec of those years would ever accuse her people of having been asleep. They rose eagerly to the challenge of playing host to the most powerful men in the world — the ones who, together with Josef Stalin, were taking the measure of Adolf Hitler, Benito Mussolini, and the Japanese.

The city was decked with flags, and the restaurants teemed with patrons in the uniforms of three countries. The atmosphere for the most part was one of carnival, in the course of which plans were laid for the bloodiest and deadliest battles of the Second World War, battles that would ravage Italy and France and Belgium and Holland, until finally Germany was laid waste and forced to yield without conditions.

Along with the leaders came enough advisers and back-room boffins to fill the Chateau Frontenac Hotel, which was the staff headquarters for the conference. Security was of a kind never seen before in Canada, though by today's standards it would be classed as minimum. The people of the city opened their arms and hearts to the visitors, and swarmed around the fringes of the conference, hoping for glimpses of the great, applauding Cordell Hull and Anthony Eden and General George C. Marshall. Nobody cheered for Mackenzie King, but then nobody cheered for him anywhere, ever, and he had been booed by Canadian troops when he visited them in England to cheer them up.

Churchill and Roosevelt were holed up in the Citadel fortress, secure both from the enemy and ourselves, and the briefings at the end of each day were sparse, though Canada's Davidson Dunton did a better job as spokesman than his British or American counterparts and was rewarded after the war by being named president of the Canadian Broadcasting Corporation (when heading the CBC really meant something).

Keyserlingk's solution to the dearth of hard news was to go out and buy a map of the world and pin it to the wall of his suite and proceed to hold his own briefings each day, complete with pointer, pins, and bits of string, while the rest of us took notes and rushed to our typewriters with the bogus tidings, exclusive on the wires of UP and BUP. We decided arbitrarily what segment of the global battlefields would provide the day's agenda, and we made up what Churchill and Roosevelt were presumed to be doing. It was a zestful business, and it gave me an appetite for foreign correspondence that sustained me for the next fifteen years. About six of us took part in this war game, calling ourselves the Commandos of the Clarendon, after the name of the hotel that was press headquarters. Our number included Merriman Smith, the hotshot UP man at the White House, who was famous for always saying "Thank you, Mr. President" at the end of presidential press conferences.

The result of all this chicanery was that each day we were putting out a file of news, background, and speculation that nobody else had, which made us the stars of the conference coverage and drove our competitors to distraction in their quest for the demanded matching stories. The ever-present censors were there, but our reports bore so little resemblance to anything they knew about that our stuff passed through unmolested. It would be nice to think it was confusing to the enemy and may have led Hitler, Mussolini, and Tojo into major miscalculations about Allied intentions.

We saw Churchill only twice, and he was out of sorts both times, though the cheers of the crowd when he appeared at the Quebec City Hall seemed to brighten him up. Roosevelt was much the sunnier of the two and managed to be congenial towards the host, Prime Minister Mackenzie King, something Churchill never bothered to do.

After the conference, Churchill went trout fishing in the wilds of Quebec and then proceeded to Niagara Falls with his daughter Mary. A few of us went there to lie in wait, and when he finally arrived we were told that we could approach him as he stood at the brink of the falls and that three questions would be permitted.

Harold Fair, known as Fanny, was selected for the first question, since he represented Canadian Press and hence had priority. As it turned out, his one question was all that got asked.

"Mr. Churchill," he said, "have the falls changed much since you were last here in 1904?"

The great man looked at Fanny Fair with an expression that said this was a peculiar question to put to a man who held the destiny of the world in his hands. Then, glowering, he took a long puff on his newly lighted cigar, turned ponderously toward the raging waters, gave the entire panorama a slow scan, and then returned his gaze to the questioner.

"The main principle," he intoned, "remains the same."

There was a telephone booth at the end of the road, and we all sprinted for that single phone. The others, including the unfortunate Fair, were older than me, so I got there first, hurled myself inside, slid the folding door shut, and called the office in Toronto. I dictated the quote and then kept talking while it went out around the world on UP wires. The longer I tied up the phone, the longer we had the exclusive, and we got congratulations from all over. Partly because of this exploit, an offer came in from Reuters to become a war correspondent, and this led, among other things, to a subsequent encounter with Winston Churchill on the occasion of his peeing into the Rhine, of which more later.

Before parting from BUP and Keyserlingk — who eventually accepted the awful fact that the Soviets were going to come out of the war as winners — I had to endure the company of a protégé of his who was appointed central division manager in Toronto, which meant he was my boss, since I was only bureau manager. (Like all news services, UP made up in titles for what they pinched in salaries.) Cliff Dowling's presence had a very jangling effect on my nerves, and it is safe to assume that my presence had the same effect on him. It was especially trying when he read over my shoulder while I was writing a story directly onto the teletype — which was our custom to save time as well as paper and typewriter ribbons.

Relations between us worsened until one day I was taking details over the phone from a correspondent at the Toronto *Telegram*, which was pinching a story from CP wires about the capsizing of a motor launch in Lake Simcoe, loaded with Sunday School kids. CP said at least a dozen of the children had perished, so we made it fifteen to put ourselves ahead on the story, and everything was moving well until Dowling loomed up behind me and started reading over my shoulder and wondered if we had the death count high enough, adding that the copy didn't seem to have enough punch the way I was writing it.

I just kept pushing the stuff out on the wire, and I wished, to myself, that my tormentor would drop dead — whereupon there was a thump on the floor behind me and when I looked around, he had. The poor man was lying there, cold as a mackerel.

I finished up the paragraph and marked it "more" and called the police, and when they had taken poor Dowling away I made a resolve never to wish anything like that on anybody any more. It is a pledge I violated only once, years later when working for Reuters in New York City. There was an Australian colleague named Alf King, who was senior to me and was always throwing his weight around, as Australian men are inclined to do. In the handling of our news reports he always insisted that we put the interests of Australia ahead of anybody else's, and for some reason this idea is particularly offensive to the Canadian psyche. Our English colleagues used to joke that if it had not been for our common ties to Britain, Canada and Australia would have long since been at war with one another, a suggestion that I have heard from various military men who have witnessed the rare occasions when Canadian and Australian troops have been in the same vicinity. The only truly non-abrasive Australian man I have ever known was Chester Wilmot, the BBC correspondent who wrote *Struggle for Europe* and went to his death in the first jet-age crash when a Comet airliner exploded over Yugoslavia. I have never understood how Australian men and Australian women can come from the same country, for they don't talk the same language and Lord knows they don't look the same, representing Beauty and the Beast.

Whatever, Alf King burst into a conference just when we were about to sign a client to a new Reuters contract, the news service business being 90 per cent contracts and 10 per cent news, and he made such a commotion that we almost lost the client. And I wished he would drop dead. In the morning we got a phone call from his grieving widow.

I kept the secret to myself and haven't used the death wish since. I'm not even sure it works any more.

2/London, Bombed

My recruitment with Reuters was arranged one day in Toronto when I first met Tony Cole, a gargantuan Scotsman who looked like a combination of G. K. Chesterton and Egypt's King Farouk. There are two kinds of Scot, rogue and dour, and Tony Cole was a rogue. Canada's misfortune has been to be populated largely by the dour kind during the nation's formative years, and generations of Canadians have paid the penalty in the form of laws, customs, and prohibitions that have inhibited the country's growth.

Walton A. Cole was anything but dour. Having matured early in Aberdeen, he had made his way to London, where by dint of ability, energy, and chicanery he rose to a dominant position in the Press Association, the national news agency. There, among other things, he saw to it that Winston Churchill's speeches got on the wire during the prewar years when Churchill's stock was low. The two men had an understanding, based on the unspoken assumption that Churchill would do anything for publicity, as would most men in British public life.

Cole had made himself such a hot item in Fleet Street that in 1943, at the age of twenty-nine, he was appointed editor of Reuters and given the job of rebuilding that ancient agency's tattered fortunes. The once-proud name had been dragged through the propaganda mud and it was widely assumed that Reuters was an arm of the British government, which to all intents and purposes it was. The newspapers of Britain had taken over the ownership, the newspapers of Australia had bought a piece of the action, and connections with the Foreign Office had been severed. Then they hired Cole, and Reuters was never the same again.

On the first of his many round-the-world dashes in the middle of the war, he rolled into the United States, where he blustered the *New York Times* and the Chicago *Tribune* into buying the Reuters' service.

Then he sold them some time on Reuters' leased circuits for the movement of their own copy, and before they knew what had hit them, Cole had the basis for a North American operation.

He hit Toronto on the fly, and by invoking King, country, haggis, the Archbishop of Canterbury, and cases of Scotch whisky, actually managed to persuade Canadian newspaper publishers to pay him something for his news service. Whereupon he set about hiring some Canadians to serve as war correspondents to replace those of the old school who had been killed, maimed, or were incapable of churning out the kind of stuff he felt would shake the cobwebs out of the place.

When I first encountered him, he was gobbling a huge plate of veal kidneys in the dining room of the King Edward Hotel, and he invited me to order a plate of the same, which he appropriated and ate with relish while promising me fame, if not fortune, if I would throw in my lot with him and go off to war. Cole had a big, droopy walrus moustache, and with kidney juice dripping from it he was an inspiring sight, proclaiming that he was assembling the greatest staff of correspondents ever dispatched to the battlefields of the world. We would not only write history, we would make it; and when the war was over, the world would be ours.

All of this, plus the prospect of $50 a week, was heady stuff, though I protested that I was near-sighted and that Keyserlingk had pulled strings in Ottawa and with the Toronto draft board, insisting that without me at BUP in Toronto to help direct the flow of news, the war might be lost. Cole waved all this aside and said I was just the boy to write about Canadian troops in action, and he promised bylines galore and my choice of foreign postings when the war was over. We made a deal while he ate three dishes of ice cream with butterscotch sauce, topped off by French pastries. And that was only breakfast.

Thus it was that I became the only draft dodger who wound up landing in Normandy at H-hour on D-day, wearing a uniform so new it still had the creases in the trousers, and wondering who to ask for directions without getting killed, either by our side or the Germans. In the meantime, Cole went off to India or South Africa or someplace, leaving me to wrestle with all the pullings and thrustings needed to pry me loose from conscription — the local board arguing that if I was expendable from the Toronto job, I was expendable to peel potatoes in the army, myopia and all. But finally I was certified to proceed to Britain and to the prospect of a certain, if glorious, death.

Days later, it was down to Halifax for a tearful parting from loved ones and then the boarding of the troopship *Ile de France* with 11,000 others, and me the only one in civilian clothes. My gaudy herringbone tweed topcoat was the hit of the trip, and the troops kept insisting that I pace the decks so that everybody could dream of home, which I was glad to do even though the *Ile de France* almost spilled me overboard with her pitching and rolling at top speed, which was her way of outwitting the U-boats, since she was running without escort.

Once in London, I was thrown into the melée of the Reuters newsroom and the whole business of wartime Fleet Street, which wasn't that different from peacetime Fleet Street except that you could get killed in it, the Baby Blitz being on at the time. Cole explained that the immediate assignment was to hype the news and churn it out by wireless to as much of the world as would swallow it. If a story lacked zing, we were supposed to put it in, making a two-pronged attack into a three-pronger, especially if it was on the Russian front. This was called "topspin."

We kept urging correspondents in the various war zones to put more colour into their copy, and one of the Old Boys became so weary of this that he wound up sending us a dispatch from North Africa, the lead paragraph reading: "As I write this, machine-gun bullets are beating a devil's tattoo on my tin hat."

Meanwhile, I had made the acquaintance of the chief accountant of Reuters, a dry stick of a man by the name of Walters, who had a wry sense of humour and actually sat on a high stool at a tall slanting desk and wore celluloid cuffs and collars. Shortly after my arrival in London, I had turned my first expense account in to him, covering the trip from Toronto to Halifax and the voyage on the *Ile de France*, and he had called me in with pursed lips to deal with my sums.

He informed me that Reuters had been moving people about the globe in war and peace since old Baron Reuter flew his first pigeons back in the 1830s. He said he could pull out the expense accounts for war correspondents back to the Crimea, not to mention the frontier campaigns in India, the Opium War, the Civil War in America, the relief of Mafeking, the First World War, Spain, Manchuria, and everything up to this moment in the Second World War — and never in all those years had there been an expense account as incredibly inflated as mine. He had me there, and besides I was still having trouble with pounds, shillings, and pence, so we reached a settlement after a lengthy parley and Cole told me later that whatever I tried to get away with, not to try to put it over Walters.

Later, when we became good friends, Walters let me know that he had a soft spot for Canadians because his daughter lived in Canada, and he let it drop that his opening speech to me was par for the course for new recruits to the agency, designed to put the fear of God into them in all future expense dealings, a technique that had served Reuters well on the budgetary side for more than a hundred years. Walters said he actually enjoyed dealing with all the barbarians Cole was hiring, especially the Canadians and Americans who were, for him, a refreshing change from the Old Boy network, whose members brought little imagination to the work of expense accounting, many of them having private incomes of their own.

Cole's first action on being appointed editor of Reuters had been to hire a number of Scots, all of them rogues only a small step removed from savagery. They collided in the newsroom with a number of Cockneys (who had been taken on from the racier shops in Fleet Street) including the chief news editor, Sidney J. Mason. This was carrying things too far for at least one of the old-line management types, a gentleman named Moloney, who proceeded to make a quiet trip to his native Ireland where he hired seven scholarly school teachers as war correspondents, with instructions to report to the newsroom in London. Moloney didn't tell anybody about his coup, so there was no advance warning when these seven Irishmen reported for work at 85 Fleet Street. The air was filled with Scottish and Cockney oaths when it became clear that none of the newcomers could type and that they had no previous reporting experience whatsoever.

A special desk was set up for them in a remote corner of the crowded newsroom, and an instructor was put to the task of teaching them to type, and they became known as Moloney's Revenge, much to Tony Cole's discomfiture. It was just about the only time anybody in Reuters put anything over on him, and it wasn't long before Moloney was gone, though his revenge lived after him.

Eventually, the whole lot of Irishmen went off to the Middle

East, and the last we heard of them was that they had created a nasty scene at the military airport in Cairo, where they were put under arrest on suspicion of being Nazi agents. I think they all wound up in Burma, and several of them actually sent in dispatches, but nobody was sure who they were from.

Cole's ruffians fared better, except that one had to change his byline, it being felt in Reuters that "Moses Appel" was a bit too much for the global file. So they changed Moe's byline to Melvin Apple. (He switched back when he returned to Canada after the war and became a big shot in the Zionist movement, promoting Israel bonds.)

Another of the gang was Marshall Yarrow who, like Appel, was a former deskman on the Ottawa *Citizen*. He had the distinction of seeing his Reuters dispatches published in India under the byline Field Marshal Yarrow, which gave him quite a jump on the rest of us. Yarrow was worldly wise and always gave the impression that he knew a lot more about Cole than the rest of us did, and that if we knew what he knew it would make our hair stand on end. But he never told us what it was, and maybe it was just that the two of them always looked like conspirators when they were together. My own suspicion was that it had something to do with the black market, either perfume or nylon stockings.

Wartime London was probably the friendliest and most uninhibited city the world had ever seen, and anybody who was there should be forgiven any and all transgressions, real or imagined, committed usually on the assumption that death was at hand. We didn't have much money, but we didn't need much because most of the pleasures to be had were not of the money kind, and the beer was cheap, and so were the theatres and the taxis and just about everything else.

There was a flat in a row of old houses near the Notting Hill Gate underground station, and I shared it with two old friends from Vancouver, Jack Scott of the *News Herald* and Reg Moir of the *Province*. Both of them were in public relations with the forces, and both shared my total ignorance of anything to do with the military, having never heard a shot fired in anger, or even for practice. We had three narrow beds in one big room looking out on a park where an anti-aircraft battery had set up its guns, and with the Germans coming over most nights the guns were busy, shaking the whole block to the point where we were moved to join the rush for the tube station sleeping quarters every time the sirens sounded.

As things turned out, we left the house only once, since the way out led past the door of Mrs. Howard, the landlady. It was her custom to keep her door open so that we couldn't smuggle any women upstairs, and she sat there in her parlour, rocking and knitting. When we invited her that first time to join us in the run to the public shelter, she snorted and said she had spent her whole life above ground and Hitler wasn't going to get her to budge in any direction, unless he blew her upward. The three of us brooded about this all the way to the shelter and all the next day, and when the sirens went again and the guns opened up, we stayed put in our big room and drew lots to see who would sleep in the bed underneath the big wall mirror, it being assumed that in the event of a hit, whoever was in that bed would proceed into the next world spangled. It wasn't until months after we left that a V-1 buzzbomb levelled the whole neighbourhood. We asked around after the war, but we never did find out what happened to Mrs. Howard.

I was supposed to be in training for my coming role as a combat correspondent, but Cole said that part would be easy and the important work was on the various desks in the newsroom. As a result, I never did get near any troops, and the day of the invasion of Europe (that was what we called it then, but the PR guys changed it later to "liberation") was getting closer. Finally, I suggested to Cole that it might be a good idea for me to get a uniform, and he referred me to Chief Accountant Walters, who said it would be best if I got one second-hand at the Moss Bros used-clothing emporium, because things were cheaper there. So off I went to Moss Bros, where I got myself fitted out with a serge dress uniform with leather buttons and a cavalry greatcoat down to my ankles and a Sam Browne belt and calf-high officers' boots in pebbled leather and a pair of waterproof veltschoen shoes and a sheepskin jacket and a knee-high pair of fleece-lined Wellingtons. Later on I would acquire a naval duffle coat and a U.S. Army steel helmet, and thus dressed for battle would strike terror into friend and foe alike. But that first day, when I walked out of Moss Bros in my cavalry greatcoat (which I never wore again) I was the newest-looking military figure in London. My officer's cap was so stiff that when an army friend of mine spotted it he ripped it off my head, tore the wire ring out of the insides, and threw what was left into the gutter where he stomped on it, returning it to my head in what he deemed to be operational shape.

Lacking any training in how to face death, my main worry was the prospect of being killed in battle. But Cole continued to talk about the great things we would do after the war when Reuters would stand astride the world news business like a Colossus. This tendency to think ahead stayed with him for the whole of his life. He was still doing it when, a victim of his overindulgence in food, drink, and work, he choked to death in his Fleet Street office in the last great London smog in 1964. They held a big memorial service for him in St. Paul's Cathedral, and all the dignitaries came and the *Times* ran half a column on the obituary page, but they didn't mention how he broke his arm when he fell into the reflecting pool at the Taj Mahal or how he got himself cartooned into the Dick Tracy comic strip as an arch-fiend or how he saved the Chicago *Tribune* contract by drinking the managing editor of that paper under the table.

Nor was there anything about how you would have lunch with Cole at risk of coming away hungry because he would eat your food as well as his own, having first asked, "What like is that?" before reaching across with his fork. And if it was his favourite meal of pig's knuckles, he would pick them up in his hands and gnaw them, fat and all, ending the ritual by sucking the marrow out of the bones with shrieking slurps that would freeze other diners in their seats, evoking visions of barbarian hordes charging down the valley, bent on rape and pillage.

Cole was fifty when he died, an age that carried off a singular number of my idols and friends, giving me an unease about that particular milestone that endured until I was safely on the other side. There were four great Canadian war correspondents, and of the four, only Ross Munro survives. The others — Lionel Shapiro, Ralph Allen, and Matthew Halton — all came through the shot and shell but died in their beds at fifty, and my world has been a lonelier place without them. Especially without Matt.

3/To Normandy with Matt Halton

My first glimpse of Matthew Halton was on a train heading from London to somewhere in Scotland, destination unknown. Without any warning, every correspondent designated for the D-day landings, wherever they might take place, had been rounded up by the intelligence people, given half an hour to pack, under guard, and whisked aboard a train heading north. We learned later that this was an exercise to fool the German spies into thinking the invasion was under way, the assumption being that war correspondents were the most visible component of the Allied force, some of them being more famous than the generals.

Aboard that train were Ernie Pyle and Alan Moorehead and Wes Gallagher and the seven men who would be landing with the Canadians, most of whom I was meeting for the first time. They weren't very hospitable to the new boy, especially when they learned that I didn't know the difference between a major and a colonel, and had never been "in the field."

Before we left London I had spent an evening with a young subaltern named Pierre Berton, who had arrived from Vancouver on his way to conquering the world. When I told him I was a war correspondent, his question was "Are you any good at it?" I had to tell him that, not yet having gone to war, I didn't know, but I could type fast. Berton snorted and said something about my looking him up if I ever became famous.

Matt Halton was very famous indeed, and he seemed the most kindly disposed of the Canadians, though he told me later that, in a letter to his wife, he had written with a shudder of meeting this "fat boy from Canada" and wondered about the idiocy of sending the likes of me on such a mission.

The whole trainload of us were taken to a commando school that had been set up at Troon in Ayrshire, where we were held for a week under armed guard and incommunicado, leaving the German spies to comb the island for us in vain. The only time they let us out was in a convoy of buses, in which we were transported to the Johnnie Walker blending plant at Kilmarnock, where we saw and smelled the various whiskies flowing in wooden troughs down into the mainstream, the whole place permeated with the most marvellous effluvium. The stuff was tightly rationed and they didn't give us so much as a tot, but it was nice to know it was there. We were trundled back to London with the same lack of ceremony that had marked our leaving, and I suppose the spies were surprised to see us in circulation again.

The next time we were summoned, it was the real thing, but again we weren't permitted to tell anybody or even to say good-bye. A young woman of my acquaintance was in the British Auxiliary Territorial Service (Action! Traction! Satisfaction!); she chauffeured brass hats around in limousines, so she heard the news, and when I got to the flat in Notting Hill Gate to pick up my stuff, she was there. Neither of us said a word about where I was going. Neither of us had to. It was a very bittersweet good-bye, and hours later I was in a hotel on the Isle of Wight — and there was Matthew Halton greeting me, somewhat superciliously I thought, with the news that the two of us would be going on the landings together.

"Where?" I asked.

"Normandy," he replied.

"Exactly where is that?"

"Oh, God," said Matthew. Then he added, "Our objective is Caen."

"The Riviera?"

"No, Caen. Caen!" Matt squinched his face the way you have to do to get that French nasal sound, wrinkling his nose and baring his teeth.

"Never heard of it," said I, "but it's nice to be going there with somebody who has."

From that moment, Matt warmed to me and we remained fast friends for years after the war, until in his late forties he set out to do once again all the things he had enjoyed in life before, as he put it, "the Old One gets me." And it killed him. But oh, he was marvellous company, and oh, the stories he told about Spain and the war and the desert and El Alamein and boyhood in Pincher Creek,

Alberta, and Sicily and Italy, and he talked the way he sounded on the radio, the way that made him for homefront Canadians the voice of Canadians at war.

That night we sat in on a briefing and were told that we would be landing at a place called Graye-sur-Mer and that we would be with the reserve brigade of the Third Canadian Division, which meant that we would be going in an hour after the initial assaults. Then we were shown photographs of the beaches and the shore defences, which seemed to indicate that the whole operation was suicide, because nobody could possibly get through such barricades.

Matt and I shared a room that night and talked until dawn, when we boarded the ship that would carry us across the Channel, a comfortable craft that had been on the Irish Sea ferry service before the war. It had a lounge and a piano, and I asked if anybody minded if I played. So it was that we sang our way into sight of Normandy, one of our companions insisting on repeated choruses of "Can it be true, someone like you could love me, Louise?"

The infantry landing craft were lowered like lifeboats as soon as we were close enough to see the church steeples, and Matt and I climbed down a rope ladder to take our places with the soldiers, each of us lugging a portable typewriter and carrying between us a big flat basket of carrier pigeons to take our dispatches back across the Channel. The gunfire that accompanied our run into the beach wasn't just the first stuff I had heard fired in anger, it was the first stuff I had ever heard fired at all, except for those anti-aircraft batteries in the park at Notting Hill Gate. Amid the din, Matt was musing about the historic aspect of the event and marvelling that here, in the biggest military operation ever to take place in the world, fully one-fifth of the land, sea, and air forces of the Allies came from Canada, and that an equal proportion of the arms and equipment were Canadian-made. He got an inspiration out of that which fed the tone of his broadcasts and dispatches for the rest of the war. But what I was most interested in at that moment was which of us was going to carry the pigeons when the ramp went down on the beach.

As it happened, the ramp didn't go down on the beach at all — we ran aground about twelve metres out — and the ramp went down with a splash and the soldiers started jumping out with their guns held high above their heads, and the water was up to their necks. I put my typewriter on my head and the basket of pigeons on top of that, and jumped, wondering what would happen if my feet didn't find bottom. They did, and I struggled to the shore, keeping the typewriter and the pigeons dry. But the rest of me was drenched to the skin.

The assault troops had cleared a path across the beach through the minefields, and one of the military beachmasters barked oaths at us to keep moving and head for the dunes. So we did, not pausing to look at the bodies lying on either side, where the men had fallen in the assault. At the dunes we found a passage that led inland past a field filled with dead cows, lying on their sides and starting to bloat. The sight and smell of swollen cows, their legs projecting from their grotesque bodies like sticks of wood, would be with us for the rest of the long Normandy battle.

Right then, the problem was to figure out where we were and what to do, and eventually what to write. I assumed Matt would know, but he kept muttering about it being a time to live and not a time to work. I subsequently discovered that he always got into that mood during historic moments, and I subsequently concluded that probably he was right. But there on the morning of D-day my news-agency instincts told me that I should file a dispatch, at least announcing the arrival of our troops in Normandy, along with my own.

We came to a farmhouse, where an elderly Frenchman was standing on the front steps, peeing. I had heard that the French were uninhibited about peeing in public, but the sight struck me as incongruous, with the battle having just swept through the area and the sound of gunfire being clearly heard from not too far away. The old man beckoned us to join him, though I didn't need to pee just at that moment, having done so during the wade ashore. Matt broke into his fluent French and after a brief exchange said that monsieur was inviting us inside for a drink.

Inside, we had our first sip of Calvados, the Normandy applejack which, when our troops discovered it during the weeks ahead, almost cost our side the battle before the authorities put a ban on it. Our eyes were watering when our host brought out bowls of strawberries and cream, following which he produced a photograph album and proceeded to show us pictures of himself, in full military uniform, taking part in the Madagascar campaign of 1895. I could see that Matt was having a hard time keeping a straight face. And when we got outside, monsieur having invited us to return and spend the night with him, we both laughed and said that nobody would believe we had approached Normandy playing the piano and then wound up eating strawberries and cream, and looking at old photographs, and being invited to sleep that night between sheets. Matt and I were the only two men in the entire Allied armies to wind up June 6 in featherbeds.

In the morning, we made our way to Courcelles, where a huge building that had been one of General Rommel's forward headquarters had been commandeered as our first Canadian press camp. On the way there, I remarked to Matthew that we had been ashore for twenty-four hours and hadn't seen the war, except for the bodies lying around. He said that it was always like that but as soon as we found our headquarters and had a base of our own, everything would fall into place. We could then start writing our dispatches — on tissue paper, which would be censored with scissors and then sent off in little capsules harnessed to our pigeons. Since nobody knew more about war corresponding than Matt Halton and nobody knew less about it than me, I took his word for it.

Everybody at Courcelles was glad to see our pigeons, and the correspondents sat down and began to write their dispatches, and the censors set to work with their scissors cutting out the good parts. The tattered remains, looking like player piano rolls, were then stuffed into the capsules, and we went outside into the courtyard to launch the first of the pigeons. They had to be launched in pairs, male and female, for some sexual reason known only to pigeons. So we followed the instructions that came with the package and prayed that the birds would make it across the Channel to their home loft in Southampton, from where the news would be forwarded to a waiting world. Hopefully.

The first pair of birds circled the courtyard four times to gain altitude and then flew straight inland, in what we gauged to be the general direction of Berlin. For sure, they went in the direction of the German lines, as the sound of gunfire told us. We stuffed two more capsules and launched two more pigeons. Same result — they wanted no part of that Channel crossing.

We had thirty-six of these creatures in all, and by the time we had launched thirty-four of them, without a single bird venturing in the direction of the water, it was dawning on us that we would be better off to have refrained from launching them at all and to have eaten them instead. They were fine plump specimens, and the British ration packs, which would be our only approved food in the days ahead, were filled with sawdust sausages and a substance that was labelled "tea" but threatened to remove the enamel from our teeth.

For the launching of the last two pigeons we elected to go back to the beach, a few hundred metres distant, so that our winged couriers could at least see the water over which it was their assigned task to carry our historic messages. The beach was littered with wrecked vehicles, and streams of tanks and trucks were being landed, and cages had been set up for the prisoners who were arriving in impressive numbers. Amidst all this, we loaded up the last two pigeons and launched them into the air. They made one pass over the breakers and then swerved inland, disappearing in the general direction of Germany. Whereupon I shook my fist and, in an utterance that became part of journalistic legend, shouted, "Traitors! Damned traitors!"

It has always bothered me that when they made the movie about D-day, based on Cornelius Ryan's book *The Longest Day*, they depicted the Reuters man uttering that cry in effete English accents, assuming that anybody who worked for Reuters must be a Limey. That was a Canadian cry, and it came from the heart.

That night we slept in a bomb shelter because the Luftwaffe was giving us a pretty good peppering. And the following day, when some of our jeeps arrived, the Germans dropped shrapnel bombs on them, flattening most of the tires and putting a jagged hole in Lionel Shapiro's tin hat, which was on the seat of one of them. Shapiro wore that scarred helmet with pride for the rest of the war and was so inspired by it that he subsequently wrote a book called *The Sixth of June*, which made him a million dollars and was turned into a movie starring Robert Taylor.

By now we had wireless communications and our dispatches were getting out, and soon messages started coming back from Cole in London that I was writing great stuff and that my future, together with that of Reuters, was secure. So encouraged was I that when, a week later, we moved our press camp to a chateau in Beny-sur-Mer and the Germans drew a bead on it with their artillery — setting the place on fire and causing us to jump out the windows for our lives — I put in an expense account reporting complete loss of kit.

Walters eventually paid the whole thing with only one whimper: he deducted the value of a set of gold cuff links I had listed, ruling that nobody should have taken gold cuff links into the Normandy beachhead in the first place.

Matt Halton continued to be fascinated by my lack of knowledge of military matters, and I soaked up as much as I could from him and the others, all of whom had covered the Italian campaign. As the days passed, we were joined by other correspondents who had missed the "draw" for D-day, and we covered the battles that led up to the eventual capture of Caen, which was supposed to have fallen in the initial assault. Matt did one of his most colourful broadcasts on the battle for Carpiquet airport, including a countdown to the artillery barrage and a description of the attack. He kept repeating it over and over to the rest of us, stepping up the tempo each time, until a colleague suggested that if Halton kept refighting the battle of Carpiquet, one day he was going to get killed in it.

Each night, we would decide where we were going the next day to get near the fighting. As Matt would put it, "We leave at sparrow fart, and we will face death." He really did talk like that. Between his own dramatizations, he would recite Shakespeare or Keats, especially the lines from "Ode to a Nightingale" that go: "Darkling, I listen, and for many a time, I have been half in love with easeful death." He would repeat the words "Darkling, I listen" over and over again with awe, as though in wonderment that anybody could write better stuff than he himself.

Ever since those days, whenever I see broadcasters being frazzled by the complex technicalities of their trade, I think of Matt Halton, and especially of the battle to capture two villages named Gruchy and Buron, on the approaches to Caen. A series of random attacks had failed, and when a set-piece operation was planned, Halton went forward with his bulky, spring-wound 78-rpm disc recorder, thus installing himself on the start line of an advance that would take the infantry across open fields in the face of heavy German fire — from automatic weapons, artillery, and mortars, with the added hazard of mines buried in the soft Normandy loam. It was the kind of assault that infantrymen have nightmares about and the kind that correspondents avoid, with their priceless option of going where they choose to go. Only the combat photographers had no such option, because they were regular soldiers. That is why so many of them became casualties.

The theory of the correspondents was that being in the heat of an all-out military action doesn't help you to write about it, because the infantryman's view of things is so narrow and because the chance of witnessing classic acts of heroism, the stuff of combat journalism, is so slight. It is better to do it afterwards by interviewing survivors and getting details like home towns and names, which are difficult to obtain when the action is hot. One army photographer, Captain Frank Duberville, who took the classic pictures of the Canadian assault landings at Bernières-sur-Mer on D-day (the pictures that have appeared in anthologies ever since) got a rocket from his bosses in London because the film wasn't accompanied by captions giving the names and home towns of the soldiers shown in action.

However, Halton wanted the sounds of battle, and the only way to get them was to be there. Up before dawn for the attack on Gruchy and Buron, he recorded the cacophony of the opening barrage by Canadian artillery, the response of the German guns, the whistling explosions of incoming shells, the shouted commands to attack, and the staccato firing of automatic weapons as the troops advanced in the fashion of World War I.

Halton advanced part way with the troops, winding his recorder which was carried by his soundman, Art Holmes. When the German mortars drew a bead on him, he dived into a narrow gulley, where for ten minutes he was in the eye of a firestorm, unable to make any movement except to keep winding the recorder and watch the metal stylus carve the sounds into the wax. The mortaring ceased when the Canadian troops overran the German positions, at the cost of more killed and wounded than they had suffered on D-day, and Halton came back across the field, where I, having watched the proceedings from a nearby orchard, met him and asked him why he looked so exultant.

He glowed. "I have just recorded the sounds of battle as they have never been recorded before! The SOUNDS of BATTLE!"

We drove back to the press camp, where Matt set up the recorder to play back the sounds. And there was nothing on the disc. Nothing. The machine had malfunctioned and there had been no link between the microphone and the stylus. Soundman Holmes was mortified and apologized to Halton, who trembled for a moment in his disappointment and then said, "Well, I suppose we shall just go again."

So he went — again and again. But none of the sounds he captured ever matched the ones he had lost, though they might have done if he had had the recorder with him the day the Allied bombers dropped their loads on our own troops, along the Falaise road. The use of heavy bombers in close support of infantry was an experiment that failed so spectacularly it was never tried again. The Polish armoured division bore the brunt of the blockbusters, and this very nearly impelled those gallant warriors to turn their tanks round and use them on the Allies (which, in the light of the sell-out of Poland after the war, they must have wished devoutly that they had). Halton was caught in that bombing and took refuge in a gravel pit, along with several fellow correspondents. When they returned, dishevelled and coated with mud, their dispatches reflected so much of the infantrymen's bile about birdmen that the censors suppressed the lot.

The immediacy and reality of Halton's battlefield broadcasts was something new in electronic journalism, and they served to stimulate the war effort, a goal which the rest of us pursued without question. Halton's advantages were his instinct for the theatrical show-business aspect of broadcasting and his hatred of Nazi Germany, born of a deep understanding of its meaning, which few of his colleagues possessed. The best of his battlefield work has been played and replayed through the intervening years, and it retains a freshness and vitality unmatched by any other accounts of war. It was propaganda — everything done by all of us was propaganda, though we might not have admitted it or even realized it at the time. Halton became the first of the great media celebrities. When summoned home to help with the sale of victory bonds, he was a bigger box-office draw than Billy Bishop.

In terms of bravery, he would admit, as all of us would, that we could not compare ourselves to the infantry, because we took our combat experiences in self-administered doses. On one of these occasions, the red-headed Ralph Allen and I went forward to visit a corridor that had been driven into the German lines beyond the Caen-Bayeux road at a place called Cheux. Allen was the star correspondent for the Toronto *Globe and Mail*, a broody genius not given to emoting, except through his writings. We arrived at the precise moment of withdrawal from the corridor under a heavy German counterattack, and it was my first experience of our troops running the wrong way.

The Germans were using a new weapon called a Moaning Minnie, a mortar rocket with a siren on it that wailed as it came at you, the object being to induce paralysis at the receiving end. We took about twenty salvos of these, huddled behind a low stone wall, and after ten minutes Allen, a brave but not foolhardy man, stuck his right leg out from behind the wall and shouted, "All right, you sons of bitches, take that leg and leave me the rest!" He kept his leg outstretched until the mortaring ceased, when we joined the troops in running for it, helping with the wounded along the way.

Unlike the soldiers, we dined in comfort that night. Allen won $100 in the press camp crap game, and we dubbed ourselves the Cheux Cheux Babies and marked it all down to high adventure.

4/A Touch of Hemingway

Canadians always have been good at war and have given splendid accounts of themselves on the battlefield, even though the homeland is one of the few places on the face of the earth that lacks the scars of armed combat. Our hallowed battle places exist in other lands, on other continents, where we have fought the foe and dreamed of home and told ourselves that we were standing on guard.

And many died — vast cemeteries are full of their graves, neatly marked and covered with flowers, conveying none of the horror of bodies strewn about or blown apart, or bloated in stinking ditches amid the grinding of the tank treads and the fumes of the exhausts. We gave a hand to the wounded and took down their names, and we recorded the exploits of the dead but ignored their sprawled corpses. These men had ceased to exist, except for the people far away at home who would be getting the telegrams and who must never know the way they looked or how they died, only why, in the cause of freedom, which is what we wrote about in our dispatches.

Combat correspondents were as much a part of the war effort as the men with the guns, or those in ships and planes and munitions factories — we were the cheerleaders, the morale boosters, filling in the details from the front to go with the "big picture" written in hotel rooms from headquarters briefings. Usually, the soldiers were glad to see us, eager for the chance of a name in the paper or even a mention of the unit in action, though the censors always took that out. And when the Black Watch of Montreal attacked along the Falaise road in the breakout from Normandy and the entire regiment was cut to pieces, with only a handful of stragglers surviving, we were not allowed to report what regiment it was.

The boys from the farms were the best infantrymen — best to be with, best to talk to, best scroungers and best fighters, skilled at crawling on their bellies. They were from New Brunswick and

Nova Scotia and Quebec and Ontario and the prairies, and they had battlefield smarts in their bones. It was as rural people that we fought our wars and cared for our guns and kept our machines running with baling wire and parts acquired by stealth in the dark of night. It was country soldiers who could come off a battlefield with their helmets filled with eggs and then brew up American coffee pinched from the Yank unit on the flank.

Canadians fought in the Second War in British uniforms, with British weapons, and under a British command structure, eating British rations and drinking British tea and usually gagging on British cigarettes. They loved Britain but had no affection for the British soldier, nor did they have much time for the Americans, and they would as soon have fought the Australians as the Germans. The Germans were respected, and tales of heroism at the front usually involved the fanatical bravery of young German soldiers, fighting on with their limbs blown off, with weapons far superior to our own. Canadian fighting soldiers, when they thought about it at all, regarded themselves and the Germans on a par, with everybody else somewhere below in fighting skills, and if they gave an edge, it would be to the Germans.

In their combat attitudes, Canadians were more sensible than the Americans and less sensible than the British. The soldiers themselves developed distinctly Canadian airs and even walked in a distinctively Canadian way, not as tight-assed as the British nor as loose-limbed as the Americans. Among Canadian officers, though, the British mode prevailed in the field, just as it did in the air force and the navy, where clipped accents were developed which dogged their users at home for the rest of their lives. Our politicians, meanwhile, fought constantly with their British counterparts and got on best with the Americans — a foretaste of Canada's postwar fortunes and fate.

After Hong Kong and Dieppe, most of our Second War battles were victories, but we came out of them without heroes, preferring to look up to other leaders with the bigger buildups, like Churchill and Roosevelt and Eisenhower and Montgomery and Alexander. Yet it can be said that the Canadian identity, as we know it, came out of the two world wars. Certainly, the wars did wonders for the Canadian sense of humour.

The telling of funny stories about war is in a sense an obscenity, since it can make war sound attractive to those who haven't experienced it, which would be criminal. It has been argued that romanticizing war has assured, through the ages, that succeeding generations indulge in it, to relieve boredom and to stimulate the senses and unburden the masculine urge for blood sports and violence. Soldiers don't talk much about war, even when they gather in one another's company. We storytellers are the worst offenders, excepting those few who catch the feel of death and convey something of it to the uninitiated and the unblooded. Few soldiers understood the larger picture during the fighting, and most history books cause war veterans to scratch their heads in puzzlement. Soldiers remember that the enemy fought damn well (or fucking good, in the language they used) especially if it was the Germans, and that is what made their own Canadian combat medals mean something. It was the same against the Japanese in the Pacific and against the Chinese in Korea.

The "liberation" battles, as we called them, meant more to us than they did to the French — over whose farms, towns, and cities we were fighting — and for most of whom the war had ended, in the combat sense, in 1940. Today, no trace of our war can be seen in Normandy, except for the parts that have been preserved as tourist traps like Omaha Beach, and the only French monuments or plaques you now find are those from the First World War.

But there are the cemeteries, ours and the Germans'; and my wife found it offensive when on a trip to Europe, long after the war, I insisted we visit the German burying ground on the road from Caen to Bayeux and sign the visitors' book in memory of the young men who had fought so fiercely. There were no flowers on these black-crossed graves, and mine was the only signature in the book that was not German — mostly parents, brothers, and sisters of the fallen.

When we visited the Canadian cemetery at Bretteville-sur-Orne, where four thousand crosses stand over the graves of those who fell along the road from Caen to Falaise, I asked my seventeen-year-old daughter Lucinda to notice the ages of the dead soldiers and to remember that they were not the *old* men she had seen in Remembrance Day parades at home. They were kids like her, and they came to Europe carrying packsacks the way young Canadians did today, with Canada flashes on their shoulders, but without the freedom to go where they pleased. They went where they were told and they fought as they were told, and it was because of them that we were able to travel freely today.

When we entered that vast cemetery, Lucinda could not believe the number of crosses, and she asked in all innocence what so many Canadians had been doing there and what the purpose of it was. When I said it was to fight Nazism and the idea that the Germans were the master race, she could not take it in, because the Germans were now our friends and obviously no more evil than anybody else. I said it was Hitler, and she had learned about him, as she had about Churchill and Roosevelt and Stalin, but she had not been told in school that the Canadians had any direct part in the fighting, so how did it come that so many Canadians had been here?

I realized that any account I could give of the motives that brought us here would not satisfy her, though it had satisfied us at the time. So I fell silent and invited her to look at the crosses, and the first one we came to marked the grave of a soldier who had been seventeen years old when he was killed; underneath his name and the date and place of his death was carved this message: "Well done, son. Mummy and Daddy." Tears welled in my eyes, and I had to turn away to regain composure, and Lucinda asked me what would ever cause parents to say that about the death of their son. It was the mood of the time, I told her, people felt that way. Driving away from the cemetery, I reflected that one of the reasons people had felt that way was that we who reported on the war had glorified it and made ourselves part of the propaganda apparatus required for the waging of total war.

I never did get the meaning of it through to my daughter, and I do not suppose members of her generation, or succeeding generations, will ever grasp it or care about it. In other ages, wars succeeded one another, and each generation got its fill. Now, because of the nuclear balance of terror, we have people in their fifties who have never been "summoned to the colours," whose heroism has never been tested, medals never won nor worn. Thus blessed, it is perhaps forgivable to recall the funny side of war before the last of us who recall anything about it are gone.

We had been in the beachhead for what seemed like years when word came that the troops of General George Patton had broken out from the American side and were swarming southward along the coast in the direction of Brittany, at the start of a giant sweep that would carry them eastward to Paris and points beyond.

"Let us," said Matthew, "go motoring."

So he took a jeep and a driver, and I took a jeep and a conducting officer named William Cornforth, and away we went. Captain Cornforth was a former assistant manager of the Chateau Frontenac Hotel in Quebec City, and besides speaking fluent French he was the best scrounger in the Canadian army. Which is to say there was nothing he couldn't produce if you gave him time and asked no questions.

Cornforth had lost everything in the burning of our chateau, one of the German shells having entered his bedroom window, passed across his bed, and exploded in the wall closet where all his clothes and loot were neatly stashed. The impact turned his bed completely over and threw him out of the second storey window stark naked; and such was his state of shock at this rude awakening that he tried to climb back up the wall to recover his effects — changing his mind only when another shell arrived and blew a segment of the wall out of his hand. Two days later, by begging, stealing, looting, and pillaging, he was the best-equipped officer in the beachhead.

Armed with Cornforth, our two-jeep motorcade rolled merrily westward through the town of Bayeux, where we stopped for a snack at the Lion d'Or Hotel and had some ripe camembert and fresh fruit and red wine, with Matt giving the instructions.

"First," he said, "put a bit of the cheese into your mouth and lay it on your tongue."

Pause for effect.

"Now," his voice took on an almost conspiratorial tone, "take a bit of the pear and let the juice flow around your mouth."

Done.

"Now, quickly, a sip of wine!"

Awed silence as we swilled the mixture around and let it slip down into our gullets.

"Never," marvelled Halton, "never let the peasants know how good is the wine with the cheese and the pear."

We drove for many kilometres through battle-shattered villages and towns until finally we came to countryside that had not been blasted and we were on Patton's trail. There were live cows in the fields, houses that still had their roofs on, and in some of the villages there were men and women waving bouquets and little boys shouting "Cigarette pour papa" and "You jig-a-jig my sister?"

It was the start of our days as liberators, and when we came to the town of Granville-sur-Mer we saw, for the first time, big hotels and restaurants and shops. We held a counsel in the main square, in the course of which Matt elected to press on for Mont St. Michel, while Cornforth and I decided to stay in Granville for the night. We agreed to meet in Mont St. Michel the following day, though I had not the faintest idea where or what the place might be.

Having found rooms in the biggest of the beachside hotels, Cornforth and I set off to explore the town, which had been vacated by the Germans only the night before. With wonderment we encountered bars that were dispensing liqueurs, sweet stuff like Creme de Cacao, which seemed a nice change from the Calvados that enabled you to appear sober, but denied you the use of your legs.

Midway through the evening we spotted a long lineup of American GIs, and upon asking what it was that they were lined up for, we were informed that this was the local public house — the first to be encountered by the Allied troops on the breakout from the beachhead. Doubtless there had been what my father used to call "houses of ill perfume" in the beachhead towns as well, but they had all been blown to smithereens or taken over by the military police, and we had heard of none that was open for business. This one obviously was, so out of curiosity we went to the head of the line, observing in the process that quite a few of Patton's spearhead troops had decided to spear something more enticing than the retreating Germans.

They were letting the soldiers in three by three, at two-minute intervals. When the door opened, Cornforth shouted something in French that caught the ear of the madame, whereupon she beckoned us inside, to the shouted protests of the American soldiers waiting in line. Cornforth was the first French-speaking military man to appear in Granville, and madame was so excited to find somebody who could tell her what was going on that she unleashed a flurry of French on him, whereupon Bill turned to me and said, "She wants to have a chat."

"Great," said I, "I'll wait."

"No," said Bill, "she wants to know if you will take over the cash register while we have some tea and talk."

"Certainly," said I, "provided she tells me how to go about it."

Another flurry of French and Bill translated. "There are three girls here, and madame would like us to know that they saw the

Germans off only last night and it was a big party and the girls are quite tired."

Looking at them, I could see they were. One of them was tall and thin, and the second was short and thin, and the third was medium-sized and very pale. Their smiles seemed forced, and I remember that their slippers were frayed.

Madame pointed to three buttons on the desk beside the cash register. "Each button rings a bell in one of the rooms," Cornforth translated.

"Deux minutes," said madame.

"They only get two minutes each," explained Cornforth.

"No suck," ordered madame.

Cornforth blushed. "No funny business. Straight fucking."

"Got it," said I.

As she and Cornforth headed for a corner of the parlour I saw her whisper to him, and he shouted, "One more thing. The prices go up fifty percent every half hour."

I turned to my task. Let them in three at a time. Assign them to the girls and watch them go upstairs. In two minutes, ring the bells. See that they come downstairs without delay. Admit three more. Raise the prices every half hour.

Thus it was that I got to run the cash register in a whorehouse, a matter that has given me considerable cause for boast ever since. And when I think of grace under pressure, and courage in the face of challenge, I think of those three frail Frenchwomen who must have accommodated at least thirty Germans each the night before and were now taking on even more Americans apiece than that. And apart from the fact that they were getting paler, they seemed to go on and on. I wondered if it wouldn't have been more humane had they stayed in the bedrooms without having to make all those trips up and down the stairs, but evidently that was the custom and they did not complain until about six price increases later, when their knees seemed to be buckling — at least, the tall one's did.

It must have been about four o'clock in the morning when there was a loud pounding on the door and it turned out to be the U.S. military police. When I answered, the lineup seemed to be as long as ever, and there were shouts of protest when the police announced they were closing the place. They did, too. There were three of them, and when they came in they went upstairs with the girls and they stayed longer than two minutes, because I didn't know whether to ring the bells or not. When they came downstairs the girls looked really pooped and madame agreed that, while the police had no authority to shut her shop, the girls had had enough and she proposed that we all have some breakfast.

So we had a big feed of bacon and eggs, and Bill and I slept virtuously in the parlour for the rest of the night, the first men ever to pass a night in that establishment without sampling its wares.

The following day, we set off for Mont St. Michel. If you don't feel like a pilgrim on your way to Mont St. Michel, you will when you get your first sight of the place, which for us was a quickly caught glimpse through a gap between two cottages on the coastal road driving south from Granville to Arromanches. I first thought it was some sort of mirage, or something flicking in my imagination, inspired by Walt Disney or his mentor and architectural role model, mad King Ludwig of Bavaria. Then it became visible again, and it remained in sight for almost all of the drive, which carried us in a great loop southward and finally swung us onto the long causeway, which twice a day in those days was engulfed by tides almost as high as those in the Bay of Fundy.

Through the centuries, hundreds of thousands of the curious and devout have made this journey, and Henry Adams has classed Mont St. Michel with Chartres Cathedral as the greatest architectural wonder of Europe. In our ignorance, we didn't realize our luck in having the Mont to ourselves in the height of summer, a time when it would normally be clogged with tourists. We were, without knowing it, among the few to see it serene and quiet in July for perhaps the only time in its ten centuries of existence.

The causeway was deserted, the Germans having crossed it for the last time three days before in evacuating the Mont, which they had used as a rest area, not bothering to erect fortifications of any kind. As the Allies had refrained from bombing it, everything that represented the last six hundred years of its building still stood atop the great rock, the ramparts spilling down its sides to the tiled rooftops of the houses huddled inside the wall at the base.

We parked our jeep above the high-tide mark and walked through the gates onto the steep, cobbled main street of the walled town, the metal plates on our boots sending echoes among the ancient buildings. Souvenir shops were on every side, but they were shuttered and locked. Not a soul did we see, not a sound did we hear except for our own footsteps. Our reverie was marred only by the thought that maybe the Germans had booby-trapped the place or left a sniper or two behind.

We had an appointment with Halton, but there was no knowing where he was in the vast spiral of stone. Though one could imagine him climbing to the topmost spire and standing there spouting Keats, or words of defiance at the Nazis, or shouts of encouragement and affection to the French.

As it turned out, he was not far away and he was doing none of those things. Our upward passage through the narrow street brought us to a restaurant, the Hotel Poulard, outside which was parked a huge open-topped touring car filled with guns of all sizes. It was one of those big Mercedes staff cars that we had seen in propaganda pictures during the thirties, and it was painted in the camouflage pattern which to our eyes gave everything German a sinister look (I have never discovered whether our paint jobs had the same effect on them).

Was this an enemy general on the lam? Or one who had been left behind? The car blocked the road to an extent that we had to clamber over its flaring fenders to get by. We looked in wonderment at the machine guns and rifles and anti-tank bazookas and pistols that were stacked on the seats and on the floor, together with belts of ammunition and loose bullets strewn around. Never having held a gun in my life, much less fired anything beyond a .22 in the cadet corps, I couldn't be sure what make the weapons were, but it seemed to me that they were German — they were too nicely finished to be the kind of junk our soldiers carried. Obviously, whoever had this car, friend or foe, was a person of some consequence.

From inside the restaurant, whose windows proclaimed that it was the home of the most famous omelettes in France, came the sounds of roistering. So we went in, and there we found Matthew seated at a big round table with a group of American correspondents. He hailed us and made the introductions. Ernest Hemingway. Robert Capa.

I blinked. Hemingway?

He and Halton had, I knew, been colleagues years before on the Toronto *Star*, and they had been together in Spain. I had heard Matthew speak of *The Sun Also Rises* as the book he admired most, the one he would rather have written than any other, and I would have expected such an idol as its author to be treated with awed reverence. But as soon as we took a place at the table and the conversation resumed, Halton and Hemingway were raising their voices at one another.

What had happened, as we pieced things together later, was that Halton had told Hemingway of his admiration for his works, and while Hemingway was basking in the glow of appreciation (aided by the warmth of the cognac the Germans had left behind) Halton had added that there was just one thing he didn't think Hemingway handled very well in his books, and that was fucking. Seeing Hemingway's annoyance, Halton had then tried to mollify him by saying it wasn't that Hemingway's passages on fucking were bad, it was just that they weren't up to the standard of the rest of his writing, and maybe it was because Hemingway hadn't done as much of it as he had of the other things he wrote about.

This exchange had taken place just before our arrival, which was why we found ourselves witnessing the spectacle of Hemingway banging his fist on the heavy oak table, causing the omelettes to quiver and jiggle in their pewter plates, while he shouted, "Nobody knows more about fucking than I do! And nobody writes about fucking like I do! And any fucker who fucking well says I can't write about fucking is a fucking liar. And you, Halton, are full of shit!"

At this point, Hemingway and a companion stalked out of the restaurant, threw themselves into the open car full of guns, and roared away over the cobblestones and out of the gate, and we saw them no more.

We asked the others what Hemingway, as an unarmed war correspondent, was doing in an open car with all those guns. Apparently he and General Patton were old friends, and when Patton's troops captured the staff car from the Germans, the general ordered it turned over to Hemingway, who was to have anything he wanted. What Hemingway wanted was weaponry and ammunition, for it was his declared intention to get out in front of Patton's spearhead and put his guns in the hands of French resistance fighters. This was a variation of Halton's thesis about it being a time to live, not a time to work, and it seemed a suicidal project at best and sheer bluster at worst. We shook our heads, and Halton guided us to our hotel, where we were the only guests.

"Matt," I said, "don't you think you were kind of rough on Hemingway, especially since you think so much of his work?"

"That's just it," said Halton. "That's just it. A man who writes so well about everything else should be able to write better about THAT!"

It was weeks later that we learned that when Patton's spearheads rolled through Chartres on their way to Paris, they were greeted in the shadow of the great cathedral by the best-armed resistance unit in all of France. And there at their head was Hemingway, aflame with the grape and laughing like a billygoat.

We never did hear what happened to the car.

5/Liberating Europe, along with the Monarch, Winston, and Monty

Halton went off for a week to assist in the liberation of "his" Paris, but the rest of us missed out on that because the Americans didn't want to share it with anybody except the French, and especially not with the armies under Field Marshal Montgomery, which included ours. During the great pursuit across Europe, the Canadians got most of the dirty mop-up jobs along the Channel coast, involving prolonged sieges. But some important places fell with scarcely a struggle, and one of them was Rouen, which I entered with Matt Halton and Bill Cornforth.

As liberators, Matt and Bill were especially good companions because they could speak French. And as Matt was a charmer and Bill a scrounger, we were sure to make the most of the gratitude of the inhabitants — except those whose homes had been blown to rubble in the liberating process, which tended to moderate their enthusiasm. Our troops were in hot pursuit of the fleeing Germans and so many places were freed so fast that the residents, who were huddled in their cellars and shelters, often didn't know the war had passed by until somebody gave them the word. When they emerged into the daylight, they found only a rearguard, among whom were the war correspondents who, having no military duties, were free to give their full attention to the human side of liberating.

I developed a kind of palms-up wave, copied from Queen Elizabeth on her visit to Canada in 1939. Cornforth favoured a prizefighter's handclasp above the head, and Halton blew kisses. Thus we came into Rouen just as the people were pouring out onto the streets and into the vast expanse around the cathedral, whose lacework spire had looked down on the burning of Joan of Arc. Inching the jeep forward, we accepted the plaudits of the multitude, while Halton explained that we had to press on to the front, where possible death awaited. But finally it became impossible to move forward, and several burly men lifted us bodily from the jeep and carried us inside a bistro to join the liberation revels there.

A huge round table had been set up, and big red-faced men were sitting around it, drinking and singing. The most massive of them introduced himself as the president of the Rouen Butchers' Association, explaining that these were his fellow butchers gathered for the celebration. We agreed to join them for a drink, not realizing that this meant joining each of them individually — and there were twenty-six butchers round that table. After several good hookers of a better class of cognac than we were used to (the butchers had kept bottles hidden away throughout the occupation), the president rose to make a speech of welcome, in the course of which he said that the Canadians were especially welcome in Rouen because in 1937 the city had been honoured by a visit from Yvon Robert, the world-champion wrestler from Montreal, whose performance in the local ring was still warmly remembered by the thousands who had packed the arena to see him.

"We honour," he said, "the land of the great Robert!"

We drained our glasses to the bottom, whereupon they were promptly refilled, and Cornforth rose to his feet to make the response in his best Quebec French.

"A special surprise!" he said, or I think that's what he said, my knowledge of our other maternal language being imprecise. He rattled off a few more words and then pointed his finger at me, shouting, "Vive Robert!"

At this, the butchers rose as one and gave a mighty cheer, draining their glasses, while Cornforth pulled me to my feet and told me to acknowledge the applause.

"What the hell did you say?" I hissed.

"I told them it was strange they didn't recognize the champion and that you were Yvon Robert, and how glad you were to be back. Take another bow."

I flexed my muscles and stuck out my chest and, with my well-known reticence, climbed up on my chair so that they could get a better look at my superb physique.

The president of the butchers' association was transported and jumped up on the table.

"We hail the return of Robert!" (Cornforth translated and I waved.) "And I inform Robert that I, the amateur wrestling champion of northern France, would be honoured if the great Robert would wrestle with me in an exhibition."

"He wants you to rassle," mumbled Cornforth. "You'd better take him on. Bow some more."

I bowed and everyone rose, and we were swept out through the door into the crowded street, where the president climbed into our jeep, and from the front seat — in a voice that shook the cathedral steeple — announced to the mob that Robert had returned and that we were proceeding to the arena where as a special added attraction of Liberation Day, he and Robert would wrestle an exhibition, without charge.

Through the streets of Rouen we went, picking up people along the way, and by the time we got to the arena there must have been three or four thousand of them milling around. To my considerable horror, I realized that there was a ring set up in the middle of the big hall and chairs all around, which soon became filled with cheering townspeople. It didn't do much for my morale that they were chanting, "Robert! Robert!" They were on Robert's side all right, but he was far away and I had only seen him wrestle a couple of times and I doubted I could remember his moves, let alone duplicate them.

Cornforth agreed to be the referee, and that was my first piece of luck. My second was that the president was pissed to the gills. And my third was that I myself was feeling no pain, even before the president laid his horny hands on me.

Cornforth blew the whistle and the president and I closed with one another, and he gave a bearhug that squeezed some of the cognac out of me, at both ends. I blew my breath in his face but he didn't flinch, and the only thing I could think of doing was to fall on my back, which meant bringing the president down on top of me. Momentary unconsciousness followed, and when I recovered my senses the president was lying on the canvas beside me, a look of affection in his eyes. Cornforth leaned over and whispered that the president wanted to know if I was all right.

"No," I gasped.

Cornforth caught the president's eye and shook his head.

The president lay still.

I lay stiller.

The crowd was hushed. Cornforth declared the bout a draw, and an enormous cheer filled the hall. The president and I then took our bows, and the butchers gave us a guard of honour to escort us out of the arena, with Halton mumbling something that sounded like "It's magnificent, but it's not war."

The butchers insisted that we should visit the homes of each of them in turn, which to the best of my recollection we did, calling in at a couple of slaughter houses on the way, at one of which they filled my tin hat with tripe, a prized delicacy of the region. We wound up at the home of the president, where he insisted we should be his honoured guests; and after I had climbed into bed, I looked up and there was the president with a giant set of iron dumbbells which he laid reverently on the bed beside me, "in case Robert should want to exercise during the night." It was at that moment that he made out a card declaring me to be honorary president for life of the Rouen Butchers' Association, an office that I have filled with satisfaction, if not distinction, ever since.

As we drew near Germany, some men of even greater distinction arrived. During the closing stages of the war in Europe, the "theatre" as it was called was visited first by The Monarch and then by Winston Churchill. Word that King George VI was coming caused a considerable stir among the British and Canadians who were bogged down in Holland, and nobody rose to the occasion more valiantly than the commandant of our press camp in Eindhoven, Colonel William "Tug" Warrener.

The war correspondents were a source of constant despair for Warrener because of their resistance to discipline, and especially because of their lack of military bearing and the carelessness of their dress. When he called his charges together to announce the impending arrival of the King, he said he was going to whip the reporters into a unit of which he and the free world could be proud. Uniforms would be cleaned and pressed, and new gaiters would be issued, and boots would be polished, and haircuts and shaves would be inflicted, and we would learn to stand in line at attention, and at the airport we would hold our positions to be inspected by The Monarch if he chose to approach us, and the first man who broke ranks or sought to interview The Monarch would be gunned down on the spot.

There was a lot of grumbling, but on the morning of the King's arrival Warrener looked us over and pronounced that God knew he had done his best, and we all proceeded to the airport where a roped-off compound had been prepared for the press. Warrener stood in front of the column, baton tucked under his arm, head held high, chin outthrust as the royal DC-3 rolled to a stop. The door of the aircraft swung open, the steps dropped into place, and King George VI descended on the soil of liberated Europe for the first time.

Warrener saluted smartly, and as he did so Walter Cronkite of United Press vaulted over the rope barrier and made a dash for the King. Cronkite was known to be fearless, having dropped into Holland by parachute to cover the Arnhem operation, so I followed and so did everybody else, and poor Warrener was left rooted to the spot, uttering shouts of "Scum!" and "Back, you bastards!" while we swarmed around King George and bombarded him with questions. Nothing like this had ever happened to the King before, and he seemed both amused and bemused, lost for words amid the din. He stammered something, but nobody could make out what it was, so we never did get a royal quote.

We did get rid of Colonel Warrener, though. Babbling incoherently, he had to be led away. We saw him no more and went back to dressing like the ragtail bunch we were, and Cronkite and I got through the Dutch winter without freezing to death, aided by occasional warming visits to Brussels.

Spit and polish didn't matter much for Churchill's visit, because of his preference for the siren suit that made him look like a walking barrage balloon. Our forces had just completed the crossing of the Rhine, and Churchill's battlefield odyssey was to begin at the Canadian army headquarters of General H. D. G. Crerar, who had fifteen divisions under his command at the time, including the cream of the British army. (It was a source of anguish for British correspondents that they had to file dispatches datelined "with the First Canadian Army" when they were writing about the exploits of their own troops, but the Canadians regarded this as sweet revenge for all the years they had been described as Brits.)

Crerar's immediate superior was Field Marshal Sir Bernard Montgomery, and Monty sent word ahead that whatever happened, there was to be no liquor in Churchill's vicinity. Crerar's staff chose to spike the order and arranged a small bar in a room through which Churchill would have to pass on his way to the map room, where he was to get a briefing. But when Montgomery (who was leading the early morning parade to the map room) spotted the bar, he reached in and slammed the door shut. Trouble was, just before Monty slammed the door, Churchill caught a glimpse of the bar.

Winston Churchill never was one to enjoy early rising, so he was in a surly mood anyway, and the fact that Montgomery, the teetotaller, had denied him the chance of an eye opener threw him into a sullen rage, which lasted throughout the briefing and during the morning's tour of gun emplacements and battlefields. Lunch was offered at the headquarters of General Guy Simonds in the Hochwald Forest. It was not for nothing that Simonds was regarded as the keenest of the Canadian general officers. Quickly perceiving Churchill's mood, he told one of his junior officers to take one of the big tin tea mugs, fill it with whisky, and place it in front of Churchill without comment. This was done, and when Churchill took a sip of what looked like tea, his eyes brightened on the spot and he took two more long draughts. The effect was that of the sun breaking through dark clouds, and there was a magic change in the mood, with Churchill becoming more and more ebullient as the lunch proceeded.

He granted us a press conference, and when Montgomery tried to cut in, Churchill waved him off. Then the motorcade proceeded in the direction of the Rhine, with cheering troops lining the roadsides and Churchill giving them his V-sign. That's not all he gave them, though. Having had so much to drink, the great man had to have a leak. In fact, he had to have one every twenty minutes, which meant stopping the motorcade while he alighted from the staff car and anointed the nearest ditch, to the delight of the soldiers looking on, all of whom craned for a look at the great man's vitals, while Montgomery fumed and snorted.

Monty must have known that Churchill was getting stimulants from somebody, but Simonds's battle plan carried the day. With wondrous symbolism, the concrete dragon's teeth of the Siegfried Line were peed upon, and from the amphibious vehicle that carried him across the water, Winston Churchill pissed into the Rhine.

Five years had passed since Hitler did his victory dance in the Forest of Compiègne on the body of prostrate France. But, to me, Churchill's victory gesture seemed much the more satisfying of the two.

6/Cleaning Up with Cronkite

The Russians waited for three weeks after they captured Berlin before giving the Allies the high sign to come on in. Then in we went, making a beeline for Hitler's shattered marble chancellery and for his bunker where, with the British historian Major H. R. Trevor-Roper, we dug up the ground around the entrance, looking for pieces of Hitler's bones or any evidence of what had happened to him. According to the Russian version, his body had been burned following his suicide, but we found nothing. We did find another exit from the bunker, and when I wrote about it as a possible escape route for Hitler it fetched a denunciation from my press colleagues, led by Chapman Pincher of the London *Daily Express*. To this day, I have never fully believed the accepted story of Hitler's end, though Trevor-Roper certified it to be true at the time.

Berlin was the most ruined city we had seen since Caen, of which it had been said that there was so much rubble that even the rubble had rubble on it. To all the damage caused by the bombings was added the damage caused by shellfire, which isn't the same thing at all, and because the buildings of Berlin had been so massive, its ruins had an awful majesty unmatched by the remains of other cities.

We were forbidden to fraternize with the Germans, so our human contacts were entirely with the British, French, and Russian troops, the most notable thing about the Russians being their apparent disinterest in anything around them except the prospect of grabbing everything in Germany that they could load onto their trucks and take back home. They had uniforms of every description and vehicles that were hitched one to another like the old Bennett buggies of the Depression. It wasn't unusual to see one lorry towing four others, each of them loaded to the gunwales with household furnishings of every kind.

There was no "East" or "West" Berlin at the time, and only the beginnings of zones of occupation, so we could go wherever we liked. But the main attraction was the chancellery, most of which was still standing, though the Soviet shells had blown it full of holes and broken the brown marble walls into slabs and splinters. Some of the splinters we took as souvenirs, along with gold-flecked pieces of tile from the floor, and we scooped up German medals that were piled in a corner of what had been Hitler's office. We sat at what had been his desk and gave mock Nazi salutes, and we squatted on what had been his personal toilet, which no longer flushed.

Our press headquarters was the Hotel Am Zoo on the Kurfurstendamm, and when I asked one Sunday about the Berlin zoo itself, I was told it could be visited, though there wasn't much to see. Hitler's Germans were ahead of the world in many things besides synthetic fabrics, autobahns, and Volkswagens, and one of them was the Berlin zoo, which was the first in the world to abolish iron bars and cages for the animals, substituting moats and giving an impression that the animals were in their natural habitat.

I went there with Basil Gingell of the Exchange Telegraph Agency of London, a gentle Englishman who had commandeered a Mercedes sedan in which he and I were able to drive about Berlin. The zoo was a forlorn-looking place and seemed to be devoid of people and animals, but finally we sighted, among some trees, the biggest elephant either of us had ever seen. He approached the edge of the moat opposite us, looking so very sad and so very lonely that I pulled a mouth organ out of my pocket to play him a tune, something I had often done for cows at home.

No sooner had I played the first notes — I think it was "Darling Nelly Gray," though I can't be sure as some people say everything I play sounds like "Darling Nelly Gray" — than the elephant proceeded to develop the largest erection imaginable. Perhaps erection is not the right word, for this enormous tube drooped lower and lower until it touched the ground, a remarkable achievement since the elephant's legs were a good two metres in length.

"I say, old boy," said Basil, his voice reflecting mixed wonderment and disapproval, "perhaps you had better stop playing."

But that elephant's eyes were riveted to mine and they seemed to be saying, play on. As I lit into another chorus, the elephant reached between his forelegs with his trunk and felt around for his penis (though penis seems too petty a word for such a gigantic dong).

80

Seizing it in his trunk, he began to sway back and forth in rhythm, I swear, with the music, and over his face came a look of contentment that I doubt he had shown since the first bombs fell on Berlin. Or maybe he had passed the entire war in this fashion, being uniquely equipped for the business.

"Good Lord!" exclaimed Basil as the elephant came to his climax and there issued a stream that could only be compared to an oil gusher or, in wartime parlance, a flame thrower. It was aimed in my direction and it very nearly carried the full distance across the moat.

"Disgusting," snorted Basil. "Remarkable, but revolting."

For myself, I have always felt good about the incident, though it has caused me to be cautious ever since about playing "Darling Nelly Gray."

Basil's commandeered Mercedes also took us to Nuremberg to cover the war-crimes trials. The three-day drive there was reminiscent of my visit to Mont St. Michel in that we seemed to have the whole countryside to ourselves. We wound through mountains, dallied in villages, slept in feather beds, dined on roast goose and farm sausages, and ignored the ban on fraternization, discovering in the process that rural Germans seemed to be human beings and not unlike the farmers at home. As in rural France and rural Belgium and rural Holland, it was brought home to us that farmers are indeed the most stable elements in society and the least affected by war, even when it sweeps over them, killing their livestock and laying waste their fields. When that happens, such emotions as they display seem to be directed at both sides in equal measure, and there isn't a farmer, friend or foe, who won't swap you some eggs if you have anything to offer that he values as barter.

Nuremberg was occupied by the Americans, in what Basil called the "spam and jam" zone, such was his distaste for the rations on which American troops were fed and upon which we had to subsist for the duration of the trials. Walter Cronkite had been assigned to cover the trials for the United Press, and he and I congratulated ourselves on our good fortune in being at Nuremberg and agreed that there was no place in the world we would rather be as witnesses to history.

God knows, it wasn't because of the city itself, which was a more pathetic ruin than Berlin, if that was possible. We could visit the vast amphitheatre which had housed the Nuremberg rallies, and beside it the remains of what Hitler had planned as the world's largest assembly hall, and we could walk down the broad avenue where his troops had marched and where his aircraft had landed, and we gaped at what was left of ancient buildings and castles that had been blown apart. Amid the wreckage, the famous toy factories of Nuremberg were struggling to resume production, reclaiming used tin cans and any other pieces of metal they could scrounge, and we bought some of the clockwork toys they were turning out — replicas of U.S. Army tanks and trucks.

The Nuremberg trials were designed to establish for all time that it was a crime to start a war, and this was the main charge brought against the top Nazis who were in the dock, headed by Deputy Führer Hermann Goering and including the former Deputy Führer, Rudolf Hess. But the trials had been under way for less than a month when the nature of the proceedings changed from the crime of war to the crimes committed in the course of waging war. The British and Americans, whose people had suffered least, tried to keep to high principles; but the French and the Russians, whose people had suffered most, insisted on justice based on revenge. In the end, the main point that emerged was that it is a bad thing to lose a war and that if you are going to start one it is as well to win.

This was scarcely a new idea, so the global import of the trials faded and we became immersed in an endless recital of atrocities committed by German troops, the point of the trial proceedings being to implicate the German high command and ensure that all the accused in the dock would hang for a lot of specific murders, rather than for inflicting war upon the world.

There were, however, moments of comic relief — descriptions of Goering playing the role of a Caesar, wearing a toga and with his toenails painted red, proclaiming that Germany's Japanese allies were "lacquered monkeys who need to feel the knout." At moments like these, Goering would rock with laughter, and so would the British and Americans, but through the whole of the proceedings the French and the Russians didn't laugh at all.

With the realization that what we were seeing was the victors extracting emotional payment from the vanquished, the element of history was removed from the proceedings and we began to go stir crazy and wish that we were somewhere else. To keep our spirits up, we organized several feasts, one of them to mark the birthday of Scottish poet Robbie Burns. Burns is a hero in the Soviet Union, so the Russian press corps turned out en masse for the dinner, including their woman interpreter who seemed better humoured than the rest of them — until British prosecutor Sir David Maxwell Fyfe rose to propose the noble toast and did it in such thick Scottish accents that the interpreter, unable to understand a word he was saying, burst into tears and fled the room.

To keep from going bonkers, Cronkite and I became the clowns of the Nuremberg press camp, which was situated in an ornate baroque castle owned by the Eberhard Faber lead-pencil family. We called it Stalag Stein, after the village whose centrepiece it was, and dubbed the camp commandant "the beast of Stein." He was an American officer, Colonel Medary, who wore a silver-plated steel helmet in the fashion of General Patton and ran the camp with such an iron hand that the Soviet correspondents refused to submit to his tyranny (or maybe it was our tomfoolery) and set up a camp of their own in a villa on the other side of town.

Although Cronkite came from Kansas City, Missouri, and I came from Saint John, New Brunswick, we knew all the same songs. And we did the same Colonel-Stoopnagle-and-Budd imitations and laughed at the same jokes, and he faked playing the bull fiddle while I faked playing the mighty gaspipe organ. We were both mistaken for Germans — he because of his name, and I because of my oversquare head. Meanwhile, we organized things like toenail-growing contests, with Ossian Goulding of the London *Daily Telegraph* declared the winner upon submitting a stupendous specimen, which he later admitted was a slice of a ping-pong ball.

While these things were going on, we were reporting the trial to an audience that was increasingly preoccupied with other things, mostly the emerging problems of peace — or, more correctly, non-war. The only lasting thing I kept from Nuremberg was an admiration and affection for Cronkite that has carried on through the years and is now shared by millions. Walter's wife Betsy sums it up whenever we meet by explaining to those present that "Charlie and Walter won the war together." Over the years, the response came to be that we didn't know *anybody* had won it.

Looking back, it seems strange and perhaps even obscene that those of us who were charged with conveying the Nuremberg proceedings to the world could have become so cynical so quickly. One of our problems was the policy of non-fraternization, which forbade so much as speaking to the Germans whose country we were occupying and whose former rulers were on trial. We were supposed to nourish hatred, and with most of the Nuremberg defendants this was not difficult as the evidence unfolded.

But the chief defendant was Hermann Goering, the rotund, rollicking air ace of the First War, the only one of Hitler's hierarchy with a sense of humour, which he managed to sustain through most of the proceedings, with the unlikely and inappropriate result that we found ourselves growing fonder of him than we were of the four-nation prosecutors who were making the awful case against him and his colleagues.

After all, the men in the dock were there as the personification of evil, the agents of the horror which has since become known as the Holocaust. We had visited the concentration camps and seen the ghastly sights, and we knew about the atrocities inflicted not only on the Jews but on villages in France and Belgium and Holland, where hostages had been shot out of hand. We knew, too, that Canadian prisoners of war had been shot — and British and American ones — and that there would be military trials to bring the offending German soldiers to justice for their crimes. But it had been drummed into our heads that Nuremberg was going to be something more than a murder trial. When it changed so quickly into the biggest murder trial ever held, we faltered, and Goering's peals of laughter, often at his own expense, were disarming.

I know that the Russian and French correspondents did not falter. They chronicled every horror in complete detail for the full eleven months of the trial. The German correspondents, too, did their work assiduously, as the occupying powers insisted, for one of the main purposes of the Nuremberg trials was to bring the sense of overwhelming guilt home to the German people so that they would never make war again.

The atrocities against the Jews did not dominate the Nuremberg proceedings in the way they have come to dominate most latter-day retrospectives and recollections of the Second World War. During the fighting, we had never thought that our armies were struggling to free the Jews from persecution and death at the hands of the Nazis. We thought, if soldiers ever think of such things, that the fight was to prevent the Germans from taking over the world.

And at Nuremberg there was the uneasy awareness that one of the four powers sitting in judgement was Red Russia, with her own history of atrocities — past, present, and doubtless to come. The Soviet prosecutors laid no stress on Hitlerite crimes against Jews — they had sufficient evidence to keep them busy of crimes against the peoples of the Soviet Union, about 20 million of whom were estimated to have perished at German hands. The French prosecutors took a similar tack. As for the American and British prosecutors, rather than concentrating on the Holocaust, they saw it as their job to concentrate on the crime of war itself.

It is a measure of their failure, and the failure of those of us whose job it was to chronicle the proceedings, that the crime of starting a war is no more clearly recognized across the world today than it has been through all the centuries of bloodshed. What has so far saved us from a third world war has not been any new code of human conduct but the balance of terror, the fear of obliterating the whole of humankind with no prospect of victors and vanquished.

7/The Long Way Home: Rio de Janeiro

Tony Cole had said when the war ended, "Now the hard work begins," his point being that, in the journalistic sense, covering wars like the one just finished was child's play — all blacks and whites and good guys and bad guys with a minimum of complexities, especially when you were on the winning side and "the only good German was a dead one." No more.

Covering the peace would be different. We would have to switch our minds on and make assessments sans propaganda and sans emotion and sans most of the things that made for combat correspondence. Above all, we had to make money against the competition.

After my four months at Nuremberg, Cole offered me the choice of going to India, China, Poland, or Brazil. The prewar news cartels were breaking up, and in India and China, Reuters would have to defend its old monopolies. Poland was fighting ground. And Brazil, once part of the French domain governed by the Havas Agency, would be a place where all the world agencies would be struggling for dominance. Reuters wanted it, along with the whole of South America. So Cole sold me on Brazil. To get there from London in 1946, you flew to Shannon and then to Lisbon, and on to Dakar and Liberia, and across the South Atlantic to Belém, and down to Rio de Janeiro, stopping at each place along the way.

The Shannon stop provided a chance to drive up to Galway to check on the origins of Lynch Law, an episode that put the family name into every one of the world's languages in a not very flattering way. In the heart of Galway town I came upon Lynch's Castle, a grey stone pile with various coats of arms on the walls and a skull and crossbones under the window out of which the first lynching had taken place. The building housed a branch of the Leinster and Munster Bank, and in the banking hall there hung a large scroll on which the dreadful details were emblazoned, bearing the signature of Monseigneur Hines, the rector of Galway University. I inquired after the whereabouts of the eminent cleric and was told he lived at the Galway Country Club, on the town's main square. When I announced myself there, a tiny white-haired leprechaun of a man came floating down the wide mahogany staircase and threw his arms around me and said Glory be to God, had I come all the way from the New World, and how grand, and would I join him in his chambers? I did, and from a wall of books he took down a huge tome and reached in behind it, producing a bottle of John Jameson's Irish Whiskey, from which he poured each of us a full tumbler and pronounced blessings on our meeting. He asked if I wanted the story in English or in the Gaelic and I said English, so he took a long gulp of "the cray-ture," as he called it, and commenced.

In 1492, the mayor of Galway was James Lynch, the office having been passed down in the family from father to son for a hundred years. He wasn't only the mayor, he was the magistrate and the sheriff and the laird and the big merchant. His trade went beyond Ireland's borders, one of his connections being with a family named Gomez in Seville, and it was decided that his seventeen-year-old son should go there for the summer to broaden his horizons. When the boy returned, he brought with him the seventeen-year-old son of the Gomez family, and a big party was arranged, with the whole town turning out.

At the party was young Lynch's sweetheart, and the Spaniard caught her eye, and in the course of the revels he lured her away from the castle. Young Lynch sensed their absence and went in search of them, discovering them locked in hot embrace on the shore of Galway Bay, whereupon he threw himself on his Spanish guest in a fury and slew him, after which he fled to the hills.

The young lady rushed back to the party to report the awful event and Judge Lynch, having viewed the body of the Spaniard, organized a posse and went in quest of the fugitive. The boy, seeing the search party headed by his father, gave himself up and was thrust into the castle dungeon, whence he was brought to trial, Judge Lynch on the bench.

The verdict was guilty, and the sentence was death by hanging. A gallows was erected in the garden of the castle, but on the appointed day nobody could be found to act as hangman, the sentiments of the townspeople being entirely on the side of young Lynch. The boy himself was confident he would survive. But his mother, whose maiden name was Blake, had a premonition of disaster and rode forth into the countryside, rounding up all the Blakes she could find and urging them to come to the rescue. They responded, and so did most of the townsfolk, a crowd assembling that filled the garden and the street outside the castle.

Judge Lynch was not deterred. Rope in hand, he descended to the cell and asked his son if he had any last words. The boy stayed silent, so the father took him by the arm and led him up the stairs to the door that led to the garden. When he opened the door he saw the crowd, heard the shouts for the boy's freedom, and immediately banged the door shut, bolting it from the inside. He then led his son up the winding staircase to the castle tower. Looking down on the crowd below, he saw his wife, surrounded by the Blake kinfolk, and heard her shriek that their son's life should be spared.

"Farewell, my son," intoned the judge, looping the noose around the neck of the boy and pitching him out the window.

The mother was struck dumb at the sight of her son dangling on the castle wall, with his father holding the rope in his bare hands. As the son's life choked away, she pronounced a curse on the House of Lynch, that every male member of the family for evermore should bear on the back of his neck the mark of the hangman's knot, which they have. (It only emerges in moments of passion, Monseigneur Hines assured me.)

Thus it was that while Judge Lynch *was* the law, he took the law into his own hands and became immortal. Following this sombre event, he locked himself in his bedroom and was seen no more, withering away and with him the family fortune.

No other Lynch ever became mayor of Galway. Indeed, there have been scarcely any Lynches in the whole of that part of Ireland to this day, said the good rector, refilling our glasses and lapsing into Gaelic incoherence. But wasn't it interesting that the present mayor was a Blake, and the magistrate was a Blake, and the big merchants in town were Blakes, and a Blake was the president of the Galway Country Club? The Lynches had scattered to the four corners of the earth, and he was sure I would find some in Brazil. With this, he gave me the blessing and I went on my way with a carton of his written works, all scholarly and all in Gaelic.

Thus encumbered, I arrived in Rio de Janeiro, the most beautiful city in the world, to set about retrieving Reuters' fortunes and, in the process, learning things about Canada that I had never dreamed of. Brazil is the only country ever to regard Canada as a colonial power, a distortion caused by the fact that the head offices of Brazilian Traction, Light, and Power were in Toronto. From the moment of my arrival, I was plunged into the circle of "the Light" and the Canadian who was the most powerful man in Brazil, and the Canadian ambassador who sought to change all that.

The powerful Canadian was Major Ken McCrimmon, whose job it was, by hook or by crook, to make sure that the Light retained its hold on everything that mattered in Rio de Janeiro and Sao Paulo, particularly the power supplies, telephones and telecommunications, and public transportation. In particular, it was McCrimmon's task to fend off the threat of expropriation and to guarantee that the profits could be remitted outside the country.

The Canadian ambassador was a buzzsaw of a man named Jean Desy, whose chosen mission was to wipe out the impression of Canada as a colonial exploiter and oppressor, and put in its place the idea of an Athens of the North, a land of Latin culture where everything that mattered happened in French and where the people felt themselves to be soulmates of all the Latin people in the world, especially the Brazilians.

At home in Canada, the era of William Lyon Mackenzie King was coming to an end, and in Quebec the era of Maurice Duplessis was in full swing. My own ideas of Canada had been freshly minted in the war, and it has been truly said that nothing so brightened the image of Canada as wartime service overseas, with its yearning for a homeland that from a distance seemed to be all of a piece. The experience dissipated whatever faint impression we might have had of the two solitudes or the urgency of the English-French question. We had contributed mightily to victory in the war, had won an honoured place at the council tables of the world, and were a model for less fortunate peoples. To bring these attitudes to Brazil was assurance enough of culture shock, and it was compounded by the conflicting impressions of Canada offered to the Brazilians by McCrimmon the WASP buccaneer and Desy the French Canadian diplomat.

McCrimmon took me under his wing immediately and told me some facts of life he thought I ought to know, not only about Brazil but about Reuters and its place in the propaganda scheme of things. He spoke plainly about it, as he did about everything, and explained how, when France fell in 1940, there had been a danger that the Germans would take over the entire Havas news monopoly in South America. So Reuters had stepped in, with the full support of the British Foreign Office and the Anglo communities in the various republics, hiring the huge staffs that Havas had built up over sixty years and ensuring that Allied propaganda got a hearing throughout the continent.

Now that the war was over, the French had re-entered the field with their new agency, Agence France Presse, assembling new staffs everywhere and leaving Reuters saddled with the old. I knew we had 180 people in Rio de Janeiro and another 180 in Sao Paulo, and I knew that my job was to slash those numbers in order to make the service pay. Cole had told me that, but he hadn't mentioned the extent to which Reuters had operated openly as a subsidized prop-aganda agency of His Majesty's Government, with help from men like McCrimmon. As a distinguished veteran of the First World War, McCrimmon had considered it no more than his patriotic duty. He told me that one of our patriotic duties now was to keep an eye on that rascal of a Canadian ambassador Monsieur Desy, who not only had some peculiar ideas about Canada but was suspected of aiding the French in their efforts to establish Agence France Presse as the do-minant news service in Brazil.

The problems inherent in all this almost engulfed me at the start of the assignment. Almost, but not quite. The spell of Rio de Janeiro is such that it dulls the mind for heavy problems, and the spirit of the native Cariocas is infectious, at carnival time or any time. There is a kind of delicious corruption in the air, compounded by the stupen-dous scenery and the outpourings of the human spirit, and the effect can be so entrancing that everyday problems fade in importance.

Yet Brazil's problems are, of course, very large. Poverty and privilege live side by side, as they do in every society, but Latin American poverty is more blatantly apparent and more likely to outrage the visitor than the kind of mass misery one beholds in the cities and countrysides of Asia and Africa. This, after all, is the New World, once a supposed refuge from the miseries and tyrannies of the Old, yet the plight of the Brazilian masses, when first I moved among them, made me weep.

But it was here that we were going to live and work, and if the Brazilians weren't crying, why should I? The adjustments were not too difficult with so much laughter around, the trick being to put your social conscience on hold and relax and enjoy the pleasant parts, as tourists can do. The communities of resident foreigners can club together and isolate themselves from the native miseries, or "go native" themselves in the sense that they adopt the habits and philosophies of the well-to-do. In this comatose state, it is possible to enjoy.

There are smart ones who avoid this illusion and keep their wits about them, and two of the smartest in Rio de Janeiro were McCrimmon and Desy. McCrimmon was in his sixties, ruddy of face and round of belly — the personification of a Toronto Tory, which is exactly what he was, larger than life. He lived in a huge mansion in the suburb of Copacabana, surrounded by servants. He also had a huge estancia in the mountain resort of Teresópolis, where he ran a herd of cattle and consorted with such neighbours as Sir Henry Lynch, the match king of Brazil who grew orchids as a hobby and was reputed to have been a master spy for England. Sir Henry looked like my Uncle Dave back in Saint John, and I reflected when I first saw him that it was nice that one of our guys had made it.

Nobody ever called McCrimmon anything but "the Major," and everybody spoke of him with awe, except for Desy, who tried to pretend he didn't exist. One of the Major's great advantages was that he always appeared to be three sheets in the wind, which most of the time he was, creating an effect that lulled his opponents in any deal into a false sense of superiority. In fact, his senses were unimpaired at all hours of the day and night, which was remarkable when you witnessed his daily regime, as I was privileged to do as his newest protégé.

His breakfast consisted of half a mickey of Scotch, poured into a cocktail shaker from bottles which he imported himself (in order to avoid the annoying habit the Brazilians had of boring tiny holes in the bottoms of the bottles, draining out half the contents, and substituting water to bring the contents up to full measure). Into the cocktail shaker McCrimmon's bodyguard — he always had two, fully armed — would break four raw eggs, shaking the mixture into a froth before pouring it into a giant tumbler, the seething contents of which McCrimmon would quaff with relish to get himself started for the day.

He would then proceed to his office in his chauffeur-driven limousine, and after a couple of hours of consultations with his minions and informers, hearing of plots and hatching counterplots, he would walk with his armed guards to the downtown bar known as Dirty Dick's, where he would meet supplicants and friends over several rounds of drinks before tucking into a heavy lunch, complete with the finest wines of his own choosing. A few post-lunch drinks and it was back to the office for more affairs of state, and then home for a late afternoon snooze before greeting his dinner guests, who might include anybody from President Dutra on down through the hierarchy of people who ran Brazil. That meant pre-dinner drinks, and then the most sumptuous of dinners to be served anywhere in Rio, following which the serious drinking would commence and continue until midnight and beyond.

And through all this, the Major would never lose sight of the main reason for his existence in Brazil, the safeguarding of the interests of the Light, making sure that he was never taken by surprise and that he never lost the initiative. This meant knowing where all the multitude of skeletons were concealed in that city full of closets — who was taking graft from whom, who was sleeping with whose mistress (nobody, it seemed, ever talked about wives), who had just made a suspicious million in gambling or real estate, and what horses were highly regarded for the next day's card at the jockey club.

Through it all, McCrimmon would talk about old comrades and ask about old colleagues like George Drew, who was premier of Ontario, and he would join in the singing of the old wartime songs and play the buffoon. But if you looked closely, you could always catch the glint at the back of those bleary eyes.

Although the Light was reviled, as it deserved to be, the Major commanded a respect accorded to nobody else in Rio de Janeiro, Brazilian or foreigner, and it was a respect based on fear. A good man to have on your side, especially when it was brought home to me that he could easily have wrecked my assignment if he had wanted to, and could have brought the whole Reuters apparatus down as well.

Jean Desy was quite another matter, a hard man for me to get to know and a harder man for me to get to like, a knack that I never did master. He was unenthusiastic about my presence and gave the impression that the last person he wanted to see in Brazil was a Canadian of the English persuasion, posing a possible threat to the edifice of an all-French Canada that he was trying to instil into the Brazilian mind. He had even arranged to have an agent in McCrimmon's camp, having persuaded Brazilian Traction to hire Montreal journalist Jean-Louis Gagnon and send him to Rio de Janeiro as a public relations man for the Light. Gagnon subsequently had a remarkable career in Canada as an editor, bureaucrat, diplomat, and mandarin, but as a PR man for the capitalistic exploiters in Brazil he was a washout, caught between the piratical world of the Major and the fantasyland of Desy.

The Brazilians thought Desy was splendid, and they relished the idea that North America contained not only the vulgar Yankees but a land of intellect, music, literature, philosophy, all Latin style. Besides preaching his gospel of Latin Canada all over Brazil, Desy illustrated it by producing the evidence. Quebec musicians came by the score. Quebec poets flew down to read their works. Quebec authors were feted. Orchestras and dance troupes came. Paintings by Quebec artists were hung all over Rio de Janeiro, and posters proclaimed the beauties of Le Beau Pays du Nord. In Desy's presence, nothing was allowed to be said about the awful fact that there was another Canada where English was spoken and where the barbarians lived. Thus did Desy wage his own quiet revolution thirteen years before the real one in Quebec. And the hell of it, for those of us from the barbarian side, was that it worked.

One of the ambassador's greatest pieces of flim-flam came with the visit to Rio de Janeiro of the cruiser *Uganda*, the pride of His Majesty's Canadian Navy of happy memory. Desy was not of a military turn of mind and he was not overjoyed at the prospect of a shipload of unruly Anglos swarming into the city. He gave instructions that on no account was the ship's band to play Anglo airs and that Quebec music was to be featured — an order that caused a crisis among the musicians, who had no Quebec songs in their martial repertoire. At Desy's receptions ashore, such French-speaking members of the crew as could be found were put on prominent display for the Brazilian dignitaries, and any suggestion of Canada's ties with Britain, or with the Royal Navy, were played down. Desy breathed a sigh of relief when the *Uganda* sailed out of the harbour, her White

Ensign flapping defiantly in the breeze. At least, he mused, they hadn't got out the Union Jack. (It was perhaps a coincidence that the *Uganda* was subsequently rechristened H.M.C.S. *Quebec*.)

Neither McCrimmon nor Desy, with their respective distortions of what I imagined Canada to be, had anything directly to do with the first of my appointed tasks, which was to dismiss two-thirds of the people on the Reuters payroll so that we could get down to the business of making money. There were some good people on the staff, but along with them was an array of uncles, nephews, brothers, and cousins, who had records of service stretching far back into the prewar French regime. Under Brazilian labour laws they had tenure, so it cost money to fire them, and every month I sent to London for huge remittances to pay the dismissal costs. We could only afford half a dozen sackings a month, but it wasn't long before I became the most despised man in Rio de Janeiro.

I had the feeling I wasn't much more popular in London, especially as the money for the firings had to be accompanied by more of the company's treasure to cover bribery and corruption. It was one thing to get our news into Brazil by wireless, translate it into Portuguese, and deliver it by uniformed messengers to the newspapers. But it was another thing to get it published against the competing news services. The only way to do that was to grease the palms of the editorial staffs, which we did on a regular basis. On the day following our payoffs there might be nothing but Reuters news in the papers, whereupon AP, UP, and AFP would get busy and we might not get another item printed for a week. The French agency even gave out automobiles to key editors, something nobody else could match.

Despite McCrimmon's expert guidance, I never did master the art of patronage Brazilian style, though God knows I tried. You needed it in everyday life as well as in business, as when the water meter at our house became clogged with debris and I dismantled it, and when I put it back on the pipe, I got it backwards. As a result, the dials spun in reverse for a month. When the inspector came to read the meter he found it registered considerably less than it had the month before, so he called me outside and accused me of tampering and said there was a heavy penalty for such an awful offence. I offered him a 1000-cruzeiro bill and asked if that would help, and he said he had some other calls to make on the street and that if, when he returned, the meter at least was in the correct position we might have something to discuss. I worked feverishly with my pliers and got the job done just before he returned, and he nodded with approval and accepted an additional 500 cruzeiros and nothing more was heard from the water utility people.

Our street, the Rua Constante Ramos, was the main route to the hospital Fernando de Morais, which catered to wealthy Brazilians and foreigners, and was the only hospital in Rio de Janeiro that handled maternity cases. The ambulances bringing Brazilian women to their accouchements had big bells on them, which they rang for emergencies. Since every impending birth was an emergency, the bells rang loudly going past our house, and the decibel count was raised by the Brazilian mothers-to-be giving their prenatal howls of "Ai, yai ai, yai ai!" The people who lived next door to us had a parrot perched outside their front door and the only sounds that parrot ever learned to make were those of the ambulances. So even when there wasn't an emergency, we were treated to a constant parroting of "Ding, ding, ding, ding, ding!" and "Ai, yai ai, yai ai!"

We had two years of this, and I sensed that either I was going to go Brazilian or that it was time to leave. The deciding episode involved a day when none of our news got into any of the papers. Since we had bestowed our weekly largesse the day before, I had inquiries made of the recipient editors, only to be told that none of our news had been delivered. When I summoned the messenger who had been on duty, he didn't wait for me to confront him with the evidence.

"Senhor," he said, "I am a Brazilian, and you are a Norte Americano, and you are not going to understand what I am going to tell you."

"Tell me," said I.

"Well, senhor," said he, "you will realize that yesterday was a beautiful day."

"So it was," I agreed.

"I put my messages in my pouch and I stepped outside onto the Avenida Rio Branco and looked up at the sky, which was blue."

Indeed, I agreed, it had been an ideal summer's day, in January.

"I realized," he continued, "that I had a choice. I could either spend the day delivering our messages to the newspapers, or I could go to the beach. Believe me, senhor, I thought very hard about it. When I reached my decision I took the messages and I threw them into

Botofogo Bay and I went to the beach and it was the best day of my life. But you, senhor, would not understand that."

The trouble was, I understood it perfectly well, and in my heart of hearts I knew that the wretched messenger had made precisely the right decision. Even though he might be sackable without compensation, I couldn't find it in my heart to fire him or even to deliver a severe reprimand.

There was something infinitely beguiling about the Brazilian approach to life, at both the personal and official levels. When Brazil played host to a summit conference of the Organization of American States, every public works project in the country had to be halted so that there would be money to pay for the do, which was held up in the mountains at the Hotel Quitandinha and attended by such hemispheric dignitaries as President Harry Truman and General George Marshall.

They gave Harry and Bess Truman an aquamarine as big as a baseball, with a portrait of the president and his wife glued to the bottom so their faces shone up through the stone. The conference accomplished nothing — OAS conferences, like our own federal-provincial ones, never do — but this one was marked by the unexpected appearance of Evita Perón, the wife of the president of Argentina, who dropped in on her way home from Rome, where she had been to see the Pope. The current joke was that when His Holiness asked her how she had felt when Perón asked her to marry him, she replied that she was so surprised she fell out of bed.

Evita arrived demanding head-of-state treatment, but since the OAS under Washington's prompting was cold-shouldering Argentina at the time, she was denied official status and her request to address the conference was refused. Her response was to throw one of the most violent tantrums ever seen in Brazil, a land where tantrums are part of everyday life. Having trashed one of the biggest and fanciest suites in the hotel, shredding the Dorothy Draper decor in the process, she left, hurling imprecations over her shoulder.

When it came time for me to leave Brazil, there arose the business of reselling to the landlord all the furniture he had made us buy when we moved into the house in Copacabana. He told me to find new tenants and sell the stuff to them, subject to his veto. After he had turned thumbs down on three prospects, I got the idea that he was a crook, an impression confirmed when he suggested that we just leave all the furniture in the house and depart. The London head office said that in view of the sums involved I should stay in Rio de Janeiro until the cost of the furniture had been recovered. I was at my wit's end until I explained my predicament to Major McCrimmon, who said he thought perhaps he could be of assistance.

There then ensued one of the most brutal and effective squeeze plays I have ever been party to, of which these were the main ingredients: McCrimmon decided that our house would be ideal as a guest house for VIPs of the Light. He would pay us in full for the amount the furnishings had cost us. He would retain our excellent cook, Nysaya, and our housemaid, Zeni, despite the latter's lamentable tendency to break out in rashes because of the bleaches she applied to her skin, seeking to lighten her complexion so that she could move up a notch in the social scale. Even as McCrimmon spoke, his henchmen were calling on the landlord to inform him of these arrangements, subject to certain conditions, which were that if the landlord didn't agree, the electric power would be cut off both at his home and at his offices, and his telephones would be removed, and various other unpleasantnesses would be visited upon him and his family, including widespread publication of his personal habits, which had unsavoury aspects even by the standards of the Brazil of those times.

The landlord was given twenty-four hours to consider the terms, but it didn't take him that long to agree, and shortly we were on our way, after McCrimmon had given me some guidance on how to get clearance from the income tax people, who were demanding large sums in imagined back taxes before my departure. I handled it the way I had handled the matter of the backward water meter, and upon passing over a few bills I was witness to the inspector not only marking the amount "paid" but tearing up my entire file and depositing it in his waste basket.

I left Brazil with an everlasting feeling of gratitude for McCrimmon and an everlasting mistrust for Jean Desy. In the end, neither of them won the battle for the hearts and minds of Brazilians, just as neither of their philosophies has carried the day in their homeland. Desy's vision of Canada did not outlive his stay in Brazil, though he carried it with him on subsequent postings. I had one memorable encounter with him when he was our ambassador to France, at a time when our relations with President Charles de Gaulle were at their lowest ebb. It was the twenty-fifth anniversary of the D-day landings in Normandy, and de Gaulle had ruled that no Canadian cabinet minister, or dignitary of any kind, would be admitted to France to partake in the observances. Indeed, he would have been happy had there been no observances at all, but token ones finally were permitted, and at the Canadian cemetery at Beny-sur-Mer, the presiding officer was Ambassador Desy, who saw to it that the entire ceremony, including his own speech, was in French.

This, like the entire Brazilian episode, took place before the realization came upon me that Desy was merely reversing what French-speaking Canadians had gone through for a century, and that the sentiments he represented would test Canadian nationhood as it had never been tested before, even by enemy forces in two great wars. I don't think that even today I could accept Desy as the spokesman for our fallen warriors in France, but I think I might come down on his side, rather than McCrimmon's, in the Brazilian situation.

McCrimmon wound up a loser in the end, because the Light's days as a colonial oppressor were ending. The company gradually became Brazilianized, and its hold on the gullets of Brazil's two largest cities was broken. It saddened me, though, that when McCrimmon tried to dispose of his own mansion in Rio de Janeiro to the Canadian government, to serve as the residence of the Canadian ambassador, the deal was scuppered in the Canadian House of Commons on the ground that a million dollars was too much to pay. After all, the Major hadn't quibbled when I needed a buyer, and but for him I might be there yet.

But why not want a life in Brazil? Why love the place as I do and not want to live there? Mainly because of the poverty. The country, after all, offers as many challenges as Canada — in size, resources, and population diversity. It was said when I lived there that its brightest years were in the future, and cynics added that they always would be. Today it is no different, despite all the progress. Brazilians carry on their backs a load of poverty that is almost a chronic illness. As with China, the size of the country, and especially its huge population, are handicaps that it seems can never be overcome.

At the time of my stay in Brazil, the country had virtually no middle class — there were the rich, and there were the poor, and nowhere in the world were the contrasts between their lifestyles more extreme. Brazil prided herself on having no racial discrimination, yet it was obvious that the blacker you were, the poorer you were, and in the so-called "parliament of the people" there were no blacks at all. Out of the racial mixture of blacks, Indians, and whites, there was supposed to be emerging something called the Brazilian race, something new in the world.

The agony of it all, for the masses, was brought home to me during a state visit to Brazil by the president of Chile. As it had for the summit meeting at Quitandinha, the Brazilian government slowed down its public works projects in order to find the money for the huge receptions that were staged. These were climaxed by a grand ball at the presidential palace, one of the most glittering affairs ever held anywhere in the hemisphere. In a setting of royal palms and reflecting pools and great beds of flowers, a feast was staged that consisted of strawberries flown in from France and caviar from Iran and beef from Argentina and exotic fowl from Belgium, from which only a few delicate slices were taken from the breasts before new birds were brought to take their places.

The finest wines of Europe were there in abundance, and most of the male guests were in gaudy uniforms of all emblazoned kinds, and the women were resplendent with great strings of pearls woven into their towering coiffures. Most of the wearers of the Paris gowns were mistresses, for it was not the custom in Brazil for wives to be brought to parties, even great ones, and the mistresses of Brazil were the long-limbed beauties who spent their days on the beaches and their evenings in the pleasure domes, with hours in between for the beauty parlours. (Brazilian men who could not afford individual mistresses of their own formed consortiums and shared in the care, feeding, and housing of a single woman, each contributor having his allotted day and night.)

The vast garden in which the grand ball was taking place was ringed by a high iron fence, and outside that fence were the people, the black people, young and old, with their faces pressed between the iron palings, watching silently. The sight of those faces will be with me forever. It took all the gaiety out of the occasion. It rendered Brazil impossible to enjoy, unless you could close your eyes to the hopeless squalor.

The same feeling struck me on subsequent visits to Venezuela and Mexico, and above all to Peru, where once, in Lima, I visited a medical clinic run by some Canadian doctors in the squatters' settlement housing sixty thousand people. The clinic operated one day for adults and another day for children, and this was an adult day. An Indian mother appeared in the lineup with a one-year-old child carried papoose-fashion on her back. When it came to her turn at the table, she explained that it was not she who was sick but her baby, and as she swung the child off her back to be examined, the doctor and two of the attendants proceeded to give her a savage dressing down that caused her to cringe with fear. She apologized, amid tears, and begged forgiveness for breaking the rules. Then, putting the child again on her back, she trudged away, and the last seen of her and her pathetic bundle were those big almond eyes of the child, clouded with fever.

When I remonstrated with the doctors for being so harsh, they shrugged and said it had to be that way, because if they had tended to a child on adults' day, every parent of a sick child would have come storming in and there would have been chaos. It was also explained to me that since Peru had the highest birthrate in the world, and since the poverty was so extreme and so insoluble, it would be no favour to anybody to cut down on the rate of infant mortality, which was the only way the population balance could be kept.

To live in countries with these kinds of problems is difficult. You have to be able to enjoy breast of guinea hen with two thousand black eyes staring at you through a fence, or with two big eyes looking from a sick child who has been denied treatment because it was the wrong day. It is easier to cut and run, and come home, grateful to have been exposed to things that make our own problems seem soluble, or at least manageable. It is perhaps a selfish solution. I would only say in my own defence that in the intervening years I have tried, without much success, to awaken Canadian interest in the peoples of Latin America, and particularly in the people of Brazil, with whom, it seems to me, we have more potentially in common than with the peoples of Africa or Asia.

My first formal photo, 1923, with my sister Virginia and my mother.

Jimmy Archdeacon (left) with my father and new 1931 convertible, Saint John, N.B.

Mother with me and Virginia, visiting Boston in the car we called Lizzie, 1932.

Above: Andy Merkel
looking to seaward,
Halifax, 1939.

Tony Cole in Toronto,
1943, at the start of his
battle to make Reuters
respectable.

Mary Churchill with
her father Winston at
Niagara Falls, 1943.
"The main principle
remains the same!"

Matt Halton at work.

In my Moss Bros uniform, London, 1944.

Interviewing wounded soldier of the Royal Winnipeg Rifles at the battle for
Carpiquet Airport, Normandy, 1944. Reading my notes is my conducting
officer and friend, Bill Cornforth.

Churchill visits the First Canadian Army in the Reichswald, 1945, the day Monty hid the booze.

On Parliament Hill, home ground for twenty-eight years.

NDP leader David Lewis laughs at our song about his 1972 campaign plane "BumAir." Background: Mrs. Sophie Lewis, Ron Collister (then of CBC), and me.

With Pierre Trudeau and Joe Clark at our annual dinner, the year I was president of the Parliamentary Press Gallery. I am explaining jokes to Trudeau, who seldom got them.

Election campaign
1972, the day Margaret
Trudeau bolted from
the official car and came
back to the press bus
"for the fun." Told she
was upsetting apple
carts, she said, "Goody,
goody!"

Hosting Prince Philip
at a banquet of the
Canadian War
Correspondents
Association, Café
Royal, London.
Background left is
Ralph Allen, who
could outwrite us all.

With Prince Charles
on his first tour,
Yellowknife, N.W.T.,
1972.

Order of Canada
investiture, 1977, by
Governor General Jules
Léger. Citation said:
"MUSICIAN?"

Toast to the Queen by Governor General Jules Léger at Parliamentary Press Gallery dinner. Prime Minister Trudeau abstains.

114

Left: In full cry at the podium — "At the sound of a chairman clearing his throat, Lynch is on his feet."

Right: Salmon fishing on the Miramichi, with guide Tommy Munns. The blameless sport.

115

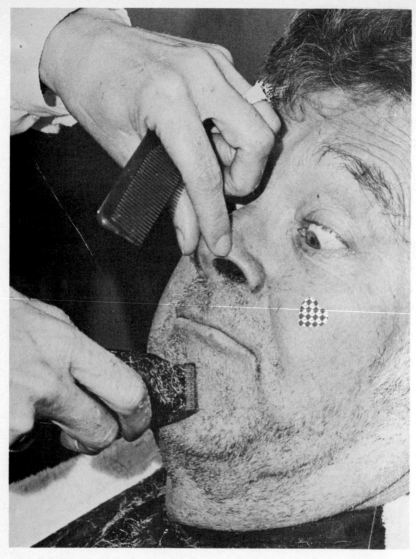

Her Excellency Lily Schreyer phones me with the code word announcing the 1979 election: "Shave!" I comply with the vice-regal command.

The Blue-Eyed Sheiks, as portrayed by the Press Gallery players. Left to right: me as Peter Lougheed, Ron Collister as Allan Blakeney, Bruce Phillips as Dave Barrett, and Geoff Scott as Thumper Don Macdonald. "The gas we have today, we just won't fart away!"

These things used to cost $1.50. Now it's $150, but you get teflon and stainless steel.

Peter Fleming, the maestro of the National Press and Allied Workers Jazz Band, conducts an "amen" at our Hamilton Place Concert in aid of the Hamilton Symphony Orchestra. The "poor man's Canada Council" strikes again.

My symphonic debut, with Mitch Miller and the Winnipeg Symphony Orchestra. We're playing "The Road to the Isles."

Charles
My favourite handicapper
Brian
June 15 83

New face in town. I predicted that Brian Mulroney would win the
Conservative leadership in 1983, and the night before he did, this picture was
taken. Mulroney called it "Faith, Hope, and Charity." The man in the middle
is Fredericton real estate tycoon Don Gardiner, one of Mulroney's mafioso
from the St. Francis Xavier University connection.

Grand Master of the Loyalist Day Parade, Saint John, N.B. I referred to the
United Empire Loyalists as the original welfare recipients.

PART THREE

Politicians

1/My Own Canadian Home

Before I left Brazil, Reuters had offered me a variety of choices. I could return to London, with the prospect of an administrative career at headquarters. Or I could have a posting to Rome and a continuation of the foreign correspondent's life. Or I could go to Ottawa to open a bureau there, now that Canada meant something in the world. My choice was Canada, the place half the people in the world seemed to want to go — the blessed land where, it was said, nothing bad ever happened, and nothing exciting.

In 1947 there was excitement galore, and for me there hasn't been a dull moment since, though oftentimes it has seemed I was the only person who wasn't bored. If I'd gone to Rome instead of Ottawa, I would have spent all these years pondering Italian politics, about which nobody cares a fig, including the Italians. Twelve elections later, my understanding of Canadian politics is imperfect, to be sure, but whose isn't?

I have become convinced that politicians are more stimulating, and certainly more varied, than diplomats, and that world affairs are best viewed through the filter of domestic interests. The truth about politics and politicians continues to be elusive, but the quest keeps one out of the pool halls, and though so many of Canada's dreams have been broken, there remains no place on earth I'd rather be. I might have served my homeland better perhaps had I laid aside my pen and wrung a few necks. Or if somebody had wrung my own.

But they didn't, and I didn't, and I have stayed on in Ottawa working for the biggest newspaper chain in the country and haranguing people and politicians on TV and radio and from a thousand podiums, and loving the country more each year, and revelling in the manifold joys of Ottawa, the most livable-in capital city in the world and one of the most beautiful. Reporting turned to punditry, and mouth-organ playing by the fireside turned to harmonica performances with symphony orchestras, just as singing in the shower led to full-throated bellowing from the opera stage at the National Arts Centre.

Millions of words and five million kilometres of travel later, I am not sure that I understand Canada or Canadians any better than when I started, though the fascination remains, and an eight-year stint in the United States only sharpened my appreciation of what we have here.

One of the difficulties about understanding Canadians is that they don't understand themselves and don't particularly want to. Politicians have wrestled with this riddle since Canada's beginnings and are no closer to a solution than when they started. Canadians, of course, tend not to understand their politicians, which is one reason why we have no national heroes, old or new. In this century, Canadians have understood only three of their prime ministers: Sir Wilfrid Laurier, Sir Robert Borden, and Louis Stephen St.Laurent. The rest were either grossly misunderstood, like Lester Pearson and John Diefenbaker, or they brought to the office an aura of mystery that shrouded their real selves, as with R. B. Bennett, William Lyon Mackenzie King, and Pierre Elliott Trudeau.

There wasn't much to know about Arthur Meighen and Joe Clark, whose time in office was reckoned in months, though it was said of Meighen that he possessed the finest intellect of any man in public life, ever. Nobody ever said that about Joe Clark, though he had a better head on him than any of us gave him credit for, even if it made him top-heavy when he swam.

My only contact with Arthur Meighen came in his twilight years, when I was new to the business of oratory and had responded to a frantic summons from the Empire Club in Toronto, whose scheduled speaker, Max Freedman, had cancelled out. The year was 1957, and I was the CBC correspondent at the United Nations, and I was to talk about Canada's potent place as a world power of the second rank, which we were at the time. The head table guest list included Arthur Meighen, and I approached him humbly to express gratitude that an orator of such great repute should have come out to hear me speak.

"I didn't come to hear you speak," he growled. "I came to hear Max Freedman speak. But since I'm here and I'm hungry and the weather outside is foul, I have decided to stay. I hope you'll make it worth my while."

I lurched into the room with my knees wobbling and made the speech, and Meighen was good enough to come forward to me afterwards and say he was glad he had stayed. After that experience, no head table has ever awed me. I never did get to hear Meighen speak, though it was said of him that he could bring eloquence to a reading of the telephone book.

Once, when he was sailing back to Canada from a visit to Australia, he received a cable from a club in Vancouver inviting him, on his arrival, to speak to them about the works of Shakespeare. Meighen accepted, only to find upon putting to sea that there was no volume of Shakespeare aboard the boat. He fell back on his own recollections of the bard, which were total, and upon arrival in Vancouver delivered a speech that was breath-taking in its scope, complete with quotations and citations that were flawless.

My favourite saying of Meighen's was uttered in the lobby of the Chateau Laurier Hotel in the days when Ottawa had two English-language daily newspapers. Meighen had bought a copy of the *Ottawa Journal*, and after scanning it he threw it on the floor, snorting, "Dammit! Whichever Ottawa paper you buy you wish you had bought the other one!"

Laurier is remembered principally for two things — having said that the twentieth century belonged to Canada, and having purchased a newspaper from a boy named John Diefenbaker at the Prince Albert railroad station. It is not clear whether either of these things ever really happened, but Diefenbaker himself saw to it that the episode involving him and Sir Wilfrid was told and retold from platforms across the land, ensuring that it became part of his legend, which was the only kind of legend Diefenbaker cared about.

There was, of course, much more to Laurier than that, and Senator Grattan O'Leary, a great spouter himself, never could decide whether Laurier was a greater speaker than Meighen, or the other way around. In Montreal, I once heard O'Leary speak for two hours and twenty-five minutes about Laurier's eloquence, at the end of which he hurled himself back into his head-table seat with such force that the chair toppled over backwards, depositing him into a crevasse between the dais and the back wall of the Windsor Hotel ballroom. We had to lift him out with ropes.

Borden was a dull, ponderous Haligonian who ranks with St. Laurent in terms of sincerity, honesty, and straightforwardness, which is probably why he is so dimly remembered, despite the fact that he saw the country through the preliminaries to the First World War, the war itself, and the immediate aftermath. The only man I know who heard Borden speak is Senator Eugene Forsey, and his imitation of Borden's voice gives the impression that he used the monotone delivery of Ontario Premier William Davis, only louder. Everybody, of course, had to speak louder in those days, there being no artificial aids to audibility, and Borden's single note was delivered with a low resonance that could carry any hall in the land and was good for a country mile in the open air.

Borden and St. Laurent were two of a kind in that they were gentlemen of courtly manners, approaching the deviousness of high office with distaste. St. Laurent permitted himself to be used by the Liberals in the Uncle Louis role, a piece of flim-flam that worked from 1948 to 1957 when the Liberals squeezed the last drop of energy out of St. Laurent and, in their own words, "ran him stuffed."

St. Laurent's years were Canada's best, in terms of global prestige, economic progress, and general well-being. He even brought in balanced budgets and paid off a small part of the national debt. He put in place social programs that set Canada on the way to becoming the most highly socialized country in the developed world, not excluding the Scandinavian countries.

Yet he is dimly remembered, and the things we recall most vividly about him are that he had a very stiff golf swing and that his wife kept preserves under the bed in their Ottawa apartment before she fled to the sanctuary of their Quebec City mansion. And that he had the grandeur to sweep through a crowd of reporters, looking neither to left nor right and ignoring all questions, making the scene seem an affront to public dignity. We called him "sir." Everybody did, even his arch-enemies such as Conservative Leader George Drew and Quebec Premier Maurice Duplessis.

The two towering figures in St. Laurent's cabinet were the great diplomat, Lester Pearson, and the tsar of the postwar economy, C. D. Howe. Each of them contributed to the Liberals' glory, and each had a part in the downfall of the St. Laurent government, Howe in the 1956 pipeline debate and Pearson in the break with Britain over the invasion of Egypt and the Suez Crisis.

Those two events ended twenty-two years of Liberal rule under King and St. Laurent, the whole period being known as the "Mackenzie King era," since the St. Laurent years were shaped by King's heirs and assignees, including St. Laurent himself. Lester Pearson once told me that he never made a move or a decision without sensing King's eyes burning into the top of his head, counselling caution and an avoidance of risk.

I find it difficult to measure which of two prime ministers, Mackenzie King or John Diefenbaker, was most responsible for Canada's subsequent and present difficulties, but let's start with King, who was ending his long reign when I first came to Ottawa in 1947, by way of Brazil. The publication of his diaries has made him a more interesting man in death than he ever was when alive. He was the dullest of our prime ministers in terms of personality, and the least accessible — my request for an interview on first arriving in Ottawa resulted in a request for written questions, and weeks after these were submitted I received a table of King's speeches over a six-year period, in which I was told the answers would be found.

My first encounter with King had been in Vancouver in 1940, when he passed through during the federal election campaign which put him in office for the whole of the war. The press corps accompanying him consisted of only two men, Clyde Blackburn of the Canadian Press and Norman MacLeod of British United Press; and Willie (as everybody called him behind his back) slipped through town with no fuss or feathers, hardly anybody noticing. He was like one of his own ghosts, a spook, and at the time we didn't even know he was running the country with a crystal ball.

There was nothing prepossessing about King, either in appearance or manner. He was rotund, and he didn't so much walk as roll along. So far as I have been able to ascertain, he made no memorable utterance during all his years in office, other than "Conscription if necessary, but not necessarily conscription" and his call to Canadians to "put on the full armour of God" in the name of temperance, when he watered the liquor to 70 proof as a money-raising device. All governments, provincial as well as federal, have cashed in on that measure ever since.

King was the least heroic of men, a fact totally ignored by the Liberals when they raised that statue to him on Parliament Hill, depicting him as the statesman supreme, in the futuristic mode. Franklin Roosevelt was able to abide his company and called him Mackenzie, but Winston Churchill dreaded every wartime meeting with Canada's prime minister and would go to any lengths to avoid an evening at Laurier House, the Ottawa mansion that King had inherited from Sir Wilfrid's widow. Yet we are told that Churchill kissed King, at King's request, at their last meeting.

In his approach to money, King was mean and miserly, and most content when others were paying the bills or bestowing largesse upon him. The stone walls that came to grace his Kingsmere estate were built by an Irish craftsman who did most of the work for $30 a month and his keep. King's faithful valet quit after years of service when he realized that the ancient suit of long underwear he was mending for his master consisted more than 50 per cent of the patches he had put in with his darning needle. King cadged meals from his country neighbours and encouraged one woman of his acquaintance in her project of opening a country tea room, until she realized that his calls were intended primarily to partake of free tea and cakes.

He had little sense of style, and less of good manners. On one occasion during the war he did invite a small group to the Kingsmere farmhouse to celebrate a victory, and one of them was his neighbour, Duncan Campbell Scott, the unofficial poet laureate of the time, who said he would write a poem to mark the occasion.

When the party assembled, King announced that his beloved dog Pat had learned a new trick, and he called the animal into the parlour to demonstrate.

"Pat!" he commanded. "Lie down and roll over."

The dog sat motionless.

"Pat!" he commanded. "Do your new trick. Lie down and roll over!"

No response.

The command was repeated, again to no avail. King sighed, patted Pat on the head, and said: "Pat will do the trick later. Very well, Scott, let's have the poem!"

On one hot summer weekend he summoned members of his staff to Kingsmere and put them to work in a stifling upstairs room while he himself sat outside in the sunshine. A plea from the prisoners resulted in permission to set up a table in a distant corner of the garden, where they continued their work in silence. One of them, Jack Pickersgill, sneaked a cigarette, thinking the indiscretion would not be noticed as he was well downwind of King. But on Monday morning in the East Block office, when King was asked how he had enjoyed the glorious weather in the country, he frowned.

"Pickersgill," he said, eyeing the culprit, "*Smoked!*"

King's hold on the Liberal party was uncanny, and he instilled in his followers the idea that the Liberals governed by Divine Right, a philosophy that remains deeply ingrained in Grits to this day. He spoke endlessly in the House of Commons, and we joked that we had combed his speeches for a single sentence as short as Lincoln's Gettysburg Address. Outside the House, he was a man of few words. The thing I remember most vividly about him was that he had masses of black hair growing out of his ears.

The only time I ever saw King display a sense of humour was at the annual dinner of the Parliamentary Press Gallery, where he was a featured speaker, along with Governor General Viscount Alexander and Conservative Leader John Bracken. At the time, word of King's retirement was being eagerly awaited, but he was hanging on so as to pile up enough days in office to ensure his record as the longest-serving head of government in the British Commonwealth. It was the custom in those days to measure superlatives in Commonwealth terms — the Bank of Commerce building in Toronto was the tallest in the Commonwealth (a lot of people still said "Empire"); the Royal York was the biggest hotel in the Commonwealth; and the Sun Life building in Montreal had the largest area of any building in the Commonwealth.

The Press Gallery dinner was an off-the-record affair at which the distinguished speakers could let down their hair. I had written a song for the occasion, dealing with Louis St. Laurent's long wait as the designated successor. It went to the tune of "Good King Wenceslas":

Good King Willieslaus looked out,
And called for Louis Stephen,
Said, "I think it's just about
Time that I was leavin'."
"Sire," said Louis, nothing loath,
"If you feel that way, sir,
'Twould be better for us both
To do it right away, sir."
"Not so fast," said Willieslaus,
"I was only thinking,
Too much haste might hurt our cause,
That would be just stinking."
"Sire, a mouthful you have said,"
Quoth the contrite Louis,

And he trundled off to bed
Muttering, softly, "Phoo–oo–ey!"

Everybody in the audience, including Viscount Alexander and the British high commissioner, Sir Alexander Clutterbuck, sang lustily, dragging out that final "phooey" with great feeling. Then Willie rose to his feet — and announced his retirement, to the great consternation of his listeners, all of whom were deeply into the sauce and unprepared for a news development of these proportions late on a Saturday night and at an off-the-record dinner. After a hasty consultation, a note was sent to Willie at head table to ask if his announcement was on or off the record. He nodded that as far as he was concerned, it was on.

But all the telegraph offices were closed, and there were no papers until Monday, and broadcasters in those days didn't deal in newsgathering. All eyes turned to R. K. "Andy" Carnegie, the bureau chief of the Canadian Press in Ottawa, who was himself nearing the end of a distinguished career and, like his fellows, was considerably sedated by the grape so late in the evening. Despite his protestations, he was conceded the big "scoop," whereupon he had to withdraw from the festivities, open up the CP bureau and find an operator to punch out the news that Willie was going. It gave King one of the few laughs of his life, though his diaries show how reluctant he was to leave office, and how much he regretted doing so once the deed was done.

St. Laurent was kept waiting while a leadership convention was arranged, to be held in the cow barn at the Ottawa Exhibition Grounds (and even after St. Laurent won, Willie crowded in a few more days). At the convention, Willie put the evil eye on the two men who dared to challenge St. Laurent: James G. Gardiner and C. G. "Chubby" Power. There was a spontaneous floor demonstration for one of the brightest and certainly the most ambitious of the younger ministers, Paul Martin, and Martin actually trembled with mortification at the unplanned and unseemly display. He must have wished, in the light of the subsequent frustration of his leadership ambitions, that he had let the movement mushroom. But he made a great show of suppressing it, and St. Laurent had an easy victory.

King was a hard man to love, and nobody did love him, but he played the game of politics with rare skill and ruthlessness, demonstrating that it is truly the art of the possible and, in the process, establishing what can be called Willie's Law, which is that Canadians do not seek heroes in high places. There is no doubt that the secret of his political longevity was his caution and avoidance of extremes, plus his ability to surround himself with outstanding ministers, any one of whom might have made more of a mark without their fear of King's restraining hand, and any one of whom might have steered a better course for Canada than he did.

By postponing problems, rather than facing them, he saved himself time and again. But he laid up a series of woes for his successors, notably on the French-English question. Perhaps even more significant than that was that he created the illusion of Canada as a settled, well-run country where nothing interesting ever happened — an image that was held not only by the rest of the world, but increasingly by Canadians themselves. The impression that our politics are dull has endured in the minds of Canadians, despite the coming to office of such inspiring figures as John Diefenbaker, Lester Pearson, and Pierre Trudeau. Having been on hand for all of twenty-five years — some of the most exciting years in Canadian political history — I still hear Canadians groan that it is "bor-ing." And I put the blame on Willie.

Politically, he had run his course by the time he decided to retire. The Conservatives had brought in George Drew — the hearty, extroverted premier of Ontario — as their national leader. Drew, and a great many others, took it for granted that he would be the next prime minister, and he set to work in Ottawa putting the tools of office into place and holding weekly press conferences, something Canadians had never experienced at the summit of their political affairs.

Drew promised open government to replace the cloisterlike approach of King, and there didn't seem to be much that the austere St. Laurent would be able to do about it. But once in office, St. Laurent began to manifest qualities of warmth and humour that he had not shown as King's Quebec lieutenant in the then almost apolitical portfolios of justice and external affairs. He had always had a good hold on the House of Commons, and now, in the unexpected guise of everybody's uncle, he toured the country patting children on the head and kissing babies and talking good sense and prosperity, making Canadians forget not only the Dirty Thirties but the war years as well.

Never had the country seen so able a cabinet; never had prospects for the country seemed so bright; and down went Drew in the wave of votes for the indomitable Uncle Louis, he of the stern visage and twinkling eyes. Hand in hand with Lester Pearson, St. Laurent helped found the North Atlantic Treaty Organization and took a leading part in the Colombo Plan to aid what came to be known as the Third World. Canada assisted at the birth of Israel, and there was a weaning away from the British tie and an embracing of new bonds, economic, cultural, and military, with the United States.

At home, the social programs set in train by Mackenzie King were expanded and strengthened, and Canada emerged as one of the wonders of the democratic world. These were the glory days of centralism, when no provincial premier counted for much, except Maurice Duplessis in Quebec, who ran a totalitarian state of his own, being careful all the while to leave room for St. Laurent's brand of Quebec federalism. St. Laurent seemed as much at home everywhere in English-speaking Canada as he was in his native Quebec. And to most Canadians from outside, Quebec itself seemed to be as English-speaking as anyplace else. Certainly, Montreal was where the action was.

Meanwhile, Lester Pearson came within a single veto of being secretary general of the United Nations. He presided over a full session of the General Assembly and he flew around the world to the friendly greetings of people and statesmen everywhere, adding a unique note of folksiness to the once-staid business of diplomacy. The industries of Ontario and Quebec burgeoned under the encouraging hand of C. D. Howe, and Canadians designed and built the first all-jet passenger aircraft, only to put it aside for massive assembly lines turning out Canadian-designed fighter planes, the equals of anything in anybody's skies. The national airline spread itself across the world, flying airliners designed and built in Montreal. Distinctive Canadian warships came off the draughting boards and down the slipways, and Canadian eyes turned northward to meet the gaze of the Russians from over the Pole. Television came to Canada with the CBC as the chosen instrument, and Canadians were enthralled by wrestling and by Ed Sullivan and by live dramas by their own actors — but never by their prime minister. St. Laurent was the last leader without a TV image, though we didn't know it at the time.

There were a lot of things we didn't know at the time, including the fact that the fifties represented the pinnacle for Canada, the time when our fondest dreams for the country came closest to fulfilment. Even this is only dimly remembered today, and Louis St. Laurent is scarcely recalled at all, except by those few still around who worked with him. Quebeckers have made no place for him in their hearts or their history, and seem inclined to dismiss him as a sellout to the English or a person who was never a Quebecker at all.

St. Laurent failed to detect, much less harness, two waves that marked the end of his regime — three waves, really, if we include Liberal arrogance and the pride that goes before a fall. The other two were the approaching revolution in Quebec, and the rise of nationalism among Canadians generally. St. Laurent could have ridden the nationalist wave, as indeed he should have after his break with Britain over the Suez invasion and his cry that the days of the supermen of Europe were over. But at the time there were too many Canadians who still cherished the British tie, and too few who were ready to make common cause either with the United States or the newly emerging nations, or who weren't yet ready for the daring business, or illusion, of full, independent nationhood with no apron strings attached.

And neither St. Laurent nor the Liberals had counted on the strangest phenomenon ever to hit the dull, well-managed country where nothing exciting was ever supposed to happen. Exit George Drew, a beaten man. Exit Uncle Louis, old and spent. Enter the incredible, amazing, unbelievable figure of John George Diefenbaker.

2/The Real Dief

No man cultivated his media image more assiduously than John Diefenbaker, who was at it years before the word "media" came into popular usage. He was the lawyer of the people before he became the MP of the common man, and he jumped over so many obstacles that he used to say he should have been an Olympic hurdler.

One of the hurdles was to have the name Diefenbaker in a country whose national flavour through most of his life was essentially WASPish — except for the French element, which baffled Diefenbaker to the end of his days. He told a lot of stories on himself, one of them being about the time he was guest speaker at an affair in Vancouver, where the chairman was a car dealer by trade. During the chairman's introductory remarks, it became increasingly obvious that he had forgotten his guest speaker's name, so he padded the introduction with reams of generalities, the sweat pouring down his brow and his eyes bulging with the agony of it, until finally an expression of vast relief came over his countenance and he wound up with a flourish, saying, "Ladies and gentlemen, it gives me great pleasure to present to you our guest of the evening, Mr. John Studebaker."

A whole generation of Canadians has grown to adulthood without knowing what a Studebaker was, and future generations may have the same trouble believing that John Diefenbaker ever existed, because although he left behind such vivid memories, he left so few tangible accomplishments. You had to be there to know him.

My first acquaintance was in 1947, when he was getting ready to run against George Drew for the Conservative leadership in succession to John Bracken, who put the word "Progressive" into the party's name. But Bracken did little else, and he had agreed to step down after suitable retirement arrangements were made, including the provision of substantial rural real estate outside Ottawa.

Diefenbaker had always been a loner among his parliamentary colleagues, but he fraternized with the press, making himself a familiar figure on the Press Gallery premises and taking care to see that his speeches, and his legal cases, got reported. In his social life, he preferred the company of reporters to that of politicians, and he drank with us though never to excess, and in this wooing of the fourth estate he was aided enormously by his loving and much-loved wife, Edna.

Edna. She died in 1951 and her memory was almost obliterated by the presence of his second wife, Olive, who got all the credit for Diefenbaker's subsequent political successes, to the point where Diefenbaker even edited all mention of Edna out of his official biographies until, in his final years, he reinstated her under pressure from friends. Edna lies buried in a Saskatoon cemetery, across town from the majestic bluff atop which John and Olive Diefenbaker lie entombed high above the South Saskatchewan River, like some pharaoh and his queen.

Diefenbaker came to all our Press Gallery revels and he would butter us up about our writings. On one occasion, he suggested I should seek a career on Broadway. That was after a royal commission into incipient mutinies in the Royal Canadian Navy had recommended Canadianization of the service to "de-Limeytize" it, and we wrote:

> We'll paint maple leaves on the funnels,
> We'll feed the men honey, and jam,
> We'll fill the ships up to the gunnels
> With women who don't give a damn!

There was a jauntiness to Diefenbaker to go with all this camaraderie. And when the leadership convention came, most of the reporters were for him in their hearts, though their heads told them Drew had it in the bag.

Diefenbaker's nomination speech went badly for him, and he left the convention a beaten man, vowing to quit politics. He headed west in a state of despair, but his spirits picked up in Winnipeg where he bought a copy of the *Tribune* and found in it an Ottawa story by Southam correspondent Richard Sanburn, which took a compassionate view of his defeat and ventured the opinion that the party would have done better to have chosen Diefenbaker, ending with the prophecy that the great prairie advocate would be back and would yet come into his own.

Diefenbaker was to say that nobody, Sanburn included, would ever know what that story meant to him. He made a special place in his "favoured" mindset for Sanburn, who eventually became editor of the *Calgary Herald* and grew accustomed to getting telephone calls from Diefenbaker at all hours of the day and night. The relationship continued until Sanburn urged Diefenbaker to retire after the defeat of his government in 1963, following which the phone calls stopped coming.

Diefenbaker had a prodigious memory, especially for those who had offended him, and during his years as prime minister it became commonplace to assume that once you were in his dog house, there was no getting out, ever. The days when he would seek the company of reporters were long gone by then. They faded after he won the Conservative leadership in 1956, in succession to the unfortunate Drew, who looked and sounded so much like Mr. Ontario that Uncle Louis St. Laurent wiped the floor with him. In those days, the prime minister's office, along with his entire entourage and the Department of External Affairs, was in the East Block of Parliament, and one night, following a Press Gallery Dinner, Drew paused on his way home and relieved himself against a corner of the East Block, saying that since he'd never get inside the place he might as well anoint the outside of it.

For some reason that I have never been able to fathom, I was able to move in and out of Diefenbaker's bad books, making the transition at least fifteen times in as many years, being more fortunate in this respect than colleagues like Bruce Phillips and Charles King, whose names for years could not be mentioned in Diefenbaker's presence for fear of inducing apoplexy. Phillips's sin was to sing a song, to the tune of "Jesus Loves Me," one verse of which referred to the split between Diefenbaker and his defence minister, Douglas Harkness, over nuclear weapons. The words went:

There were rumours from George Hees,
I had Harkness's disease.

Diefenbaker thought Phillips had sung "Parkinson's disease," a reference to his trembling jowls, and his government fell two days later, and he never trusted a press man again, nor did he acknowledge Phillips's existence for many years after.

Charles King's sin was to report from an Edmonton meeting that the "Diefenbubble" had burst, causing Diefenbaker to order King thrown off his campaign train, whereupon I, as King's chief, instructed him to stay with the Diefenbaker campaign unto death. There were popular demonstrations in various parts of the country advocating "Charles King for PM," and Diefenbaker trembled so violently we feared we were going to lose him — which, at least as prime minister, we did.

One of my own transgressions came midway through the Diefenbaker regime when I wrote that signs of erosion were beginning to appear in the Diefenbaker cabinet. Two weeks after that piece appeared, French President Charles de Gaulle came on a state visit — a great occasion, with de Gaulle acknowledging the cheers of the multitudes and actually shaking a few hands in Confederation Square. Diefenbaker, as prime minister, called on him at Government House, where de Gaulle was staying as guest of his old friend Governor General Georges Vanier, and when Diefenbaker emerged after the meeting he faced a battery of reporters from France, the United States, Britain, and assorted other countries, besides Canada. He was asked what he and de Gaulle had discussed, when suddenly he spotted my face in the crowd.

"Never mind what we discussed," he said, giving that whinnying laugh he used in moments of mischief. "We are honoured to have in our presence one of the world's leading experts on erosion. Mr. Lynch will now address us on that topic."

He called for silence and refused to speak further. I blurted out a question to change the subject.

"No, no, my friend," he chided. "Give us the benefit of your views about erosion."

He kept it going for what seemed to me an hour, though colleagues said afterward it was only thirty seconds, but it indicated the workings of the man's mind. Days later, he phoned to thank me for a favourable piece on some other topic, and we never discussed erosion again, though the rot in his government continued to take its toll.

The most vivid memories of Diefenbaker are from the campaign trains, and the speeches that went with his travels back and forth across the land. He was the despair of his speech writers, for never once did he deliver the speech that was prepared for him, taking off on his own flights of oratory and fancy as soon as he sensed the mood of the crowd.

His political masterpiece was the 1957 campaign which brought

138

him into power, paving the way for his 1958 landslide which gave him the greatest victory ever scored in federal politics. It fell to my lot in the 1957 campaign to pioneer TV network election coverage, and our little CBC election crew, including Morley Safer as producer, did the first "on location" reports from places ranging from Newfoundland to Vancouver Island. Diefenbaker was given little chance of winning, so we concentrated on the invincible Grits — St. Laurent, Howe, Pearson, Paul Martin, while conveying a sense of the countryside through broadcasts from railway dome cars and the lawns of assorted legislatures. We did our first film package from the banks of the North Saskatchewan, looking across to the skyline of Edmonton, which at the time consisted mainly of the Alberta Legislature and the Macdonald Hotel. To mark the historic occasion, we built a stone cairn on the spot where I did the on-camera narration, but it was carried away in subsequent flooding of the river.

We came upon John Diefenbaker in the town of Kipling, Saskatchewan, where he was having dinner in the old wood-frame hotel. When I sought him out, I found him at table alone, and he waved me into a seat and then, pouting his lips the way he did when he had tidings to impart, informed me that he was going to win this election and become prime minister of Canada. There was nothing to do but humour him, so I did, and he went on to explain how terminal cancer had set in for the Liberals and how he was getting vivid messages from crowds across the country that his time had come. Others had heard the same thing from him and laughed it off. But something must have impelled me to pay attention, for I did a report saying Diefenbaker was sure he was winning and that something in his manner, and the mood of the people, indicated that he might just be right. My CBC masters were not very happy with that report and they cautioned me to stick to the straight and narrow, which meant the assumption of yet another Liberal victory. But I kept slipping in references to the possibility of an upset, and when we did the first network election-night broadcast, with me as anchorman and Blair Fraser as chief commentator, it happened.

Subsequent years have made it seem that the Liberal defeat of 1957 was inevitable, but the fact is that it was a sensation, the like of which none of us had seen before — or have experienced since. Everything we did in those days was television history. On that election night, we also had two commentators from Quebec named

Pierre Trudeau and Pierre Laporte, and such back-up men as Norman DePoe and Bruce Marsh, and off-camera helpers like Morley Safer and Michael Maclear . . . but most of all we had John Diefenbaker. Not on camera, for he was at his home in Prince Albert, where his tiny press corps was huddled in the Sanitary Café. But he was with us in spirit, all night long, while the plot unfolded and while we ladled out the results from the teletypes, my voice growing more excited while Blair Fraser's became more sombre. We had to wait for British Columbia to establish that the Diefenbaker Party (for that is what they themselves called it) would emerge with more seats than the Liberals, and hence had won.

Our roving television crew had given me a big, metre-long cigar, which I had promised, days before, to light on camera as soon as we had a result. Out it came, topping an evening of on-camera smoking of countless cigarettes and bowls of pipe tobacco, for in those uncluttered days it was permissible to smoke in front of the viewers. We didn't know until years later that every time somebody lit up on the screen, uncounted viewers yielded to their reflexes and lit up too, thus shortening their lives by a few gasps each time.

That cigar became celebrated, because, in the intensity of the moment, it came to signify my own joy at the election outcome, which was real enough — though I don't know to this day whether it was elation over Diefenbaker's victory or just my own exhilaration at being part of what was the political upset of the century. Whatever, after a few deep drags on that cigar, which was a cheapie and nearly caused me to gag in the fumes, the word came from the control room for me to douse the stogie, which I did cheerfully enough.

In the subsequent autopsy, it was the view of the program supervisors that the lighting of that cigar was tantamount to editorializing, which was forbidden for CBC personnel, though it was all right for Fraser as the hired gun. In vain did I argue my innocence, though the damage to the corporation's reputation was not great, since the entire country was gripped by the story itself, and so far as I could find out there were no complaints from the audience. Blair Fraser, though, was inconsolable, for he had a distaste for Diefenbaker that went back a long way and would extend for years into the future. It was a feeling that Diefenbaker reciprocated in full measure, just as he would feel that the CBC was part of a plot against him. In later years, Diefenbaker would seek to have just about everybody who was anybody in the CBC fired, and he tried vainly to get Fraser fired from his various posts at *Maclean's* magazine, including his eventual job as editor.

It took the Liberals days to realize what had happened, and they agonized over the business of relinquishing office, with Jack Pickersgill arguing then, as he has ever since, that St. Laurent had the option of remaining in office and facing Parliament. But St. Laurent finally became convinced that it was his duty to resign. So Diefenbaker came down from his beloved fishing ground on Lac La Ronge and returned to Ottawa in triumph, setting the stage for what appeared to be the demoralization of the Liberal party and the prospect of at least a decade of Conservative rule. It should have been two decades, and the story of why it wasn't is the story of Conservative mismanagement that has dogged the party ever since, marring the careers not only of Diefenbaker but of his successors Robert Stanfield and Joe Clark.

From the outset, though, Diefenbaker had a hold not only on the office of prime minister but on the hearts and minds of Canadians. Those first months in office as a minority prime minister were the happiest and most fruitful months of Diefenbaker's political life. Throughout that period, St. Laurent was a man in a trance. They had run him stuffed, and stuffed he remained, sitting silent and stunned in the House of Commons while Diefenbaker toyed with the Liberals and set about the business of governing with a master hand, sure of his every move, confident that he was Canada's man of destiny. The only hope for the Liberals was to seek new leadership, and when they moved into their convention the two contenders were Lester Pearson, wearing his fresh-minted Nobel medal for saving the peace during the Suez Crisis, and Paul Martin, whose whole life in politics had been spent preparing for leadership.

That convention was televised live from coast to coast, and it was a sign of the times that the CBC hoped the result would be decided by 9 P.M. Eastern Time, at which hour a live telecast of the opera *Billy Budd* was to come on from Toronto, featuring a cast of hundreds. A hitch developed when Premier Joey Smallwood of Newfoundland, called upon to speak while the ballots were being counted, saw the red signal lights of the TV cameras and realized he was "on." Once that happened, Joey wouldn't get off, and he ignored all signals from the television crews for him to terminate so that the result could be announced. Producer Michael Hind-Smith, who was getting frantic orders from Toronto to speed things up, panned his cameras around the audience in the Ottawa cow palace and finally found one ancient male delegate whose chin was trembling. Hind-Smith waited until the trembles were synchronized with the cadence of Joey's voice, and he put the old man's picture up on the screen and held it there. But nothing would deter Joey, and by the time he finished it was a quarter to nine, fifteen minutes from the scheduled start of the opera.

Pearson's victory was immediately announced to the cheering delegates, and he was then told by the CBC people to rush into his acceptance speech and to cut it short. For Pearson, it was the beginning of years of frustration that would mark his leadership, for he had prepared a major acceptance speech, some fifteen pages long, announcing the rebirth of the Liberal party and its early resumption of power. In response to the signalling of Hind-Smith's henchmen, he ripped page after page out of his speech as he went along, throwing the unread passages onto the floor beside the rostrum. The speech was disjointed and Pearson was unnerved, but Hind-Smith got the show wrapped up only five minutes beyond the nine o'clock deadline. And in Toronto the huge cast of *Billy Budd* swung into action and the tyrant television was served. It took Pearson years to recover his aplomb, if indeed he ever did.

His first action as Liberal leader was to go into the House of Commons and demand that Diefenbaker resign and turn power back to its rightful owners, the Liberals. Later that evening it fell my lot on live television to ask Pearson why he had made such a preposterous suggestion. The Liberals grieved at the word "preposterous" and once more I stood accused of editorializing.

Diefenbaker revelled in all of this, with everything going his way, and in a subsequent Commons debate with Pearson he pulled out a "secret document" left behind by the St. Laurent government and made what was probably his most masterful speech ever, to which Pearson could reply only with cries of anguish. On CBC that night I said that Diefenbaker "smote Pearson, hip and thigh," and again the corporate bosses had a conniption, claiming my report showed bias. My defence was that of truth, because if anybody had ever been smitten hip and thigh, it was Pearson that night.

Some days earlier, Diefenbaker had slipped on a pebble and strained a muscle in his back while crossing from his East Block office to the Centre Block of Parliament. The doctors ordered him to rest, and soon the rumours were spreading that he had injured himself more seriously than we were being told, that he would be laid up for weeks or months, and that he had a body cast that extended from his hips right up to his neck.

I put in a call to the official residence at 24 Sussex Drive and got him on the phone, things being simpler in Ottawa then than they have since become.

"John?" (A few of us still called him that, not yet fully adjusted to the fact of his being prime minister.)

"Yes, Charles."

"They are saying you are hurt worse than we've been told."

"Who says that?"

"Grits."

"What are they saying?"

"They are saying you will be laid up for a long time and that you have a body cast, and that you won't be able to work, much less lead the party in an election."

Short pause. Then: "You get right out here!"

I jumped in my car and drove around to the residence and rang the doorbell, there being no guards in those times. A maid answered and told me to go right upstairs, that the prime minister was expecting me.

Diefenbaker greeted me at the door to his bedroom and beckoned me inside, dismissing the two stenographers who had been taking dictation there. He was dressed in his pyjamas and was wearing a blue silk dressing-gown with gold brocaded squares on it.

When we were alone, he chuckled. "Now," he said, "let's hear all that stuff again."

I told him about the severity of his injuries, and the body cast and the rest of it.

He untied the sash of his dressing-gown and threw the garment on the floor. He unbuttoned the top of his pyjamas and threw that on the bed. He pulled the string on his pyjama pants and they fell to the ground, and I found myself in the full and complete presence of the Prime Minister of Canada.

"Do you see anything?" he demanded.

"Well, sir. . . ."

"Do you see any body cast?"

"No."

He faced away from me and put his hands on his hips. "Do you see any swelling back there?"

"No."

"You see that chair there?"

"Yes, sir."

"Well," he said, "I'd jump over that chair for you, just to show I'm fine, but I can't, because I've got an awfully sore back."

He then asked if I was satisfied. I said I was and that I couldn't help remarking that this method of dealing with his medical problem was somewhat different from the way they were going about it in Washington, where President Eisenhower was ailing and medical bulletins were being issued almost hourly, with great diagrams of Eisenhower's insides splashed over all the magazines and newspapers.

"There will be none of that Hagerty nonsense here," said Diefenbaker, a reference to Eisenhower's press secretary James Hagerty, who had become a media hero during the president's illness.

While Diefenbaker was pulling his pyjamas back on, I remarked that I hoped he realized I would be reporting on this encounter in full detail, and he chortled.

"Of course you will, why do you think I asked you out here?" Then he sat on the chair, motioned me to take a seat on the bed, and said, "Everything up to now is on the record. Now we'll have a chat and that will be off the record."

I agreed, and he outlined to me his plan of returning to the Commons within a week and drawing Pearson into a debate that would leave him with no alternative but to call an election, which the Conservatives would win. And so it happened, just as Diefenbaker ordained it should.

My report on my medical inspection of the prime minister, right down to the buff, led the Liberals to charge that Diefenbaker had gone bonkers, a charge that they were to repeat often in the days and years to come. But it put at rest all the rumours about the gravity of his injuries and cleared the way for his return to Parliament, fighting fit. He called the election and then went off onto the wintry hustings for the greatest campaign not only of his life but of the life of any Canadian politician (John A. Macdonald's 1878 campaign notwithstanding).

This time, the slogan was "Follow John." And this time, instead of doubters, he had allies. One of them was Premier Maurice Duplessis, who threw his Union Nationale political machine behind the Conservative party, providing candidates, money, and all the bribery and corruption needed to knock the stuffing out of the Quebec Liberals, who had started to come apart from the moment of St. Laurent's departure.

As soon as Duplessis' intention to intervene became apparent, I went to Quebec City and sought an interview with him. Moments after presenting myself in his anteroom I was ushered into his presence, whereupon he looked at me with a frown, saying I wasn't the man he expected.

"I thought it was my friend Charles Lynch of the *Ottawa Journal*," he said. "He's a good Tory and I once named a bridge after him, did you know that?"

I said I didn't, though I knew that my arrival in Ottawa had been a source of annoyance to this older Charles Lynch, who in addition to being a distinguished newspaperman was also a bagman and fixer for the Tories and for the Union Nationale — a commonplace relationship in Canadian politics and newspapering well into the 1950s. The senior Charles Lynch had even invited me to assume another name; and when I refused he reluctantly inserted his middle name into his own byline and was known from then on as Charles Ivers Lynch.

"I regard you as an impostor," said Duplessis, "but since you are here, and since there are only boring people waiting to see me" — his office was thronged with supplicants for favours — "I shall talk to you as long as it takes me to smoke one cigar."

I thanked him and asked him how far he was prepared to go to help Diefenbaker.

"Tell me what kind of a man he is," was the response.

"He is a great speaker," I said. "In their last debate he absolutely wiped the floor with Lester Pearson."

"Ah!" said Duplessis, "but that is so easy!"

I laughed and admitted that Pearson wasn't much of a debater, though he had been great at diplomacy.

Duplessis expressed his admiration for Louis St. Laurent and launched into a masterful imitation of Uncle Louis' speaking manner, complete with facial expressions and gestures. When I applauded, Duplessis beamed and said, "Not bad, eh?" I agreed that it was very good and suggested he should practise up on Diefenbaker, showing him the business of the shaking wattles and the hands on hips, elbows flapping.

"Does he actually do that?" asked Le Chef.

I assured him it was so, except when Diefenbaker was speaking French — at which times all gestures ceased and his face assumed a fixed expression, while his eyes tended to bulge.

"And the eyes of his listeners," said Duplessis. Then he changed the subject. "Do you think Canada will ever have a national flag?"

I said I hoped so, but I wondered if there could ever be agreement on its design: "There is no unanimity about whether it should have the Union Jack or the Fleur-de-lis, or both."

"My boy," said Duplessis, lighting his fourth cigar of the interview, "the only place in this world that you find unanimity is in the graveyard." Then he added, with a twinkle, "And even there, I have heard it said, at election time the dead have been known to vote in various ways!"

I thanked him and departed, and he said that even if I was an impostor he had been glad to see me.

As a result of his machinations, Diefenbaker won fifty seats in Quebec. But as Diefenbaker also swept the rest of the country, it turned out he didn't need those Quebec seats, and he never did figure out how to handle the incumbents Duplessis sent him. In the end, their presence hastened the premature end of his regime.

No Canadian prime minister has ever been given the power the voters bestowed on John Diefenbaker in 1958, and no Canadian prime minister has ever been so corrupted by it. Not that Diefenbaker overused the mandate he had been given. He either underused it or he didn't know how to use it at all. Rather than wielding power, power wielded him. It fed his ego to the point where he became incapable of meaningful communication with colleagues, and at the end of his ministry he was acting as though he had no colleagues at all, only foes and toadies. Overriding arrogance is not a fatal flaw in political leaders, and it might have carried Diefenbaker through had he been younger, or more experienced in the business of administration. As it was, he had never run anything more complicated than a prairie law office, and in all his years in Parliament as an opposition MP, he had operated as a one-man band.

What really did him in, though, as prime minister, was the humility with which he approached the House of Commons, where

146

he was wary of using his massive majority to achieve his own political ends. He had a fatal reverence for the institution of Parliament, in
which he had served so long that by the time he became prime
minister he was years past his prime. His inability to understand
Quebec caused him to throw away the gift of fifty Quebec seats
Duplessis had bestowed upon him, and caused Quebeckers to feel
estranged as never before from the national government. His eventual mistrust of all but the most fawning colleagues denied him what
should have been a decade, or maybe two, of power, breaking the
Liberal grip on what has cynically been called "the federal trough."
(Derek Bedson, Diefenbaker's principal secretary during his first term
in office, coined the phrase "trough Grits" as a response to the com-
monly used "rabid Tories.")

The people around Diefenbaker permitted him first to drift into a
fantasy world of his own and then, when he began to flounder, they
did nothing to buoy him up. The breaking point was the nuclear
weapons crisis of 1963, but by that time Diefenbaker had been
weakened, like a bull picked by the lances of the picadors. There had
been the crisis with the governor of the Bank of Canada, James
Coyne, over who was managing the money, and devalued "Diefen-
bucks" were spread like confetti across the land by resurgent Grits.
Then there was the tokenism of introducing bilingual government
cheques and also a simultaneous interpretation system in the House of
Commons, plus a Governor General from French Canada — all of
which failed to produce a response in Quebec, where, in the wake of
Duplessis' death, the Quiet Revolution was gathering strength. The
seeds of today's Quebec separatism sprouted, along with René
Lévesque, out of the 1959 Montreal strike of Radio Canada producers, an event that Diefenbaker scarcely noticed, let alone understood.

He lost touch with urban Canada, and he developed a physical
tremble that disturbed his friends and brought mockery from his
foes. Beyond cause, he fancied himself to be surrounded by enemies,
plotters, and fools. It has always seemed to me that if the John
Fishers, Allister Grosarts, Bill Brunts, Howard Greens and, yes, the
Leon Balcers, had made more effort to bolster Diefenbaker in his
moments of darkest mistrust and uncertainty, the Tory time in office
would have been greatly prolonged and might have lasted to this
day. As it was, the doubters took their toll far sooner than they
should have, aided and abetted as they were by the influence of John

F. Kennedy in the White House and his agents in the State Department and Pentagon, with Whitehall cheering from the sidelines.

Diefenbaker's final, fatal move in the governance of his country might otherwise have made him a hero — when he renounced Canada's commitment to adopt U.S. nuclear weapons. In this, he was twenty years ahead of his time. But by telling the Americans to take back their nukes, he came into open conflict with the powers in Washington, who got him in their sights and pressed the button. This provided a chance for Lester Pearson, in an action denounced by Pierre Trudeau among others, to switch from opposition to support of nuclear weapons for the Canadian army and air force. And it drove a wedge into Diefenbaker's own cabinet, impelling Defence Minister Douglas Harkness, Associate Defence Minister Pierre Sévigny, and Trade Minister George Hees to come down on the side of the nuclear commitment.

Diefenbaker's vast majority had been wrecked in the election of 1962, and his minority government had been kept from governing by an obstructionist Liberal opposition, hungry for a return to power and prepared to cripple Parliament itself to get it. In 1963 they succeeded, amid scenes of political turmoil that were Shakespearean in their dimensions — except that there was no bard to embellish them other than Peter C. Newman, who dubbed Dief a renegade.

But Diefenbaker was considerably more complex than that. His most unappealing traits became magnified in office, and while his wife Olive has often been given credit (by himself as well as others) for helping him keep his sanity, her own flawed judgement of people and events often warped his attitudes and led him into dead ends. The characteristics which he manifested through most of his life — and which propelled him into power on a wave of popular esteem — faded in office and left the man a caricature of himself, friendless and alone, with only Olive to offer counsel and comfort, smiling sweetly all the time while whispering into his ear the names of those she suspected of treachery.

Diefenbaker's most appealing feature was his westernness, and specifically the whiffs of Saskatchewan that he carried with him wherever he went and whenever he spoke. In those days, Saskatchewan wasn't such a great place to be from, and I once heard a Saskatoon woman say, half-apologetically, "Well, I'm from Saskatchewan because *somebody's* got to be from there!"

Diefenbaker's mind was stocked with anecdotes and experiences that made Saskatchewan throb in the minds of his listeners, and the broad prairie perspective was such that he could look any person in the eye, be they high or low, friend or foe, and make them laugh or wince at his choosing. He had the ego that is a prime ingredient of political ambition, but it was remarkable how many of his jokes and misadventures were recounted at his own expense. He could be thoughtful almost to the point of being cloying. He was extroverted and outreaching, though a loner in his practice of the law and, later, in his participation in politics. He was good humoured, tireless, jaunty in appearance and manner, a rustic hunter and fisherman, eloquent, a champion of the oppressed and a freedom fighter. All these things were part of the man who became Conservative leader at the age of sixty-one and prime minister one year later. In power, the dark side of the man emerged and contributed to his own political destruction, and that of the party he led.

Ironically, many of his old beguiling qualities returned to Diefenbaker in his closing years, when he revelled in his role as national sage, dying at age eighty-three full of years and full of honours, his funeral rite the most elaborate since that of Sir John A. Macdonald, and his monument in Saskatoon the most lavish ever erected in Canada to the memory of a single man. By then, people had forgotten the litany of charges that brought him down — that he was vindictive, suspicious, malicious, unforgiving, malevolent, narrow-minded, self-centred, mistrustful, arrogant, resentful, bad tempered, mean, feline, cunning and cantankerous, and a tamperer with truth. And it was possible, in later years, for Pierre Trudeau to say, from the prime minister's seat in the House of Commons, "I really love that old guy."

Diefenbaker left so little in the way of political achievements, and his leadership was so disruptive of the nation's affairs and those of his own party, that Canadians coming after must wonder if such a man could ever have existed, and what the fuss was about.

Here are some glimpses:

William MacPherson, the associate editor of the Ottawa *Citizen*, tells of visiting with Diefenbaker in Barbados during the Old Chief's final winter and finding him chortling with delight over a newly finished passage of his memoirs.

"This," he said, "will really fix Lynch at last!"

He proceeded to read MacPherson his version of my part in the nuclear weapons crisis of 1963, in which he said I had played the role of foreign agent for the government of President John F. Kennedy and had sold the government of my own country down the river for a few glasses of bourbon. It is a matter of regret that this portion of his memoirs went unpublished in the form he wrote it, because it is exciting stuff in a land whose politics are deemed to be so dull.

The whole thing had arisen out of the press briefings. One of the techniques employed by the Kennedy forces consisted of off-the-record briefings by U.S. Ambassador Livingston Merchant, who kept telling us that Canada was committed to nuclear weapons and could not renege without playing false to her allies in the North American Air Defence Agreement (NORAD) and the North Atlantic Treaty Organization (NATO). These press briefings were held in the basement recreation room of the Rockcliffe Park house occupied by the counsellor of the U.S. Embassy, Charles "Chuck" Kisseljak, and they were attended by about twenty invited members of the Parliamentary Press Gallery. As they were "for background only," none of us reported on the facts of the matter, though the briefings doubtless coloured our coverage of subsequent events, including a State Department press release denouncing Diefenbaker's version of the nuclear weapons agreement.

President Kennedy also caused the NATO supreme commander, General Lauris Norstad, to visit Ottawa and hold a press conference. And at the conference, in response to my questioning, Norstad said in public what Merchant had been saying in private — that Canada was firmly committed to nuclear weapons for her armed forces in Europe. Diefenbaker fumed, and when months later I finally wrote about the Merchant briefings, he seized on them as the clinching evidence of my treachery to my country. On national television, he confronted me with suppressing the facts of hostile activity by a foreign power on Canadian soil, and said that had there been full disclosure at the time he could have taken counter action in the best interests of Canada.

My involvement did not end there, in Diefenbaker's view. There was also my supposed influence on Harkness. The Norstad press conference had strengthened the pro-nuclear views of Diefenbaker's defence minister, Douglas Harkness, and the associate defence minister, Pierre Sévigny, both of them distinguished veterans of the Second World War. (In fact, Harkness had formed a battlefield friendship with Matthew Halton that endures between the two families to this day.)

I had invited Harkness to the annual dinner of the Parliamentary Press Gallery in 1963 — a historic dinner in that it took place on the eve of the House of Commons defeat of Diefenbaker's last government (and was, in Diefenbaker's version, a decisive factor in his downfall). My other personal guest at the dinner was Howard Green, the external affairs minister and the staunchest of Diefenbaker loyalists. He and Harkness were at daggers drawn over the nuclear weapons question, and both maintained a sullen silence as I sat between them in the parliamentary restaurant atop the Centre Block on the Hill. There was no discussion of the events of the moment, but as Diefenbaker recounted it to MacPherson years later, I pumped whisky into Harkness and taunted him with lacking the courage of his convictions. And this so filled Harkness with anger and self-pity that he blurted out "I'll do it!" and handed his resignation to Diefenbaker the following morning, thus sealing the fate of the government and enabling Lester Pearson, with President Kennedy's blessing, to assume power in the resultant election.

As a result of these incidents, said Diefenbaker, I would have my country's blood on my hands for evermore.

It was during this time of the weapons crisis that Diefenbaker had his most severe bouts of "the shakes," keeping his fists clenched to control the trembling in his hands. His head shook uncontrollably and his wattles jiggled in an effect that many Canadians found comic, and visitors from abroad found incredible, and mimics found irresistible. Behind Diefenbaker's back, serious conversations were going on about whether his judgement was impaired to the point of incompetence to govern, and in the Press Gallery we were speculating on who gets the net when a prime minister goes round the bend.

The 1963 election removed Diefenbaker from office and put him back in his natural environment as defence counsel and opposer, where he made a physical comeback, if not a political one. He made a creditable showing in the 1965 election, winning ninety-five seats almost single-handedly and denying Pearson his coveted majority. He fought valiantly, if unsuccessfully, against his removal from the leadership in 1967 and then settled down to the happiest years of his life, harassing his successors, Robert Stanfield and Joe Clark, without mercy. He made himself into a sort of national totem, hailed everywhere but listened to nowhere — apart from the short shots that TV editors and viewers found so appealing. Canadians in all parts of the country flocked to his speeches, and even the House of Commons, that graveyard of the spoken word, filled when he was on his feet.

Diefenbaker was a crashing bore when he was reading from a written text, but he was matchless when working from no text at all, or from a pile of disjointed notes, clippings, and quotes from his opponents. During his prime ministership, there had been nobody in opposition who could hold his own with Diefenbaker. Lester Pearson was hopeless as a debater. Paul Martin was all bombast, refusing to rally his energies or skills in the distasteful work of opposition. Jack Pickersgill was best, though the effect he achieved was usually more clown than clobber, and Diefenbaker loved nothing more than skewering Sailor Jack. Pickersgill's riding of Bonavista-Twillingate came out of Diefenbaker's mouth as Twisted Billingsgate, and he could convulse any crowd by saying, slyly, that whenever he wanted to hear people laugh, he needed only to say one word.

Here, he would pause, then pounce: "PICKERSGILL!"

Everybody howled, every time.

Transcripts of Diefenbaker's speeches abound, but they convey nothing of the flavour or the mannerisms or the vocal effects — from falsetto to basso profundo, with the occasional horselike whinnies and the pauses for effect. He would point the avenging finger, and he would flap his arms like a pelican venting its wings prior to takeoff. The eyes would burn and the tightly waved hair would fly and, at the height of his powers, the crowds would roar and people would clutch at his garments. As show business, Diefenbaker was prime box office when he was at his best. And though people turned away from him when he needed them the most, he won his way back into their hearts at the end of his long span, and in the words of his faithful supporter Arthur Maloney, they stood up when John Diefenbaker came into the room.

It was Maloney who fought hardest to save Diefenbaker's leadership when Dalton Camp mounted the campaign to bring him down after the 1965 election. Camp and his allies carried the day, knocking the Old Chief off his perch but failing in their main objectives — one of which, though dimly perceived and vehemently denied, was to install Camp himself as Diefenbaker's successor. It was to frustrate this knavish trick that Diefenbaker bent the last of his political energies and in the process opened gaping wounds which continue to sap the strength of the Progressive Conservative Party, sabotaging the best hopes of men like Robert Stanfield and Joe Clark, and women like Flora MacDonald.

Dalton Camp, to Diefenbaker's delight, became a mere footnote in the party's history and a non-entry in the political history of the country itself. Yet he was a man who could have filled the role played eventually by Pierre Elliott Trudeau. When Camp switched from being Diefenbaker's loyal lieutenant to becoming his principal critic, he harnessed the emerging forces of youth in the sixties, and he personified many of the hopes that had died, in the United States, with John F. Kennedy — the emotions that were to be so much a part of the impending Trudeaumania. When Camp made his move against Diefenbaker, Trudeau was not even dimly perceived on the horizon of Canadian politics, having just entered the House of Commons on the coattails of Jean Marchand and Gérard Pelletier, the new embodiments of the French Fact Militant on the federal scene. Camp got there first, and he developed the momentum with courage, flair, imagination, and, in Diefenbaker's word, treachery. That he failed in his own ambitions is one of the ironies of Canadian politics. He wound up in the despised role of executioner, while the dilettante Trudeau harnessed the forces Camp had set in motion, becoming the darling of the Age of Aquarius.

Pondering the conundrum of Camp, it has always seemed to me that had he clung more firmly to his New Brunswick roots, instead of becoming as deeply Toronto-ized as he did, he might have achieved at least some of his large ambitions. It is a curious fact that in later years, having retired to what he called his "bunker" in New Brunswick, Camp found more fulfilment than he ever did in his years as a power broker and manipulator in and from Toronto. He receded into sagedom with a twinkle, even as Diefenbaker had done before him on a grander scale. And Diefenbaker once admitted that nothing in political life gave him as much unmitigated delight as Camp's two election defeats in Toronto, after spending more money than any other candidate in the land.

Two speeches of Diefenbaker's stand out in memory, for special reasons. The first took place in 1967, shortly after his impeachment at the 'Conservative leadership convention, when the Parliamentary Press Gallery organized a dinner for him as "the newsmaker of the century." At the time, there was great speculation about Diefenbaker's future. Stripped of party office, would he seek to remain in Parliament? Would he try to start a breakaway western party? Would he support Robert Stanfield, and would there be a place for him in a Stanfield government?

I had bought tickets to the testimonial dinner for all our parliamentary staff and then was called out of Ottawa on assignment, returning a few hours before the dinner was to commence. To my surprise and indignation, I found that the Press Gallery executive of the day had decreed, without consulting Diefenbaker, that the dinner should be off the record. When I protested the folly of news people staging a dinner for the newsmaker of the century and having if off the record, I was told that everybody wanted it that way so they could enjoy the evening without having to work.

I continued my protests right up to dinnertime and took my place in the crowded room with foreboding, having a premonition of things to come, heightened by the gleam in Diefenbaker's eye and his long glare in my direction, followed by a wink. My worst expectations were met when Diefenbaker got to his feet and uncorked an hour-long speech about the perfidy of President Kennedy who, in Diefenbaker's view, had been Canada's worst enemy, ever, in the White House. It was probably the most scathing speech ever made about the United States by a leading Canadian politician. At the end, Diefenbaker cooled down and said he realized we were wondering about his future plans. Giving me another baleful stare, he said he would not be running for Parliament again and probably would not make any future appearances in the House of Commons, though he would keep his seat until the election, which was expected the following year.

This was the news we were waiting for, and as soon as the dinner adjourned I made known to my colleagues my intention to write it, quoting Diefenbaker directly. From all sides came appeals not to violate the "off the record" stricture. Only colleague Bruce Phillips agreed with me that the news came first and that we had no further need for speculation when we had heard it from Diefenbaker himself, whether we believed him or not, and I did not. Phillips filed a news

154

story to our papers, and I wrote a commentary, and when CBC producer Don Atwood saw what we were doing, he ordered an item of Diefenbaker's "announcement" included in the CBC's national TV news that night.

Phillips left on a Caribbean tour the next morning and so escaped the aftermath, which was lucky for him. Tom Gould, the CBC's chief correspondent in Ottawa, resigned on the spot in protest at the CBC quoting Diefenbaker — and went on to a profitable career with the rival CTV. Charles King, associate editor of the Ottawa *Citizen*, threatened overnight resignation rather than be associated with the likes of me under the Southam banner.

An emergency general meeting of the Press Gallery was called for the purpose of expelling me and Atwood, and there were demands that my employers be asked to dismiss me. Finally, after stormy scenes, a resolution was passed overwhelmingly for a three-week suspension of membership and withdrawal of all my parliamentary privileges, including parking, reading, eating, and attendance at the Commons sessions. Commons Speaker Lucien Lamoureux eased my pain somewhat by finding me a place in the officials' gallery and saying I would be welcome anywhere on the parliamentary premises, thus enabling me to continue my work, though no colleague would speak to me during the "exile."

There remained the ordeal of a meeting of all the publishers of Southam-owned newspapers to consider the affair and to rule on the question of dismissal. I was told to wait outside the room while my masters deliberated, and I shall always remember the sight of Basil Dean, publisher of the *Edmonton Journal*, bursting through the door, beaming, and saying, "We have decided to support you, and to hell with them!"

The only person who enjoyed the affair was Diefenbaker himself, who was quoted as saying it was good to see Lynch writhe and that it was high time we had some ethics in journalism to match those followed by practitioners of the law. But he never did complain about his "secret" speech being reported, and I think he would have liked it if the sulphurous parts about Kennedy had leaked out as well. I have never regretted what I did. The alternative would have been to present "informed" speculation about Diefenbaker's plans, under one's own signature, which may have been Diefenbaker's intent. If so, it was mischievous, because Diefenbaker's statement of his intentions bore no resemblance to what actually happened. In fact, he spoke long and often in the House of Commons during the thirteen succeeding years, and he ran in every election that came up, holding his Prince Albert seat until the day he died.

The other speech of special memory was the last one he made in the House of Commons, an ill-tempered and ill-formed intervention. The Trudeau government had moved to limit debate on a measure to conserve oil supplies during periods of national emergency, and Diefenbaker rose in wrath to note that Trudeau had referred to a crowd in Vancouver as "creeps."

"I was interested," said Diefenbaker in the Commons, "in finding the meaning of 'creep.' I looked it up and found that it is 'nervous shrinking or shiver of dread.' Certainly the way this government is postponing the calling of an election would indicate that the creeps are over there. . . . If we give the government of Canada the power for which they are asking in this bill, we might as well close the institution now. The opposition will cease to exist. . . . Creep! That is what this government is doing."

The speech tailed off into a series of rambling complaints about how Quebec Premier René Lévesque got the French Legion of Honour, and how Trudeau had informed the CBC that only selective things could be placed before Parliament, and how former Solicitor General Jean-Pierre Goyer (Diefenbaker called him "Go-Go") had squandered $10,000, and how his own questions on the Commons order paper were not being answered.

I confess that in retrospect the speech doesn't seem so very disjointed or out of place. But it did at the time, and I wrote that it was one of the least distinguished speeches Diefenbaker had ever made in the chamber and one that ill fitted his stature as Canada's senior statesman.

After Diefenbaker read the piece, he telephoned all over town, determined to reach me. He found me in the make-up room at CJOH TV, where colleagues W. A. Wilson and Bruce Phillips were preparing for a panel program. When the operator announced that Mr. Diefenbaker was calling, I told Wilson and Phillips to plug their ears, because this was going to be a beaut.

The familiar voice came through the phone like the trump of doom. "That," he proclaimed, "was an absolutely shameful piece of journalism!"

"But . . . ." I gasped.

"And to think," he went on, "how I have defended you through all the years!"

I mumbled.

"I have trusted you," he trembled, "and comforted you, and now you turn on me in this way. I tell you, you will rue this day, and I shall see that you suffer for it, and I put you on notice of that!"

Finally, I got a word in, pointing out that at least I had mentioned his many distinguished speeches of the past, comparing this latest one, however unfavourably, to his best.

"Aargh!" growled Diefenbaker. "We have no more to say to one another!"

And he banged down the phone, leaving me all a-tremble, while Wilson and Phillips shook with laughter. We agreed it was vintage stuff, and I heard later from Keith Martin in Diefenbaker's office that he threw the phone down with such vigour that it missed the cradle and went skittering across the room.

Diefenbaker did not hold the grudge. I took part in his final TV appearance the week before he died, and he bantered about my carelessness with facts and recalled my days as a U.S. spy, and we had a rollicking good time.

Days later, I was playing the mouth organ aboard his funeral train as we carried him across the prairies to his final rest.

3/Pearson, Canada's Man of the Century

The prime minister who remained most a "person" in high office was Lester Pearson. He was selfish, to the extent that he sacrificed loyal colleagues to save himself from embarrassment, a latter-day concept of "the king can do no wrong." He was stubborn in pursuit of things he believed in, notably the way he bulled through the maple leaf flag against heavy opposition, trampling not only the feelings but the emotions of those who were loyal to the ensign and its links with the British past. He was ambitious — else why would he have sought the prime ministership, elbowing his way through a field of qualified candidates?

King had stored up problems for his successors by his inaction; Pearson left a pile of problems because he was an activist and because he was prepared to make concessions to the New Democrats in return for their support of his minority governments. His social programs, plus his acceptance of collective bargaining in the public service, were based on the assumption of perpetual good times. Being a confirmed optimist, Pearson could not have done it any other way, and he assumed that the methods that had served him so well in international diplomacy would be equally effective in domestic politics.

Westerners tended to regard him as a stuffed shirt, which is odd because a less stuffy man never held public office. His opponents mocked at him for his lisp, and it is true he was no orator, though on the rare occasions when he himself was moved he could transmit the feeling. He had no knack for the memorable phrase, and when they named the new external affairs building after Pearson they searched his speeches for a line that could be chiselled into the foyer walls, finally giving up and settling for a montage of stilted sentences.

He walked funny and he talked funny, but he acted very seriously indeed, and his diplomatic achievements, speaking for a Canada at

158

the height of its world prestige and influence, made him the Canadian of the century. Yet in the last year of his prime ministership his popularity plummetted and his government was beset by scandals, forcing him to quit while he was behind and yield his job to Pierre Trudeau, who proceeded to govern as though Pearson had never existed.

Those of us who covered what turned out to be Pearson's winning of the Nobel Peace Prize at the United Nations during the Suez Crisis of 1956 remember how, as foreign minister, he ran his team of young diplomats like a football coach, sending players in from the bench. He kept the press informed of what he was trying to do at all times, using media as a weapon. He had the *New York Times* in the palm of his hand. He would invite reporters back to his hotel suite at the end of an exhausting day and would pump us about what other delegations were saying.

I have a vivid recollection of him kicking off his shoes and putting his stockinged feet up on the coffee table. When he noticed that the table had a map of the world inlaid into it, he leaned forward and pointed to the Middle East. "Where the hell," he asked, "is Sharm el Sheikh?" He had been engaged in furious negotiations all that day about the disposition of that port on the Gulf of Aqaba, without knowing where it was, though he had a vague memory of having flown over it years before.

Days later, when he had obtained agreement for the formation of a United Nations Emergency Force, he was on the telephone to Prime Minister St. Laurent to discuss which Canadian military units would be sent. The role of the force was to replace the British and French troops that had invaded the Suez Canal Zone, and it was delicate ground for Canada, since the Egyptians suspected Pearson of being a British mole. Pearson was surrounded by news correspondents when he took the call from Ottawa on a lobby phone at the U.N. He asked what units had been chosen for the peacekeeping, and when he heard the answer, he sputtered and uttered an oath.

Covering the mouthpiece with his hands, he groaned: "They've picked the Queen's Own Rifles!" Then he opened the mouthpiece and shouted: "No! No! NOT the Queen's Own Rifles. The Egyptians will have a fit."

It took Pearson two days of negotiations with his own government to get what he wanted, and at the same time he had to arrange for the purchase, in Canada, of two tons of ghee to feed the Indian contingent to the U.N. force.

"What on earth is ghee?" he kept asking. "Whatever it is, we need some fast." When he was told it was a kind of rancid butter, he passed the news back to Ottawa with all speed, and the required ghee was fast-rotted and dispatched, though we never heard whether or not it was to the taste of the Indian troops.

Pearson had a wife who despised politics, and he himself was on the verge of quitting after a mass Liberal rally in Maple Leaf Gardens during the 1957 campaign, when a young demonstrator was knocked sprawling from the platform and cracked his skull on the cement floor. In 1958, at the start of his first election campaign as Liberal leader, we were travelling with him by special train to Espanola, where he was to be nominated as the candidate for the riding of Algoma East. He invited us for a drink in his private car, and after we were assembled with glasses in hand, Mrs. Pearson was asked how she felt about the campaign.

She took a long puff through her cigarette holder, exhaled a cloud of smoke, and said, "It's all such a terrible waste of Mike."

There was a shocked silence at this candid observation, the first of many that Maryon Pearson was to make in the course of her husband's political leadership. It was later in that campaign that Mrs. Pearson made her memorable response when she was asked, at a coffee party, whether there was anything she wanted to bring up, and she said, "Yes, six cups of coffee and three doughnuts." She was also credited with the remark that "behind every successful man there is a surprised woman," and the statement, following Pearson's retirement, that she had married him "for better or for worse, but not for lunch."

Pearson bore his wife's scorn with no outward signs of annoyance, and it was assumed he enjoyed her irreverence and her barbed wit. Certainly, she was right about the 1958 campaign being a waste of his talents — Diefenbaker gave him the worst whipping in the history of Canadian politics, and Pearson held onto the job of Liberal leader only because nobody else wanted it. But by holding on, he ensured his presence when the Diefenbaker government self-destructed, and thus achieved his ambition of becoming prime minister and sitting at the summit of affairs "without," as he put it, "having to clear policy through somebody else."

The disasters that befell him as prime minister would fill several books, some of which have been written and some of which are still to come. Through it all he kept his balance and his sense of humour, though he used to wish for deliverance from writers who would plead their everlasting regard for him and then roast him alive in print. His advisers were even less adroit than Diefenbaker's had been, and he followed their advice into pratfall after pratfall, leading to the theory that Pearson was only happy when he was hanging over the edge of a cliff by his fingernails, watching his friends and associates being dashed to pieces on the rocks below.

Pearson once told me that he sincerely believed that Canada, because of its size and diversity, was the hardest country in the world to govern. He also informed me that I was a danger to the country through my writings, but he never said why. I was left to conclude that he was talking about my tendency to take the English side of what was then called the English-French dialogue, and to express undying loyalty to the monarchy in Canada. He agonized over the Quebec question and dreaded the prospect of presiding over the dissolution of Canada as a nation-state, the blame for which he laid on the hated Diefenbaker and on the procrastinations of his old mentor Mackenzie King.

Pearson was like Diefenbaker in at least one thing — he delighted in telling stories on himself. The first volume of Pearson's memoirs, like the first volume of Diefenbaker's, abounds with them. I think the humility was more honest in Pearson's case than it was in Diefenbaker's, though there are those who feel the two arch-enemies were equal in self-esteem.

My favourite Pearson story was the one he told about the morning in 1963 when he awoke to the realization that, the night before, he had been sworn in as prime minister of Canada. He rose and did his ablutions, and while he was looking in the mirror adjusting his polka-dot bow tie, wondering what the first challenge of high office would be, the telephone rang. It was a message from Governor General Vanier from his sick bed in Government House. Would Pearson come to Vanier's bedside with all speed to attend to an urgent matter of state?

Ah, thought Pearson with relish, this was it. The summit. The first big problem and the first big decision. He hastened to Rideau Hall and was ushered into the bedroom of his old friend.

"Thank God, Mike, you are here. We have this awful problem to settle."

"Ready, sir!" said the eager Pearson. "What is it?"

"It's Vincent."

"Vincent?"

"Vincent Massey, he's been driving me crazy!" Vanier indicated a pile of correspondence on a bedside table. "He's been flooding me with letters for months, and I've been passing copies to that man, but he won't do anything."

"That man?"

"Diefenbaker. He hates Vincent, you know."

"Yes, I know," said the crestfallen Pearson. "But what's the problem?"

Vanier sighed. "Vincent is building Massey College at the University of Toronto and he wants his coat of arms over the archway."

"So?"

"So the Massey coat of arms contains nothing to indicate that Vincent was Governor General. It's all ploughs and pitchforks and threshing machines. He wants the coat of arms amended."

"So?"

"So the application can't go forward without the government's endorsation, and Diefenbaker wouldn't give it, and Vincent is enraged."

"Is that all?" asked Pearson, deflated.

"All!" fumed Vanier. "Nothing has caused me more trouble."

"Well," said Pearson, "it need trouble you no more. I agree to whatever it is Vincent wants."

"It's not that simple," said Vanier. "It needs the approval of your secretary of state."

"Who is my secretary of state?"

"I believe it's Jack Pickersgill, Prime Minister."

"Well then, Pickersgill agrees."

"No," said Vanier, "it's not that simple. It has to be stamped with the Great Seal of Canada."

"Where is the wretched thing, then?"

"It is in the custody of Pickersgill."

Pearson picked up the phone and demanded to be put in touch with Pickersgill, and when contact was made, he instructed his secretary of state to round up the Great Seal with all speed and get it over to Government House in his own hands. Pickersgill got busy and arrived with the Great Seal, and the documents were processed on the spot and dispatched to London, and the Massey coat of arms was properly amended before being inserted into the wall of Massey College. Pearson said that, after that episode, he never did take affairs of state too seriously, using the Massey incident as his measuring stick.

It was Pearson's fate, as prime minister, always to have Diefenbaker chortling over his shoulder, and it may be that Diefenbaker continued to have the last laugh, even after both of them were dead. A public opinion poll asking who had been Canada's most memorable prime minister brought Diefenbaker out on top, way ahead of Pearson. It is not a verdict that I would be inclined to accept, nor do I think it will be the verdict of history. Diefenbaker certainly had more of a flair for showmanship and flamboyance, and there is no greater contrast than the manner of their leaving. Diefenbaker had the biggest funeral in modern Canadian history, followed by the odyssey of the train that carried his body to its spectacular resting place in Saskatoon, beside the multimillion-dollar Diefenbaker Centre. Pearson's simple grave can be found in a remote corner of a country cemetery, amid the simple folk of the Gatineau Valley. There is nobody to ask directions of — you have to find it for yourself.

4/My Favourite, David Lewis

I have often been asked why I have never run for Parliament, and a stock answer is that no party has ever asked me to. I add that the only party that would be worth running for would be the New Democrats, and this provokes laughter, nowhere more than in the ranks of the NDP itself.

My point is that a radical reform party would be the only worthwhile place to be in public life, and since the Liberals have stopped being one and the Conservatives by name and nature lack the disposition, that leaves only the socialists, despite the fact that I have almost always been at odds with their policies. Of course, many of their own members seem always at odds with their policies too, so that is not an insurmountable obstacle, though in today's media-oriented politics and TV elections it has become increasingly difficult to detect what the policies of the NDP are.

My admiration for the party as a vital influence in Canadian politics has more to do with people than policies, and in particular with people like Tommy Douglas, Colin Cameron and, above all, David Lewis. I am not sure how any of our "great" politicians would have fared in the politics of other lands, but I am sure that these three would have been towering figures in, say, the British Labour Party. I mean, they had dimensions — Douglas the activist, philosopher, and humorist, Cameron the doughty warrior who carried his sense of social justice like a banner, and Lewis the fire-bellied, eloquent intellectual who put his party's good and his sense of his country's good ahead of his own welfare and interests.

To me, for all the joy and stimulus I have had from Tommy Douglas, Lewis burned the brightest, though he lacked the essential political ingredient of a sense of humour, which Douglas had in overabundance. Since humour is a prime instrument of communication in our society, it was a grievous lack, despite which Lewis was one of the greatest, and perhaps the last, of political orators to grace our Parliament. He spoke with a combination of polish and conviction which was unmatched anywhere in the country, and I have sat for hours in the Commons entranced by his words and his voice, even while quarrelling with the ideas he was advancing.

At no time was I more captivated by his powers of argument and his courage than during the Quebec crisis of 1970, when more forcibly than his then leader Tommy Douglas, he stated the case against the application of the War Measures Act and braved the wrath of an aroused public. I myself was totally on the side of Pierre Trudeau and established order against the threats of the FLQ terrorists, so I could not have been more opposed to the things Lewis was saying in Parliament, on television, and before any audience that would listen.

It was perhaps the sternest test of a man whose whole life had been one of combat against the system, against injustice, against petty and enormous jealousies within his own party. Lewis fought communism and capitalism with equal vigour, and his character was fired in the furnace of dispute. He brooked no compromise, though at times he was inclined to be kindly towards me, while lamenting that my kind were beyond salvation.

His views were so intensely held that he once withdrew from a country weekend with friends because they insisted on watching the latest instalment of Lord Louis Mountbatten's superb televised autobiography. He said that he didn't want to dignify Lord Louis by his attention, since Mountbatten signified everything he had fought against.

It seemed incredible to me that when Tommy Douglas announced his intention to retire as NDP leader in 1970, the successors being talked about did not include David Lewis, the feeling being that he was too old and that his Jewishness would render him unacceptable to the broad spectrum of Canadian voters. With all the petty powers at my command, I urged Lewis to run and urged the party to draft him, there being nobody else on the political scene with anything like his knowledge and his powers of persuasion.

When Lewis himself decided to go for it, he said to me, "I'm afraid you are going to get your wish, for what it is worth." It was worth a great deal to me and to the country and to the New Democratic Party, which he carried to new heights of esteem with the people. He also, in the Trudeau minority government of 1972-74, carried the party to its pinnacle of influence, using his balance-of-power status to force his policies on Trudeau, expanding the country's social policies beyond the ability of the economy to finance them. Lewis's proposals of the time were more daring than they would have been had he been prime minister in his own right, for the simple reason that he had power without having the ultimate responsibility. The ultimate responsibility was Trudeau's, and he shouldered it with cynical cunning, destroying the political career of David Lewis in the process, since Lewis lost his seat in the 1974 election which restored Trudeau's majority.

I had long arguments with Lewis over the way he let Trudeau sandbag him, but he always said he had no regrets. We argued too over my contention that if he had been prime minister during the FLQ crisis, he would have been even tougher on the terrorists than Trudeau was. We argued, in fact, about virtually everything, including Lewis's contention that 90 per cent of workers despise their jobs. Lewis didn't despise his job, and I certainly didn't despise mine, and I couldn't visualize so large a majority of workers despising theirs, but his point was that we lived in rarified circles, his in politics and mine in journalism, and that among the blue-collar and white-collar people in the nation's workplaces, work was mostly drudgery.

His chosen lot was to improve the quality of life for the common man, and he went about it in a most uncommon way. The early part of his autobiography, *The Good Fight*, tells the story better than anybody else could do it, though the account tapers off at the end due to his illness, and his death robs us of his reflections on the most meaningful years of his political life. The same thing happened to the autobiographies of Lester Pearson and John Diefenbaker, which is perhaps a signal that we should set our political leaders to writing earlier, or else elect younger leaders (maybe Joe Clark or Ed Schreyer will give us written accounts that don't peter out halfway through — though since they themselves lack the stuff of Lewis, Pearson, and Diefenbaker, their literary potential might not be as bright).

Lewis never did enjoy our Press Gallery revels or lampoons, and he was the only politician of my acquaintance, except for Diefenbaker at his most petulant, who would come to us after we had done a satire skit on him and protest, "Surely, I'm not like that at all?"

His wife Sophie would try to jolly him out of it and say that it was all in fun for heaven's sake and that it was like the business of caricature in cartoons — "It's a joke, David!" she would say. But David never saw the point and we only made him laugh once, during the 1972 election campaign when his charter plane, christened "BumAir," survived a landing in foggy darkness amid the mountains of Vancouver Island. We made our way to Tommy Douglas's nomination meeting in Nanaimo, and at the reception afterwards we sang a song we had written on the plane about corporate welfare bums, and he got the joke, and roared.

5/Stanfield, Big Thunder

Of all the nicknames we have had for our political leaders — Willie for Mackenzie King, Uncle Louis for St.Laurent, the Chief for Diefenbaker, Mike for Pearson, Himself for Trudeau, and Little Joe for Clark — my favourite has always been Big Thunder for Stanfield. People came to call him "the best prime minister Canada never had," and I don't doubt that had he won power, as he did in every province but Quebec in 1972, he would have been in office for twenty years. Whether the country would have been in better shape is a moot question.

No leader ever had more friends in the press corps, yet no leader, not even Clark, suffered more at the hands of the press. Stanfield was lampooned for everything from the hunch in his back when fatigue overcame him to the retarded speech pattern and the joke about his droopy eye (we're trying to decide whether to prop that eye up or lower the other one). Cartoonists feasted on him, and Pierre Trudeau held him in open contempt. Diefenbaker said he had all the leadership qualities of an old boot worn backwards. His own supporters writhed in discomfort when he tucked his pantlegs into his cowboy boots or was pictured dropping a football (nobody used the shots of him catching it). One of the hazards of working in the Stanfield office was that everybody there started talking like him — rather like the time the CBC brought reporter d'Arce Fardy from Newfoundland to Toronto to cure him of Newfspeak, only to find that a week after his arrival, everybody in the CBC's speech department was talking like d'Arce Fardy.

Stanfield was that oddity in politics, a gentleman. He was even more unusual in that being a gentleman, he was a success, having brought his party from nowhere to the seats of power in his native Nova Scotia. The son of a wealthy family, he was the noblesse oblige contribution of the Stanfield family to public life. Despite his background, there was no swank in the man and none of the spoiled brat manner that marks and mars so many sons of the privileged families of the Maritimes — and of Montreal.

Working for Stanfield or covering his activities, it was possible to love the man and despair of him at the same time. The love was for a straight shooter with a massive sense of humour, especially where his own misfortunes were concerned. The despair was for the way so many of those misfortunes were self-inflicted through overcautious thinking, or through sluggishness of wit and speech at big public meetings where audiences came wanting to cheer him and went away depressed.

American visitors, listening to Stanfield, were wont to ask, "Who's the undertaker?" Much as, later, having beheld Joe Clark in action, they would ask, "Who's Howdy Doody?"

Seven years in a row, and through three election defeats at the hands of Pierre Trudeau, Stanfield defeated Trudeau at the annual Press Gallery dinner, wowing a hypercritical and besotted crowd with a string of one-liners that knocked them dead. Although the jokes were produced by Stanfield's aides, mostly by his court jester Bill Grogan, the delivery was the man's alone, proving his claim about his speech patterns that "those aren't long pauses — that's timing." Audiences hearing Stanfield at his humorous best would go away shaking their heads and asking, "Where does he keep that stuff the other 364 nights of the year?" Stanfield's answer was that humour had no place on the political platforms of the nation, and he would drone away on the need for neatness and order and fair play in the transaction of public business.

He fell for the Bank of Canada's private warnings that, if he overthrew the Pearson government when he had them on the ropes in early 1968, the effect on the Canadian dollar would be too horrendous to contemplate. So he held his fire. Meanwhile, the Liberals invented Pierre Trudeau, and in the resultant mania Stanfield was engulfed and humiliated at the polls.

He tolerated the public and private taunts of his predecessor John Diefenbaker without complaint, out of respect for the Old Chief, and thus allowed Diefenbaker to rebuild his own stature with the public at the expense of Stanfield's. "You don't call *that* leadership!" grumbled Dief, and more and more Canadians came to agree.

Stanfield committed political suicide by running in the 1974 election on his sincerely held view that only wage-and-price controls would save the economy — and consequently both the Liberals and New Democrats were able to run against the Conservatives as though the Tories and not the Grits were the party in power. And when that election restored Trudeau's majority, Stanfield chucked it in, three years shy of the decade which, as Nova Scotians knew, Stanfield needed in order to win the confidence of the people.

In retirement, Big Thunder grew in stature, to the point where he had no enemies and almost no critics in the country, the general feeling being that he would have won on his fourth try and that if he had, the course of our political events would have been more serene. Maybe. My own impression of the man was that he was happier gardening than governing and that his low-key approach to administration might have contributed to the national sluggishness, leaving everybody glassy-eyed in an epidemic of political mononucleosis.

You could talk to Stanfield about these things, and he would laugh about them more in sorrow than in anger, joining in criticism of himself more vigorously than he would criticize his opponents. Even though Trudeau treated him with open scorn, Stanfield would not reply in kind.

Stanfield's campaign for the Conservative leadership had been conceived and executed by party president Dalton Camp, after it had become clear that Camp's belling of the Diefenbaker cat had cost him his own chance for a leadership run. Camp had to choose between Stanfield and Manitoba Premier Duff Roblin, and when Roblin dillied and Stanfield dallied ("I'd as soon take up ski jumping") Camp decided to run Stanfield on the slogan "The man with the winning way." Nobody thought Stanfield would run, but during the days of indecision I met him on a downtown Ottawa street and he invited me to a cup of coffee, in the course of which he wanted to know everything I could tell him about Ottawa and about life in the House of Commons. Parliament was a mess — could anybody hope to do anything about it? I gave him all the negatives and he kept coming up with the positives, and at the end of the conversation I realized we had a live candidate on our hands.

He started slow — so slowly that the national press corps kissed off his chances. But those of us in the know — we Maritimers, that is — cautioned that fast footwork wasn't Stanfield's bag and that once he got rolling he would be hard to stop. At the 1967 convention, the Camp PR apparatus provided the pizzaz and the text of a speech in which Stanfield unveiled the promise about "improving the quality of life" for Canadians. Camp ran the Stanfield demonstration on the convention floor, watching the proceedings on TV and giving the signal for the unrolling, from the topmost rafters of Maple Leaf Gardens, of the longest vertical scroll in the flamboyant history of conventioneering.

Having won the Conservative leadership, Stanfield had to await election to the House of Commons, so he sat in the officials' gallery. And I sat there beside him, since this was during the time that I was barred from the Press Gallery. It was the most instructive period I have ever spent watching Parliament. For three weeks I was able to study Stanfield at first hand, listen to his asides, question him and respond to his own questions. It isn't true that newspapermen make their own best company.

Stanfield, it turned out, had the same handicap in politics that afflicted Adlai Stevenson in the United States. In a business where myopia can be an asset, he persisted in seeing a question from all angles, including those of his opponents. Taken together with his extreme Maritime caution, it was a fatal flaw, and grievously did Stanfield pay for it once the floundering Lester Pearson stepped aside and Pierre Trudeau strode onto the scene. As we put it in song, to the tune of "Snoopy," with Trudeau playing the Red Baron:

> There was one who stood tall against the Baron's tide,
> Unsinkable Stanfield, the Bluenose pride,
> He ate a banana and he strode out to meet
> The Gallic Red Baron of Sussex Street.
> His trapdoor was flapping, the Baron took aim,
> And Stanfield went down with his flannels aflame,
> "Curse you, Red Baron!" was his parting bleat,
> "Curse you, Red Baron of Sussex Street!"

(That became, and has remained, Trudeau's favourite song of all the parodies and sketches we have written about him. In fact, it's the *only* one he ever liked or requested to be sung on feast days.)

When Stanfield was premier of Nova Scotia he had made several deals that backfired, the most notable being the heavy-water plants that didn't produce and the Clairtone hi-fi business that moved down from Ontario and went belly up. These events gave us, after Stanfield's retirement, the material for what I always regarded as the most telling last line of any parody. This one is sung to the tune of "Farewell to Nova Scotia":

If you ever need to reach me, you know where I am,
You can call me on the telephone.
I'll be back in old Truro, where the long johns ebb and flow,
Drinking Scotch and heavy water by the old Clairtone!

For most of the years of his leadership of the Conservative party, Stanfield carried his own baggage at airports, railway stations, and bus depots. Often he travelled unaccompanied and was unmet upon arrival, even when he was guest of honour at some function. Once he flew from Ottawa to Vancouver for a luncheon in his honour, only to find that none of the other guests had shown up. Another time he went on a hotline show in Ontario, and in the space of two hours on the air, not a single person called in. He always drove his own car, and he liked to mow his own lawn and tend his own garden, resenting the intrusion when public works crews took over the maintenance of the grounds at Stornoway, the official residence of opposition leaders (which gives the Tories guaranteed tenure).

Surprisingly, he stayed in Ottawa after his retirement, instead of returning to his once-beloved Halifax, feeling more at home in the scene of his failures than in the place by the sea where he had triumphed. But he stayed out of Joe Clark's hair in a way that Diefenbaker had never stayed out of his. If Stanfield had reservations about Clark he kept them to himself, and only occasionally, when people would heap praise on him and wish for his steady hand on the national tiller, would he mumble, "Where were they when I needed them?"

6/Little Joe . . . and Pierre Elliott Who?

Since you can't get to know prime ministers after they assume high office, it is well to launch the project early when they are still people. The problem here is trying to identify who, among the political throng, might make it. Sometimes you do it by accident, as happened in my case with Lester Pearson and John Diefenbaker, who were around and highly visible for years before they became party leaders. But both Pierre Trudeau and Joe Clark came from nowhere, and they grabbed the top rung before most of us had noticed them skulking about in the parliamentary shadows. So we were left to write profiles of these two before we had really met them, lamenting that we had not cultivated their acquaintance when they were eating alone in the parliamentary cafeteria or, in Trudeau's case (as he told us), hanging around outside the National Press Club, hoping somebody would invite him in.

We had to scrounge in 1968 for information about Trudeau, but we were engulfed in the mania and we've been scraping ever since for whatever may lie behind his assorted masks. I had at the time a treasured and magnified memory of a brief on-camera encounter with him during the strike of the copper miners at Murdochville in 1957. Then he was a romantic figure of mystery, a man in a trench-coat moving around the fringes of the violence and advising the workers on their legal rights. Twenty-six years later he remains a figure of mystery, in various kinds of coats. And despite the shelf of books about him and the million photographs and the hundreds of interviews and press conferences, and all the quotable quotes, we have mostly given up the quest for an understanding of the inner Trudeau. The only thing consistent about him has been his contempt for the working press, which he had at the start of his public life and maintained to the finish. We owe him a debt for providing so much colourful copy, but much of it was dross.

Joe Clark was equally unknown when he won his party's leadership, but unlike Trudeau he didn't act as though he had something to hide about his past. The fact was that Clark had nothing to reveal, as we discovered in our frantic digging after he and Maureen McTeer held their victory press conference at the Conservative leadership convention.

I had started to take Clark's candidacy seriously only a few days earlier, when he gave an able account of himself during a television interview with emphasis on his main thesis, which was that only a looser kind of confederation could survive. He didn't look like a prime minister, and he didn't sound like a prime minister any more than Trudeau had when he first emerged (or, as some would say, throughout his long tenure). What Clark did look and sound like, to me, was western — Gary Cooper in *Mr. Deeds Goes to Town* or James Stewart in *Mr. Smith Goes to Washington*. I settled for those images and wrote them up, and I was completely wrong. It was the "Joe Who?" image that caught on, developing into "The Wimp" and Clark was denied the chance to become "The Man from High River" and became instead the MP for Yellowhead, remarkable only for having won his party's leadership on a fluke.

He was the youngest party leader in our history and he became the youngest prime minister, and the chances for high drama were great. But all were either flubbed by him or kicked away by a scornful media that saw nothing good in the man. Through it all, he was courteous but reserved. He preserved his good humour, and in the face of discouragements that would have broken most men, he carried on with a courage and tenacity that amazed, though it did not arouse, his onlookers. Of followers he had few — he had no ring of loyal courtiers to sustain him, as Diefenbaker had during his years of trial.

It became impossible to write a piece about Clark that wasn't a put-down, and he became a spectacular exception to a rule that I had long proclaimed, namely that media can't hurt a good man. This was based on my assumption that people with well-rounded qualifications for public life cannot be hounded out of it by probing reporters or cynical commentators, or even by the revelation either of skeletons or live snakes in their closets. Ability and self-confidence will surmount all obstacles, I thought, and mediocrity will stand revealed, together with fakery.

174

Among the many examples, I cited Trudeaumania; while it was magnified by the coverage Trudeau received from press, radio, and TV, it had to be generated by the man himself — his antics, his views, his body language. We couldn't have generated Stanfieldmania, not in a thousand years of attempted manipulation. Stanfield came through stolid in the prints and on the air because he was stolid, and because he chose not to show his marvellous sense of humour in public. In the end, the perceived images of Trudeau and Stanfield were the true ones, just as had been the case with Pearson and Diefenbaker, and St. Laurent and Drew before them. I would argue that the same was true of the various leaders of the CCF/NDP, from M. J. Coldwell through the fill-in Hazen Argue to Tommy Douglas, David Lewis, and Ed Broadbent.

But not Joe Clark.

As a child of the television age, he was superbly equipped to handle the same cameras that had murdered Stanfield, because he not only had a nimble mind, he actually thought and talked in ten- or twenty-second "clips." As a public speaker, on the platform or in the House of Commons, he was streets ahead of his predecessor and could debate rings around Trudeau. He had a grasp of national issues that buttressed his conviction that regional ambitions must be accommodated, and above all he had made himself that rarest of beings, a bilingual Albertan with a deep understanding of, and sympathy with, the aspirations of Quebec.

These things, plus his youth, contained all the makings of a potent political image, and it was denied him partly because of his indented chin, partly because his ears were fastened on too low, and partly because of his lack of personal or financial accomplishment prior to his election as leader. More than anybody before him, he could have been inspiring evidence of the fact that any young person in the country can hope to be prime minister and that a life in politics can open the way not only to high achievement but to glory.

Clark had won the leadership of his party without a home base, because his native Albertans refused to regard him as one of their own, or even as a westerner. The party didn't want Claude Wagner and it didn't want Brian Mulroney, and with the two glamour candidates faltering, Clark was the compromise. Peter Lougheed was dumbfounded. John Diefenbaker laughed outright. Who was Joe Clark?

We found out in a hurry that he was nobody in particular. You couldn't do a full-page take-out on him because the reference books were barren. Old friends had little to say. He was a political drone, and the only accomplishment of his life was to have been elected as a Conservative in the Alberta constituency of Rocky Mountain, unseating a Liberal named Allen Sulatycky. Clark was so little known that most Conservatives didn't realize he was a Roman Catholic until they had elected him leader. The only membership he listed in his official biography was the Hillcrest Miners' Literary and Athletic Association, and he called himself a journalist on the strength of summer stints in the newsrooms of the *Edmonton Journal*, the *Calgary Herald*, and the Canadian Press.

His weakness, as with Diefenbaker before him, was in his choice of advisers. His inability to inspire the party faithful might have been overcome by his intelligence and good humour, but there was no media build-up, and the effect was to cut him down below size to the point where only his personal courage and tenacity sustained him. That, and the support of the person who may have had most to do with his seeking and winning the leadership of the party — his wife, the remarkable Maureen McTeer.

Another of Clark's problems was his curious inability to identify with his own age group, let alone those much younger than himself, including the kids who thought so much of old gaffers like Trudeau and Diefenbaker. Clark seemed to have been born old. Yet he was twenty years younger than me. I always half-expected him to call me "sir."

On the other hand, I never knew *what* Trudeau was going to call me. But as I was only three months younger than him, I could at least sense when, how, and where he was coming apart at the seams and calculate the effects on his outlook, since he regarded his body as the temple of his mind and spent hours each day tending to its needs.

Trudeau had said at the outset of his run for the Liberal leadership that his candidacy was a joke played by the media on the Liberal party. This turned out to be one of his more accurate assessments — the joke being not only on the party he had once despised but on the country he came to love as much as so cold-blooded a man could ever love anybody or anything, apart from himself. His prime goal was to put down the Quebec separatists, but the most he did was to confuse them with his own Quebec credentials, which the separatists tried to discredit by calling him an agent of the Anglos, the line being that any Quebecker who entered federal politics had sold his birthright and betrayed his people.

Trudeau fought a holding battle against the idea of Quebec independence, an idea whose time had come and might have been brought to fruition in the 1970s but for Trudeau's position at the head of our national affairs. He couldn't put separatism down, but he could and did deflect it into a maze of dead ends. Had there been an Anglo prime minister during his long years in office, the union might have been fractured. What we got instead was a prolongation of the agony.

Trudeau blamed his troubles, and those of the country, on the rest of us, and went through his successive prime ministries convinced not only that he was surrounded by idiots but that most of the people he was governing were idiots too. It was part of the magic of the man that he never ceased to tell us so, and his put-downs were his high points, since people seemed to delight in seeing him at his worst. His don't-give-a-damn attitude beguiled English- and French-speakers alike, and nothing delighted the populace more than his scathing remarks about media.

He treated all of us with equal contempt. He felt we were ill-qualified for the work of political reporting and said time and again that we were lousy at our jobs. He manipulated media as no elected head of government had done in any country, and he reaped a media image that did him much more good than harm.

His marriage to 23-year-old Margaret Sinclair in 1971 gave his image a boost, though his approach to married life was unconventional, to say the least. Within Margaret's hearing, he lectured us on how she should be assumed not to have a political idea in her head. He humoured her and put fetters on her at the same time. He told us she was publicity shy, and it was years before the awful truth became clear.

Once, when he abandoned her at an official dinner to attend an unexpected vote in the Commons, Margaret came directly to me to take issue with a column I had written saying her ambition to be a press photographer was impractical for a newsmaker of her impact. She defended the practicality of her plan, and when I chided her for having such political naiveté, considering that she had grown up in the house of a politician father, she looked me right in the eye and said she had hated her father and had left his house as soon as she was old enough to walk out, and that she had never respected or agreed with any of his ideas until after her marriage. (Father James Sinclair had told both Pierre and Margaret that the marriage was a mistake, and he lamented privately that since he had four daughters, why did the prime minister have to pick the crazy one?)

7/Anthony Eden, Richard Nixon, American Wigglers, and Other Rare Birds

The relationship between press and public figures is a high-gloss thing, mostly devoid of warmth or human feeling on either side, and after a long career of reporting on the great, I can claim very little in the way of intimate knowledge. But I have occasionally become involved in some degree or other, however slight, with a number of the Great Ones. So let me tell you about Anthony Eden, Richard Nixon, Georges Vanier, Princess Margaret, and others, not the least remarkable being two American ambassadors named Wigglesworth and Butterworth.

Anthony Eden

I am an anglophile as well as an anglophone, and during the war I developed an abiding respect for upper-class British men in armed combat — which, I suspect, is the activity for which they are best suited. I don't doubt that they themselves share this suspicion, since they seem so little suited to peacetime pursuits.

On the battlefield, they showed a knack for making themselves as comfortable as possible under hostile conditions. Given the choice of an orchard or a chateau, the Brits would choose the chateau and risk the shells, whereas the Americans would dig in outside and sleep in holes in the ground. The Americans would let their beards grow, and the British would shave. The Americans were grim and teetotal, Boy Scouts at war, whereas the British smiled and offered the visitor a drink. The Americans accepted that "war was hell" and resigned themselves to it, even to the business of getting killed in combat. American casualties were always higher than the British, and American generals planned their battles that way. The British would go slower but arrive with more of their men alive. Americans wore steel helmets all the time while British officers often went into combat wearing cloth berets, with their walking sticks tucked underneath their arms.

I once crossed a field with a Guards officer whose troops were linking up with a force of American tanks in a pincer movement, and he warned me it might be a bit sticky. He was right, since it involved walking across the open field under direct shell and mortar fire. Straight as a ramrod, he just kept walking, and I strode beside him, trying to keep up my end of the conversation amid the explosions all around. When we approached the American tanks, every gun they had was on us and we were later told that if we had made one suspicious move, like diving for cover, we would have had it.

The same class of Brits who made such effective combat officers also dominate British politics and officialdom, and it is doubtful if any group of people anywhere in the world handle positions of authority with less grace or intelligence, in peace or war. Power, it seems to me, brings out the worst in an Englishman, and the fact that British attitudes matter so little in today's world doesn't seem to have altered things. Both at home and abroad, the highly placed Britisher tends to be a pain in the ass, to his own people as well as to others of lesser breeds.

Take Anthony Eden. He had been a hero of mine from the days of his Munich protest when he resigned as Neville Chamberlain's foreign secretary, rather than support the appeasement pact with Hitler. Handsome, dashing, and with a reputation for courage, he was a key figure in the Churchill wartime government and was thrown out along with Churchill at the war's end. He turned to travel and arrived in Brazil during my term as Reuters man there.

Eden was a director of the *Yorkshire Post* and hence felt himself in a position of influence with Reuters, a fact of which I was unaware until he told me about it, having summoned me to meet him at the British Embassy. I went to the meeting with great anticipation, but I came away shaken.

He had done his homework on me and his greeting consisted of some flattering words about Canada's war effort, followed by a flurry of praise about the Canadian way of life and capped by the declaration that if he was a younger man he would emigrate to Canada and, hopefully, make something of himself there. We were pretty cocky ourselves in those years, but this torrent of mush left me breathless, and I fidgeted in my chair.

Then Eden got to the point — had I witnessed the tremendous hospitality the Brazilian government was extending to him, and the crowds who were applauding him in the streets? I said I had seen a few paragraphs in the papers and had heard a bit of applause when he entered the Press Club, and that it was nice he was being made to feel welcome. He said that of course I knew it wasn't for him that the welcome was being extended, but for Britain and the British people.

"The people at home," he said, "deserve to know how the Brazilians feel about them. I assume you have filed dispatches about my visit, telling them so."

I confessed I had not done so, since we did not normally cover the private visits of politicians, unless something newsworthy happened, like an assassination.

"But this is news!" proclaimed Sir Anthony. "I suggest you send a dispatch at once about the welcome and the honours I have received."

I finished my drink and walked back to the office, where I banged off a cable to London saying that Eden was pressing for coverage of his visit and did they want any? The answer came back promptly: "No. Downhold harshly."

Eden's manner during this little episode turned from syrupy to offensive, and while no great man should be begrudged his moods or his bids for favourable publicity, it seemed to me that for Eden to show himself that way to a stranger was not only a monumental piece of misjudgement but also a sign of petty-mindedness. His later conduct in the office of prime minister of his country did nothing to alter my view of him.

Tricky Dick

I had covered the political convention in Chicago that nominated Richard Nixon to run against John Kennedy in 1960; I had seen him as a shadowy figure at the Barry Goldwater convention in San Francisco in 1964; and I was there when he beat Nelson Rockefeller and Ronald Reagan for the 1968 nomination at Miami Beach. But of these and a hundred other impressions of Nixon, the one that sticks in mind and craw the strongest is of a visit he made to Ottawa in 1965 as a "private citizen."

He had been set up in law practice in New York City by a group of high-rolling friends, including Bebe Rebozo and John Shaheen, the idea being either to thank him for past favours or grease the way for future ones by putting him onto some real money as a base for another run at the presidency. And it was as Shaheen's lawyer that he came to Ottawa, in company with his client, to wheedle the Canadian government into building a $16-million wharf to serve Shaheen's big oil refinery at Come-by-Chance, Newfoundland. The refinery, designed to process Middle East oil for the United States market, was the product of a sweetheart deal with Premier Joey Smallwood, parts of which were so distasteful they drove John Crosbie to resign from the Smallwood government in a fury.

Nixon had cultivated a friendship with the Newfoundland premier on Shaheen's behalf, and he had Joey eating out of his grasping hand. But Ottawa, with Lester Pearson in power, was harder ground, and Nixon found the going difficult. Pearson perceived a certain odour around all of Joey's works, and the same smell assailed his nostrils when Nixon was around. As for Shaheen, Pearson was not above accepting favours from the rich, but he preferred old-money tycoons to swarthy buccaneers.

Shaheen was one of a number of promoters who swarmed around Joey, including John Doyle, the master of the fast buck, who managed to stay in the thick of the island action, even though he was a fugitive from United States justice over a stock promotion deal. Joey always said that when a province was as poor as Newfoundland, you couldn't run it like a Sunday school and hope to turn a dollar.

On the day before Nixon and Shaheen's arrival in Ottawa, I had received an urgent cable from London, informing me that I had been granted a long-sought visa by the government of the People's Republic of China, and that I should proceed at once to pick it up at the London office of the Chinese chargé d'affaires. Canada had no diplomatic relations with Peking at the time, and I had made several applications for the coveted visa in London. Our bureau there had been making monthly telephone calls to ask if there was any progress on the Charles Lynch application, and on one occasion the response from the Chinese end was "Charles Ling who?" From that moment, the nickname for me in the Chinese context was Charles Ling Hoo.

So I had to pass up Richard Nixon's press conference on Parliament Hill to go to the foreign exchange counter of the Royal Bank on Sparks Street. But just when I got to the wicket to buy my travellers' cheques, I was elbowed aside by a small dark man with a black bag in his hand. The man thrust a piece of paper over the desk, and after reading it, the foreign exchange teller excused himself and went to the back of the department, returning with the manager.

Question from the bankers: "Just who is this Mr. Doyle?"

The man replied that if the bankers didn't know who John Doyle was, they shouldn't be working there.

Frowns and consultations behind the counter. Then: "And you want $15,000 in United States dollars, all in cash?"

"That's right. Small bills, please."

More fuss behind the counter, and after several minutes and two frantic telephone calls the money was forthcoming, in packages like the ones you see in photos of ransom payoffs or bank heists. The man didn't even count the stuff. He scooped it into his black bag and walked quickly out of the bank.

Somewhat shaken, I got my travellers' cheques and headed for the airport, having time only to phone the office and tell them about the scene I had just witnessed, adding my suspicion that it had something to do with Nixon and Shaheen's visit. I flew to London, picked up the visa and headed for Peking, by way of Moscow and Irkutsk, with a stop at Omsk. A cabled query to Ottawa from London produced nothing other than the news that Nixon and Shaheen had left for an undisclosed destination, with Joey Smallwood in tow.

I spent several days in Moscow, trying to sound out Soviet feelings about the Chinese, but the comrades were being coy and it was hard digging — they had a lot of Chinese jokes that were the same as our Newfie ones, but they wouldn't talk about their deeper feelings. Then, on the eve of my departure for the East, there was great excitement at the Canadian Embassy — Nixon, Shaheen, and Smallwood had arrived in town from Helsinki, by way of Leningrad. I tried to find them, but they were incommunicado. (Later it came out that they were walking the streets of Moscow, trying to find the deposed Nikita Khrushchev, who was reputed to be living in an apartment house across the street from the Canadian Embassy.) My travel plans were firm and couldn't be changed without jeopardizing the Chinese visa, so in a state of great frustration I had to leave without filling in the gaps in the Nixon, Shaheen, Smallwood, and Doyle caper.

Nixon subsequently invited Joey to his inauguration as president in 1968 and made one of the truest statements ever to come from his lips when he said, "There are no flies on Joey." We all knew that, and we all knew Joey's preference for fast company — the Shaheen refinery got built, and for its inauguration the promoter sailed a boatload of guests up from New York into Placentia Bay, the boat being the *Queen Elizabeth II*. But I wondered: Should what's good for Joey Smallwood be good enough for the new president of the United States? Would Nixon run the United States on the same moral principles applied by Joey to inject some juice into the Rock?

I have long been haunted by the feeling that if we could have plumbed the bottom of that $15,000 black bag and the whole Come-by-Chance scam, and the trip to Moscow, we might have saved the American people a lot of subsequent trouble. If I'd had more of the Woodward and Bernstein instinct, Washington might not have needed a Woodward and Bernstein of its own to flush the man out and nail him.

The Vaniers

It is beneath the dignity (or vanity) of Canadians to have home-grown heroes, all of us being heroes to ourselves alone, but if I had somebody I would "follow through hell," it would have been Georges Vanier. He was our most distinguished Governor General — and, by the accounts of those closest to him, I helped kill him.

I respected Vanier above all other Canadians of his time, and I loved his wife Pauline, who combined beauty and regal bearing with a heart as large as a pumpkin. In the press corps, we sometimes get closer to a Governor General than we do to a prime minister, in terms of human contact. Prime ministers don't give skating parties or invite press people to dinner. They don't hold investitures or hand out prizes. And when governments are being sworn into office, it is the GG who pours the wine and lays on the buffet.

Vanier was in the tradition of Viscount Alexander of Tunis, the last and in many ways the best of the British Governors General. After Montgomery, Alexander was the great Commonwealth hero of the Second World War. In fact, Monty had first refusal of the Canadian appointment when the war was over, but fortunately for himself and for the rest of us he turned it down when he discovered the job was toothless. Had he moved to Rideau Hall, the first crisis would have followed twenty-four hours later and the smoke would have been visible as far away as Thunder Bay, with Willie King and Monty exchanging stink bombs. As it was, Alexander accepted the job and was so good at it that they named a ski hill after him in the Gatineau.

As to our home-grown military heroes, we deglamorized them in wartime and put them aside once the fighting was over. Guy Simonds of the army, Jeffry Brock of the navy, and Wilfred Curtis of the air force, together with most of their comrades-in-arms, wound up at odds with the postwar generation of politicians in office, most of whom had stayed well away from the fields of combat. The Canadian who commanded the largest number of troops in our history, General Harry Crerar, went unhonoured and unsung after he rammed his car into a telephone pole in Hull and got his name in the papers. As for General George Pearkes who won the Victoria Cross in the First World War, although he rose to be John Diefenbaker's defence minister forty years later, none of his political colleagues took him seriously.

Vanier, also a First War hero, had a distinguished diplomatic career, while continuing his association with the army up to his appointment in 1959 as Governor General — the first French-speaking Canadian and the first Roman Catholic to hold that office in the two hundred years since the breaking of the French connection. In his military uniform he was a striking change from the semi-comic spectacle of Vincent Massey in his gaiters and cocked hat. Yet for all his soldierly bearing, Vanier had the common touch and the ability to make everybody in his presence feel equal and at ease.

His fanatical Catholicism and the agonies of soul that brought him to his knees in private moments, with wails of anguish and penitence, we did not know about until his son Jean revealed them in print after his death. The hidden side of Vanier was as impenetrable in its way as Mackenzie King's.

One of Vanier's "courtiers" was Leonard W. Brockington, a political and literary fringe figure of distinction, who called in at Government House in Ottawa with the same assumptive ease that made him feel at home when he paid his respects at Buckingham Palace whenever he was in London. Brockington was also a wartime friend of mine from correspondent days, and when I bumped into him one morning in the lobby of the Chateau Laurier, he invited me to accompany him to Rideau Hall, where he was going to give "the gov" the benefit of his views.

It had not occurred to me that people "dropped in" on the Governor General, any more than they would on the prime minister. But Vanier showed no surprise. It seemed that a visit from Brockington meant good talk about all manner of things, political and otherwise, including on this occasion a discussion of the monarchy in Canada, a subject close to both their hearts, and certainly to mine. Vanier was at pains to make the point to me, in the light of growing restlessness and demonstrations against the Queen in Quebec, that it was possible for Quebeckers and others in Canada to be indifferent or opposed to the monarchy and still be good Canadians. This was before the Crown became the fair game it is today for criticism and ridicule — indeed TV star Joyce Davidson had been driven off the CBC and into virtual exile for saying she was indifferent to the 1959 royal visit.

I myself was a militant monarchist and still am, though more muted now. I had written during the flag debate that if the Crown was to follow the Red Ensign into oblivion, I would punch the guilty parties in the nose, and Vanier said that such an attitude was neither realistic nor necessarily patriotic. Certainly, he felt it wasn't helpful.

Following this visit, I brooded a long time about Vanier's words. After all, I told myself, he was the Queen's representative, and if he was not a whole-hearted monarchist, then where did that leave the future of the Crown? The thought festered with me, and in 1967 I wrote an article for *The Canadian* magazine on the status of the Crown in Canada, harking back to the conversation with Vanier and saying that there might be reason to question Vanier's total dedication to the institution of royalty.

On the Saturday when that issue of the magazine appeared, I was skiing at Camp Fortune in the Gatineau Hills north of Ottawa, when an announcement came over the loud speaker at the base of the hills, summoning me to the telephone in the ski shop. The call was from Guy Robillard, the press secretary at Government House, who said in a trembling voice that he was calling as a courtesy to tell me the Governor General was issuing a press release sending me to hell. He read it to me over the telephone — the only press release ever issued by any Governor General attacking anybody. It read:

The Governor-General's attention has been drawn to an article on the monarchy written by Mr. Charles Lynch, attributing to the Governor-General views which he does not recall having expressed to anyone at any time.

The author concluded "that raised the awful thought that the Governor-General himself might not be a really convinced monarchist." Such completely irresponsible speculation is unworthy of comment by one whose life has been and continues to be a life of service and sworn allegiance to the monarchy.

I thanked Robillard and returned to the ski hills, but found my co-ordination was shot and that I was perspiring freely. When I got home I phoned Esmond Butler, Vanier's principal secretary, and he said in grave tones that the Governor General had gone into a fit of anger when he read my piece and was beyond being reasoned with. Esmond suggested I keep my distance for a while until the GG's blood pressure went down.

I waited three downcast days and then sought an appointment, which was granted. On being ushered into Vanier's presence, I tendered my humble apologies, which he waved away.

"You didn't give me much of an alternative, did you?" said he.

I recalled the Brockington conversation, but he waved that off too, saying that in public no doubts or reservations could be entertained about the institution whose representative he was. Had he not served the Queen faithfully, and her father and grandfather before her? Had he not insisted that his beloved regiment be known as the "Royal" Twenty-Second?

We talked of other things and shook hands warmly and I left, full of contrition, and days later I saw flags at half mast and switched on the car radio and learned that he was dead. A call to Esmond Butler left me in no doubt that the paroxism of savage anger my article had provoked had hastened Vanier's death — and when I got a summons from Madame Vanier to visit her at Rideau Hall on the day she was moving out, I went with some fear and trepidation.

Her objective, though, was to cheer me up and tell me not to brood about his anger or any effects it might have had. What had happened was God's will, and we should all count ourselves blessed for having known her husband. At the end of the visit, we both burst into tears and fell into one another's arms, and I held that great lady for a long moment before we parted, her last admonition being a repeat of a thought I had heard her express many times before —

"Try and write more about the good things that happen." Somehow, something always seems to get in the way.

Lumumba and Ellen

Canadian cabinet ministers tend to be tightwads, and no matter how often their pay and expense allowances go up, they can't be persuaded to pick up a tab and they hardly ever reciprocate all the diplomatic hospitality that comes their way in the Ottawa whirl. As for giving parties, they are poopers. The result is that whatever entertaining is done for diplomats or visiting dignitaries falls to the Governor General or to the speaker of the House of Commons, and the cabinet ministers get off scot free.

A notable exception to this pattern was Canada's first woman federal cabinet minister, Ellen Fairclough, who loved going to parties and loved giving them, even if she had to cough up some of the cost out of her own ample purse. Ellen was Diefenbaker's secretary of state, a job that gave her a special responsibility for visiting dignitaries, and she was on deck when Patrice Lumumba came flying into Ottawa.

Lumumba was prime minister of the Congo, and a strutter, and a stud. His memory is revered in revolutionary circles in various parts of the world, and there is a vast university in Moscow that bears his name, where foreign students are indoctrinated into the gospel according to Marx. He brought an entourage of thirty to Ottawa, and no sooner were they ensconced in suites in the Chateau Laurier than they sent a message to Howard Green, the austere secretary of state for external affairs, asking, "Where are the women?"

Green, a prim and proper man with a minimal knowledge of the world outside Canada and no knowledge at all of Africa, sent back word that the Canadian government did not deal in such matters. One of Green's aides, in delivering the reply, let slip on the sly that maybe the distinguished guests could try the By Ward Market, the hangout for hookers, just two blocks down the street.

Upon receipt of these tidings, Lumumba went into a snit, and when it came time for the welcoming reception in the hotel that evening, with Howard Green as the host, he refused to show up. Finally he was persuaded to come, but the party had all the makings of a major fizzle, with Congolese and Canadian men standing around in surly silence and Howard Green frowning into his perpetual glass of orange juice, of which he consumed hundreds of barrels during his years at the diplomatic trough.

Enter Ellen Fairclough. With one twitch of her finely sculptured nose, she detected that the party was dead on its feet. "Whoop-de-doo!" she shouted, "let's get this thing on the road!" And she sashayed up to the prime minister of the Congo and told him to cheer up and enjoy himself.

Ellen did everything but chuck Lumumba under the chin. She led the assemblage in song and flounced up and down the room, and she got Lumumba laughing, and the rest of the Congolese loosened up too. The liquor flowed more copiously than Howard Green would have liked it to, either in the interest of temperance or the government's purse strings, it being well known that John Diefenbaker frowned on drinking at the public's expense. But Ellen's silver hair was flying and her arms were waving like wings, and the evening was a great success, and the Lumumba visit was off to a flying start.

After the party was over, Ellen returned to her suite upstairs in the hotel, exhausted but happy, having done her duty for Queen, country, and Howard Green. She changed into her nightdress and was about to flop into bed when there came a hammering on her door. She threw the security chain into place and opened the door a crack, revealing two of Lumumba's burly henchmen standing in the hall.

"Yes?" quavered Canada's first woman federal cabinet minister.

"The prime minister thanks you for the lovely party," said the larger of the two envoys. "He wishes you to know that he finds you charming and that he will receive you now in his quarters."

"The hell he will!" said the proud Ellen, and she moved to slam the door, but one of the callers blocked it with his booted foot.

There ensued a scene in which the two men tried to unhook the chain, and when that proved impossible they tried to break it, but fortunately for Ellen's honour, and Canada's, the Chateau Laurier has strong doors and everything held against the Congolese onslaughts. The men went away, and Canada's first woman federal cabinet minister rested in peace.

In our slim book of racy political legends, it became The Night Patrice Lumumba Sent for Ellen Fairclough. Ten days later, Lumumba returned to his own country, where he was set upon by enraged mobs of dissidents who tore him limb from limb and dragged his remains through the streets of Leopoldville. That was the end of Lumumba, except for his university in Moscow. But Ellen lives on, still full of pep, and a handsome bust of her may be seen in the parliamentary corridor at the rear of the House of Commons. They should move her to the front.

George Nowlan and Princess Margaret

One of the highlights of the Diefenbaker years was the Canadian tour undertaken by Her Royal Highness Princess Margaret, and it is remembered in legend chiefly for the fact that in Victoria she danced all night with young John Turner, an event that put Turner on the political glamour road. There has been much speculation over what might have happened had Margaret and Turner wed, in terms of her subsequent career, and his. The fairy tale might have come true had the press not seized on the brief affair and exposed it to so much light that it faded.

Margaret was the glamour item in the Royal Family at the time and people still referred to her as Margaret Rose. But she was showing signs of having a mind of her own and not wanting to be led around with a ring in her nose while on tour. Her thoughts about the Turner business have never been revealed — about the only thing about the workings of her mind and body that hasn't. Nor have we ever heard from Turner himself on the subject. But it's a fact that she became more and more cranky as the tour progressed, and by the time she reached Nova Scotia she was fed to the royal teeth with the whole business.

Her host for the Nova Scotia segment of the tour was George Nowlan, in his role as the senior federal cabinet minister from the province. Nowlan was a tall, ambling figure of a man who had been a country lawyer all his life and had an easy way with people, not to mention an even easier way with the bottle. He was one of those unusual people on whom strong drink had a beneficial effect, heightening his good nature and sharpening his wits. At the time of the cabinet rebellion that toppled Diefenbaker in 1963, Nowlan was the nominee of the rebels to succeed Diefenbaker as party leader and prime minister. It didn't happen, but it very nearly did, and many of us have wondered longingly what it would have been like to have Nowlan as PM, since he had so many of the racier characteristics of Sir John A. Macdonald.

Despite his lifestyle, Nowlan was able to keep the support of his bible-belt constituents in the Annapolis Valley where, it was said, vices counted for nothing as long as they were concealed, and appearances were what mattered. Nowlan was a man of magnificent appearance.

When Princess Margaret boarded the Royal Train at Digby, Nova Scotia, for the trip through the Annapolis Valley on the way to Halifax, Nowlan greeted her warmly and joined her in acknowledging the cheers of the Digby multitude. Then the train set off through Nowlan's riding, slowing down at each level crossing so that the people assembled could get a look at the Royal Person. It was drizzling rain and it was cold, and after three level crossings Princess Margaret informed Nowlan that she was too tired to go out on the observation platform any more and that she proposed to lie down and rest.

"But Ma'am," said Nowlan, as he himself recounted the story later, "these people have been waiting for hours in the rain to see you."

"I don't care. I'm not going out."

"But you owe it to them."

"I do not."

"Well then, consider that these are my people and you owe it to me."

"I'm not going."

Short pause while Nowlan took a deep breath.

"Well then, Ma'am," he said, "in that case, it is my painful duty to inform you that if you don't go out and wave at the people I am going to take you over my knee and whale the bejesus out of you."

Shocked silence.

"You wouldn't dare!"

"Wouldn't I," said Nowlan, flexing his big hands. "Here's another crossing, and if you don't go out you're going to get it!"

She went, and the crowd cheered, as did all the crowds, all the way to Halifax.

The Worths — Wiggles and Butter

In the diplomatic world it's hard to tell who are the unhappiest about being posted to Ottawa — the Americans or the Russians. The Russians have the discomfort of constant surveillance and an unending quest for information, of which Canada has little that is worth snitching or snatching. There is the prospect of periodic ritual expulsions, and the climate isn't much better than at home and the quality of the hockey is much worse.

The Americans never seem to get adjusted. The place feels like home and people talk in recognizable accents, at least in English — except for the words *out, about, gout, boat, goat,* and *house*. Yet if the Americans relax too much and talk as they would at home, somebody clobbers them. Often they get talked about as the enemy. The money has familiar denominations, but it comes in funny colours, and people are always trying to pawn off two-dollar bills. And nobody seems grateful for blessings conferred by a benign neighbour. Although Canada is America's closest ally, she sure acts funny sometimes. For Americans in the diplomatic service, it's more fun being someplace else where you can get your bearings, even if the natives may be hostile and inclined to stone or burn the embassy from time to time.

In Ottawa, the Soviet and American embassies are neck and neck in terms of hostile demonstrations, but the Russians are the only ones to have had their embassy burn to the ground. It is widely assumed that they did it themselves so that they could get a new building where they could play games and show movies.

The most remarkable ambassador ever sent to Ottawa by the Soviets was Amasasp Aroutunian, a protégé of his fellow Armenian, Anastas Ivanovich Mikoyan, who was then at the height of his powers in the Moscow apparatus. I once asked Aroutunian why it was that Armenians did so well in the U.S.S.R. when there were so few of them, and he said, "It's because we're so much smarter than the Russians." Aroutunian's views about Russian stupidity were deeply rooted, and nothing made him more angry than to be called "the Russian ambassador." He would make a face and correct the error: "Soviet ambassador, please."

Aroutunian was an activist envoy and he believed in spreading the gospel openly and above board, talking with a frankness that was unheard of in Cold War diplomacy up to that time. In the early 1960s, he undertook a series of speaking tours in Canada, in English and French, drawing large crowds wherever he appeared and drastically altering the impression of the Soviets as dour people who went around saying "nyet" all the time. The trouble was, his principal topic was the perfidy of the United States and the danger to Canada and the rest of the world from American imperialism.

After several well-publicized Aroutunian blasts against them, the Americans cranked up their ambassador to deliver the rebuttals. His name was Arnold Wigglesworth, and as a performer he wasn't in Aroutunian's class. American ambassadors usually get appointed as a reward for political favours rendered to the president of the day and seldom for their intellectual qualities or diplomatic skills. They tend to be faceless ciphers like Wigglesworth, or roaring bulls like Walton Butterworth, of whom more in a moment. They live in splendour in a big house on the finest estate in Rockcliffe, apart from the Governor General's place. Like GGs, U.S. ambassadors usually talk blather, when they talk at all.

Wigglesworth wearily took up the cudgels on orders from the State Department, and he set about a cross-country speaking tour, blackening the name of the Soviet Union from every platform and warning the people against the blandishments of that rascal Aroutunian. At this, Aroutunian redoubled his oratorical efforts and tore strips off Wigglesworth, whereupon Canada suddenly found herself a cockpit of the Cold War, with the contending ambassadors making headlines across the land.

Aroutunian had built up a big lead in terms of public favour — Mayor Nathan Phillips of Toronto had received him with enthusiasm and dubbed him "rootin' tootin'" — but the contest clearly was getting out of hand. Before the two superpowers could dust off their nuclear weapons, the Canadian government (doubtless encouraged by the State Department) called a halt, rebuked both envoys, and told them to keep their dirty laundry to themselves. Thus ended the liveliest diplomatic roadshows ever to delight Canadian audiences, and things have been relatively dull along Embassy Row ever since. No Soviet ambassador has spoken out on any subject from that day to this.

When Aroutunian left, he went quietly, and I had a farewell lunch with him at his embassy, during which I asked him what, of all our conceptions of the Soviet Union, amused him most.

"Easy question," he laughed. "It's your idea that the U.S.S.R. is so tightly organized that when somebody pushes a button in Moscow, lights go on all over the country and around the world. The fact is that hardly anything ever goes right. I have been sitting here for years pleading for answers to cables and hearing nothing. Time and again, there have been no explanations of policies, and I have had to make it up as I go along, hoping for the best. Chaos!"

He admitted readily that a new privileged class had grown up in the Soviet Union to replace the old aristocracy and described this phenomenon as a conundrum that no revolutionary movement in the world had ever solved. Not only was there a new elite, many of whom abused the powers put in their hands, but there was the problem of how to prevent their children growing up with illusions of superiority, as was traditionally the case in capitalist societies.

"This has been one of my biggest headaches right here in the embassy," said Aroutunian wistfully. "My own son, who is seven years old, became aware that his father was the ambassador, and he started to throw his weight around with others on the staff. He became what you call a little pain in the ass. We tried everything to knock it out of him. We put him to peeling potatoes in the kitchen, but he insulted the cook. We told him that the major domo in the embassy was the real boss and that I was only a figurehead, like the doorman. He believed it for a while but then he insulted the major domo and got away with it without my knowing. Finally we gave up and we've been hoping for the best — but when I go back to Moscow he'll be going to a special school like the children of all officials, and there's no way he's ever going to think of himself as ordinary."

He added: "I guess it's a good thing he's Armenian."

We heard nothing more of Wigglesworth after he left Ottawa, though we hoped his wife finally got warm, because she had worn her fur coat even in the most sweltering Ottawa summer weather. Like Sam McGee, she was always cold.

When the Americans sent Walton Butterworth to be their ambassador, there were jokes about the two "worths," Wiggles and Butter, and the thing seemed funnier when Butterworth turned out to be a ruddy-faced, tweedy man, who looked for all the world like a British-style Colonel Blimp home from a lifetime of campaigning in India.

Butterworth made it clear he thought John Diefenbaker an utter cad over his proposal to abandon nuclear weapons, an issue that gave rise not only to Diefenbaker's defeat but to what became known in diplomatic parlance as the Butterworth Forgery. In the dying week of the 1963 election campaign, when Lester Pearson, in the words of the CBC's Don Minifie, was "coming on strong and smelling pussy," a Diefenbaker aide, at his chief's request, took our man Bruce Phillips aside and showed him a copy of a letter. It was written on official United States embassy letterhead and was addressed to Lester Pearson, and the signature was purported to be that of Ambassador Butterworth. It consisted of a single paragraph congratulating Pearson on his acceptance of nuclear weapons for Canada and wishing him well in the election.

Phillips was told the letter had come into Diefenbaker's hands via Senator Grattan O'Leary, who got it by way of Canada House in London, where George Drew was high commissioner. Everything about it seemed improbable, and we agonized over whether to put out a story about it. The decision was to ask Pearson for confirmation or denial, and his angry answer was that there could never have been such a letter and that if we used it in advance of election day he would denounce Phillips and never speak to anybody from Southams, ever again.

We did put out the story, but it didn't reverberate, since there was only one day left of campaigning. Butterworth issued a denial of authorship and Pearson won the election, and as soon as he was installed as prime minister he ordered the RCMP to investigate the matter of the letter, which Diefenbaker continued to treat as genuine, a belief he held to the end of his days. His aide and faithful friend, Gordon Churchill, still gets riled at suggestions the letter was a fake, but that's what the Mounties decided after their secret in-house inquiry, finding among other things that there was no typewriter in the United States embassy with the characteristics of the one that produced the letter.

Diefenbaker referred in speeches to "the Butterfingers affair" and he called Butterworth "old Butterballs" in private. He refused to attend any function at which Butterworth was present; and, in seeming revenge, the State Department left Butterworth in Ottawa longer than any previous U.S. ambassador, thus cutting into Diefenbaker's social life in the capital.

In our own investigation of the letter, we did no better than we had earlier with Nixon, Shaheen, Doyle, and Smallwood. I still have a hunch that Butterworth wrote the thing and that he did it with the full support of President Kennedy, whose loathing for Diefenbaker was matched by his high regard for Pearson. As Kennedy said when he was asked if he had described Diefenbaker as an S.O.B. after their first meeting, "How could I have called him that when I didn't know until later that he was one?"

Charlotte Whitton

When I came home from the States in 1958, it struck me that Canadian women were both more repressed and more gifted than their American sisters, and that Canadian men were lazier than their American brothers. So I set about stumping the country on the subject of "the natural superiority of Canadian women over Canadian men." It was intellectual superiority I was talking about, and I said that of all the Canadian couples of my acquaintance, the woman was smarter than the man in every way and her company was greatly to be preferred to that of her mate.

These speeches led to a series of columns on the subject and an article in *Chatelaine* in 1961, in which I advocated the abolition of all women's "auxiliaries" in the country, with women assuming a full share of the benefits and stresses of the rat race. This, I reasoned, would more than double our national work force, since women would add more than their numbers, in view of their better brainpower and more daring instincts.

Chatelaine treated the idea as being very far out indeed and published it with all sorts of warning signs, like the ones they put on cigarette packages. Women's audiences liked the theme but didn't know how to follow up on it and doubted that men would ever let them anyway. Men's audiences took it as a good-natured rib. Mixed audiences, especially those of husbands and wives, were thrown into turmoil, and many a husband regretted the night he ever came with "the little woman" to hear my spiel.

The suspicion existed then, as it has ever since, that I was motivated not so much by sincere conviction as by a delight in the sight, sound, and company of women, and that what I was really celebrating was the sexual aspect of their contribution to society — that it wasn't their minds I was praising so much as their bodies; and not the way they thought so much as the way they walked. It is a charge that every male feminist must face, just as every bachelor must endure the general supposition that he is gay. I have never known how to answer it, and my joy in female company was so unconcealed, if not

196

flamboyant, that it deprived me of credibility to such an extent that I abandoned the crusade years before the women's movement emerged as the force it is today.

Obviously, it was not deemed fitting for any man to tell women how to gain equality, much less that they had a duty to do so, any more than it was appropriate for any White to tell Blacks or Native people how to fight discrimination and bring their God-given gifts to the national table. As for viewing women as sex objects, I cannot plead innocent, nor can I feel guilt for the marvellous urges women excite in men, and vice versa. The Good Lord did well to arrange things that way, though it strikes me as odd that among the latter-day human species, the fancy plumage is displayed by the female, whereas in the worlds of birds and animals it is the male who is the gaudy one.

I propose to discuss only one of my extracurricular love affairs, the one with Charlotte Whitton, who was as far from being a sex symbol as a woman could be, and yet she captivated Canadians as no other woman ever has. She was, in turn, the terror of the university world, the stimulator of the social sciences, and the mayor of Ottawa. In everything she did, she was years ahead of her time, and she went about her work with an awesome conviction that roused her supporters and confounded her enemies. In most of the halls of the land, the person who held the title for drawing the largest audiences was Charlotte, the undefeated hell-raiser of them all.

Charlotte had one major flaw — her hatred of men. Her attitude in this regard both spurred her on and impeded her progress. For while she was one of the most interesting people in the public life of her time, and probably the smartest, she would have had a more lasting impact on her country and her world had she rid herself of the idea that all men were out to do her in. Doubtless they were, and perhaps it was inevitable that Charlotte would carry that chip on her shoulder for the whole of her life, sapping her energies if not her strength, and diverting her from the many marvellous courses on which she set out.

She exempted me from the general suspicion, and we revelled in one another's company, perhaps because she found me such a good listener. During the 1960s, we shared adjacent offices at the Ottawa *Citizen*, where Charlotte had become a resident columnist after her spectacular career in Ottawa civic politics, in the course of which she had achieved more national and international fame than any of the members of the federal cabinet, not excluding Prime Minister John Diefenbaker.

Charlotte is remembered mostly as an eccentric, a species more common, or at least more treasured, in civic politics than at any other level of our public life (perhaps because they can do least damage there, some of our most noble cities having survived under mayors who were raving lunatics). Eccentric she was, as anybody who bumped over Ottawa streets during her tenure as mayor could attest. She actually took pride in "her" potholes, feeling it was misuse of public money to fill them in, and contests were held in which various neighbourhoods competed for the springtime honour of the biggest and deepest hole, some of which could swallow up the full-size cars of the time without a trace of chrome remaining above street level.

Charlotte used to say that in order to succeed in a man's world, a woman had to be three times smarter than the competition. This was no problem for her. She had the best-stocked mind in the political business, and her energies were limitless and her prowess as a public speaker was such that her name on the program was enough to fill halls from one end of the country to another. Not only did she draw crowds, she never sent her audiences away without the feeling that they had attended a major happening. City Hall, during her tenure, was a livelier and more stimulating place than Parliament Hill, any day or night of the week. Besides making news, she was a walking and talking library of scholarly information about her region, her country, and her world.

Her world wasn't always the "real" world, for she had such strong views on everything that they often hardened into prejudices. Which is a way of saying that she had, to a massive degree, the courage of her convictions, and that's hardly a trait of our male politicians, or of the Canadian people at large. She was a national treasure, and when she died we should have buried her with the gold reserves in the Bank of Canada vaults.

When the voters of Ottawa finally threw her out in 1964, I gave voice to my sense of loss and recalled how many a night I had trudged home from Parliament Hill after a long, dull day and had been revived by the published tidings from City Hall — columns of them, usually with illustrations. Charlotte had been raising hell, letting loose with cap pistols, fists, tongue, and even chain saws.

On the eve of her defeat, she got a full column (plus a picture wearing her tricornered hat and chain of office) on the front page of the Sunday *New York Times*, a feat no Canadian prime minister had ever been able to perform. Nobody has ever filled her shoes — those same tiny pumps that led her to grief on the curling rink and gave the world its most unforgettable photograph of her, sprawled on the ice with her legs akimbo and a look of mixed astonishment, indignation, and amusement on her face, with George Hees doubled up with laughter in the background.

A flaming Tory (not Red, but crackling hot), she cut across party lines and Lester Pearson was once among her fans, though he regretted a joking offer to put her in his cabinet. John Diefenbaker was not a devotee while in power, and her efforts to get elected to the House of Commons threw a chill into Tory ranks, just as the Senate trembled at the news she might be appointed there. Would that she had.

The delightful possibility that she might be named our ambassador to her beloved Ireland withered after she resorted to fisticuffs against a male colleague at City Hall who, she said, had reflected upon her honour. She doubled him up with a blow to his ample breadbasket, and it was duly recorded for posterity by the cameras. These and other antics led her to be named Canada's woman of the year so many times that they finally gave the honour to Judy LaMarsh to break the monotony.

Charlotte talked so fast she frequently interrupted the flow of her own conversation, and this was one reason men found her too hard to cope with. When we had adjoining offices at the *Citizen*, she used to burst through my door when her indignation became too great to bear in solitude. She would blaze away, and it was up to me to find what she was incensed about and beam in on it, which after five minutes I usually managed to do, but by that time she was off on something else, and by the end of an hour I was pooped. It always seemed to make her feel better and I didn't begrudge the time.

"They're all trying to tree this old cat," was one of her sayings at election time, when all the supposed agencies of sanity, efficiency and finally bilingualism, were mobilized against her.

They treed her at last, because she wouldn't shovel the snow and because she salted the streets until our feet were pickled and our cars eaten out from under us. But she made "Ottawa" something other than a dirty word in the national vocabulary, and heaven knows what she might have achieved had she been a man in what was then a man's world. But then she wouldn't have been Charlotte.

PART FOUR

Stirring the Pot

1/Publish and Be Damned!

In 1977, I was president of the Parliamentary Press Gallery, and that year all hell kept breaking loose — to the point where the cell of activists who had promoted my candidacy, led by the CBC's Mike Duffy and Marjorie Nichols of the *Vancouver Sun*, considered engineering not only my impeachment but my certification for insanity.

My friends the Communist Chinese had been waiting for years to obtain Press Gallery memberships for the correspondents of their national news agency, who with the Soviet correspondents constitute virtually the entire foreign press corps in Ottawa. But the Red Chinese refused to apply for membership, because when the nationalist Chinese quit Ottawa in 1971, they left behind Dr. Li Yueh, representing the Central News Agency of Taiwan. He occupied what the comrades referred to as "the Chinese seat" in the Press Gallery, and they said they could not take their rightful place until Li Yueh was expelled, since no representative of the People's Republic of China could be associated with any group that contained a representative of Chiang Kai-shek.

Members of the gallery had long been adamant on the subject — the Communist Chinese were welcome to join, but nobody was going to tell the gallery who to admit and who to expel, especially on political grounds. I had tried on numerous occasions to explain the situation to the Chinese, in Ottawa and in Peking, but they refused to accept it, and as soon as I was installed as president of the gallery they called on me for action.

I decided to give it to them, if only to prove that the result was a foregone conclusion. I summoned an emergency general meeting on the Chinese question, proposing that Dr. Li Yueh be expelled to make way for the correspondents from Peking. This brought the immediate denunciation from colleagues that I was introducing politics into the gallery, to which I replied that to the Communist Chinese, the act of granting membership to Dr. Li Yueh was politics of the most flagrant sort. I took the One China line, based on the premise that the real China was the People's Republic and that Dr. Li Yueh had been left behind by the Taiwan clique solely to be a thorn in the side of the diplomats from the mainland.

I expected to be shot down, but not with quite the vehemence that greeted my proposal, accompanied by demands that I resign as gallery president and face dismissal by my employers. Only four votes were cast in favour of my resolution, and when it was over I conveyed the sorry result to the representatives of the New China News Agency, who expressed disappointment but thanked me for my effort on their behalf.

I prayed silently that this might get them off my back for a while and ventured to suggest that since I had taken my lumps for them, they might do something for me — namely, persuade their government, just this once, to permit them to apply for Press Gallery membership, ignoring Dr. Li Yueh. The answer was no, though I got the distinct impression that if I were to kill Dr. Li Yueh or arrange for his death in a traffic accident, I would solve the problem and be named a hero of the People's Republic.

In fact, nothing happened, and it wasn't until the Gang of Four was behind bars and a whiff of freedom swept over China that the Xinwah representatives in Ottawa agreed to swallow their pride and apply for Press Gallery membership, making the announcement at a lavish embassy dinner in my honour. As a result, they took their places beside Dr. Li Yueh, who continued to make token appearances at gallery affairs, despite the fact that his political usefulness to Taiwan was at an end.

Somewhat prior to this happy event, we received a call from the Chinese Embassy to present ourselves urgently, which we did, to be informed over the usual mugs of tea that our correspondent in Peking, John Walker, was being expelled for unsuitable conduct. Walker was away from China at the time, on a Malaysian holiday, and the charge against him was that he had typed a memo to his translator in Peking, asking that he be communicated with immediately if there were major developments in China during his absence. He noted that major events might include the deaths of either Premier Chou En-lai or Chairman Mao Tse-tung.

Walker had thought better of the memo after typing it and had crumpled it up and thrown it in the wastebasket of his office. But the translator had retrieved it in the course of going through everything in the place while his employer was away. He reported it to his immediate superior, setting in motion the reverse domino effect that governed so much of what happened in China in those times. When it got to the top of the Foreign Office, the expulsion order was issued, it being taboo to suggest in any way, shape, or form that either Chou or Mao might be so mortal as to die.

We took the matter straight to our external affairs department, where we got the backing of the minister, Mitchell Sharp, and his under-secretary, Edgar Ritchie. With their help, the expulsion order was fought right down the line, resulting in a stay of execution followed by a reversal, the first time the Communist Chinese had yielded to Western protests at one of their diplomatic decisions. Walker had to tender his apologies when he got back to Peking, and Southam president St. Clair Balfour had to do the same during a personal call to the Chinese Embassy in Ottawa, but the day was saved, though the episode gave Southams a pain in the corporate gut and contributed to our closing the Peking bureau the following year — a step I have always regretted, being deeply fascinated by China, the Chinese, and the China story.

The second crisis of my presidential year was over the question of televising the House of Commons debates, something I had been urging for years. With the onset of television as a major factor in parliamentary coverage, a serious distortion had set in with the establishment of a television studio in the basement of the main Parliament Building. In this studio, the events of the day in the Commons were being re-enacted in question-and-answer form, with TV reporters doing the on-camera questioning, and this was the way most Canadians were getting their impressions of events in the Commons.

I agreed with those who felt it would be better to televise the debates themselves, and as president of the gallery I appeared in a film advocating televising the proceedings of Parliament, as an extension of the people's right to know and as a way of ending the fraud of the studio re-enactments. An emergency meeting of the gallery was summoned to censure me and seek my impeachment. The major movers were the representatives of TV stations and the networks CBC and CTV, who preferred the tailor-made clips they were getting from the studio to the prospect of having to select uncontrolled footage from the live proceedings of the House itself.

If it had been left to the gallery membership, this battle too would surely have been lost — but the government House leader, Mitchell Sharp, was firmly committed to TV in the House, and he managed to persuade the doubters in all parties and get it installed, with the TV journalists protesting all the way. Once the cameras were in place, the actualities from the Commons became part of every newscast, a contribution to public enlightenment, if not to the prestige of Parliament itself. People may be incredulous at what they are seeing, but at least they are seeing it straight.

Having survived that battle, there remained the matter of whether federal-provincial conferences should be open or closed to the public. On this one, it is helpful to keep in mind the words of the late great editor of the late not-so-great *Montreal Star*, George V. Ferguson, who said that our system of parliamentary democracy was largely a plot against the people's right to know. Ferguson was referring to the cabinet oath of secrecy and the closed nature of the party caucuses, and the fact that, unlike the American way, new policies are not made public until they are in their final form, ready to be rammed through a docile House of Commons and a servile Senate.

In the system that has developed in Canada, "power" devolves on the growing army of appointed officials and advisers who regard themselves as the last bastion of sanity and good government. So the often ill-equipped press corps has to be constantly kicking at closed doors, trying to find out what is being planned before it becomes a *fait accompli*, or sniffing for suppressed secrets that might help the public understand what is, or what is not, going on. Pierre Trudeau once referred to all knowledge about government plans as "his," adding that publication of such knowledge was "theft." The one inviolate freedom we enjoy in our political system is that of reporting the proceedings of Parliament, though even there the MPs (meaning the government, if it has a majority) have the right to "spy strangers" and order the galleries cleared and the microphones turned off.

This freedom to report Parliament was won in other lands, in other times, and we inherited it with the vast package of manners and mores bequeathed to us by the British. But there is a persistent idea among Canadian politicians of all levels and stripes that they do their best work away from the public gaze, and that the chief function of the press is to see that governments and oppositions get due recognition for their achievements.

Parliamentary committees (like legislative ones in the provinces and municipal ones in the cities and towns) can and do slip into closed session at the drop of a gavel, and usually without the public giving a damn. If anybody is going to care about public business being transacted in public, it must be those of us who have a vested interest in the matter. If we do not persist in demanding access, who will? The alternative is an ever-increasing diet of managed news, controlled prime ministerial press conferences, and various versions of closed meetings from the perspectives of the various participants, consisting neither of news nor reality.

Consider the evolution of the federal-provincial conference, that peculiarly Canadian contribution to the democratic process, which has now been elevated to the status of a fourth level of government — after the municipal, provincial, and national — with a potential power overriding all the others. The matters considered at these conferences, and the decisions sought, can have a more profound influence on national events than anything emerging from Parliament or the legislatures. Yet there is no tradition, inherited or of our own making, that these conclaves be held in the open, and the tendency is to regard them as executive sessions, hence closed, an extension of the cabinet meetings held in the various capitals. These are not parliamentary gatherings, since none of the legislative or parliamentary opposition parties are represented. The meetings can be thrown open at the discretion of the assembled first ministers, who then bask in the klieg lights and the cameras, but the doors can be slammed just as quickly under the guise of "getting down to business."

The trouble is, it is the people's business, and the people who elect the federal delegates are the same people who elect the provincial ones. Almost always, the first ministers will have received fewer votes than the combined opposition parties, whose members have no voice in the discussions. Thus, the federal-provincial conference is a doubtful instrument of democracy at best, and an absolute violation of democratic principles at worst. It has been argued that open meetings lead only to posturing, and yet the closed meetings lead almost invariably to failure, recriminations, or compromise harmful to the public interest.

It has always seemed to me that we of the press had a bounden duty to fight for open meetings, and when it was proposed that the first great constitutional conclave of this quarter-century be held behind closed doors, I decided to resist openly. This was to be the first "summit" attended by René Lévesque as premier of Quebec, and almost every one of the first ministers had radical new ideas for reforming the federation and changing the face of the union.

So it was, the week before the meeting, that I let it be known through my writings and broadcasts that when they ordered the room cleared following the opening "photo opportunity," I proposed to remain in the conference hall until forcibly ejected. The only helpful advice I had from any quarter came from my father, who suggested that I wear my old clothes. Two colleagues, Marjorie Nichols of the *Vancouver Sun* and Ron Collister of the *Toronto Sun*, agreed to stand with me, sharing my conviction that closed meetings were no way to draw up even the beginnings of a new constitution for Canada.

When the order was given to clear the main hall of the conference centre, all the pictures having been taken, I took my place in the middle of the room and refused to move. Collister and Nichols took seats at the back. The wave of news people leaving the hall suddenly reversed itself and streamed back in, against the entreaties of the federal flacks and security officers. Colleagues thronged around me, poking microphones into my face and asking what I thought I was doing, and why. Members of Trudeau's staff urged me to "come off it." Trudeau himself kept pounding his gavel, and at one point he attempted to begin the closed meeting, and I shouted to him to let the people see what he was doing.

Suddenly, he gave a sharp whack of the gavel and adjourned the meeting, announcing that it would reconvene in an upstairs room. The acoustics in the conference hall are so atrocious it was hard to know what was happening without an earpiece, but as Trudeau headed for the staircase leading out of the hall I yelled that he had said he could live with an open meeting, and he snapped back, "Yes, but I can't live with you, Charles."

Thus, instead of being symbolically ejected as I had hoped, I was left in sole possession of the conference hall. Sole, that is, except for the abandoned members of the various delegations and the colleagues who swarmed around to vilify me for violating the press precept of non-intervention in events. I pleaded that the question of open or closed constitutional plenaries was a principle, not an event, and a principle in which we, as reporters, had a vested interest. But of peer sympathy there was none, and I discovered later that most colleagues were mad because the officials on whom they relied for leaked information were barred from the upstairs room.

The only person to speak a kind word to me that day was Lévesque, who said he sympathized with what I had done but that, for him, the timing was wrong. If he was going to walk out of the conference, as he subsequently did, it was going to be over something other than the question of secrecy.

Again, there were calls for my impeachment as Press Gallery president, but my term was just about over and the matter was not pressed. Public reaction, as expressed in letters and phone calls, was two-to-one in favour of my protest. My employers wavered, and while most editors and publishers were critical, they confined themselves to a firm request that I desist from such overt action in future, confining my protests and convictions to the written word. This I accepted in the dismal knowledge of what a dull instrument the written word can be when placed before an indifferent public, one of whose convictions is that all freedoms are part of the national birthright and not things that have to be guarded and fought for.

My main regret is that, having protested once more at the next closed constitutional conference, I didn't do it again and again and again, until the point was won. With support from professional colleagues, I might have continued the campaign — but it is hard to stand up, on a matter of professional concern, to the concentrated scorn of one's peers. In the jungle of news-gathering, I had learned never to count on the sympathy or good will of colleagues, and now I knew that the same thing applied to activism in pursuit of principle. Since then, I have valued the company of fellow journalists, but have never looked to them for anything but scorn and abuse of my writings or my conduct.

2/The Blameless Sport

Over the years, when not observing politics and politicians, I have spent a lot of time thinking of fish. Fishing has been called, justly, "the blameless sport," and it has been said that Saint Peter extends one's lifespan to allow for days spent angling. The art is universal in its appeal, and it would be called Canada's national sport except that people all over the world do it, unless they dwell in deserts, and even there, it is said, the mirages abound with fish and the tent walls ring with fish stories.

Though gentler in aspect than hunting, and a whole lot quieter, fishing has a macho aspect that is hard to fathom, especially since so many of its fine details are essentially feminine in character, such as the delicacy of tying and casting a fly, and the handling of light tackle, especially the unsnarling of a mare's nest of monofilament when fish are jumping all around. I once asked Katie Cooke, when she was head of the Women's Rights Commission, how she would approach the problem of male domination of fishing, and her ready answer was that she had no objection at all to men on fishing trips, as long as they didn't get in her way when she was casting.

Fishing brings out the worst in some people, but in my experience it brings out the best in most. Even the fish appear to enjoy it, though evidence on this score is somewhat one-sided, and I have known non-anglers wish for the sight of a fish, rod-in-fin, playing a fisherman on the shore. (The fisherman has a hook firmly imbedded in his gums, and he is leaping up and down as the fish reels him into the water, and the question is: "Who's enjoying it now, chum?")

Often the catching of fish is the least part of the game, though non-anglers laugh that thought to scorn. There are, to be sure, meat fishermen who pillage the waters. And there are those who fish for the pan, relying on their luck for their breakfast, lunch, or supper.

My respect for my father soared when, on a fishing excursion to

Kouchibouguac on the New Brunswick North Shore, he waded into a stream in quest of sea trout. Father was wearing hip rubber boots, and he went in on the slippery rock bottom as deep as he dared and had just begun to whip his fly rod when he stepped into a hole. No cry escaped his lips as he disappeared beneath the surface of the chilly fast-running water, the only thing remaining in view being his felt fishing hat, which was bobbing downstream in the current.

Then there was a boil in the water and out of it came father's head, then his shoulders, and then his torso. The rod was still in his hand, and water was streaming from him the way it pours off the antlers of a moose after a deep probe among the lily roots. Father shook his head, blinked his eyes, and sighted his hat disappearing downstream. Two flicks of the rod and he sunk his fly into the hat. Calmly he reeled it in, emptied the water out of it, jammed it on his head and waded ashore, where we built a fire and dried him out. There were no fish taken that day, but his conduct of the entire affair has always epitomized, for me, grace under pressure.

The most publicized (and self-publicized) fisherman of our time was Greg Clark, the beloved gnome with the porkpie hat and the sideburns. Having been lucky enough to share several trips with him, I can testify he was grand company, though he became something of a caricature of himself at the end, the usual price of a lifetime of celebrity. On his seventy-second birthday he proclaimed, "All your life you're led around by your cock — now at last I've got the upper hand of the bugger!"

Besides being an assiduous fisherman, he was a master at tying flies, and he distributed feathery handfuls of them to people he liked. One man he didn't like was George "Chief" Carpenter, who wrote a fish and game column for the Montreal *Gazette* under the byline "Izaak Hunter." Carpenter and Clark were both outdoor showboats, and when you had the two of them on a trip, as we often did, they tended to get in one another's way, figuratively and anecdotally. Carpenter always brought in more fish than Clark, but he always fished alone and in short bursts, raising the suspicion, voiced in low tones by Clark, that dynamite had been employed.

Journalist Ralph Allen once went fishing with Carpenter and, hearing the haunting cry of a loon at dawn one morning, he went down to the lakeshore to feel the magic of the sunrise and admire the swirl of the early morning mist on the still, limpid waters — and also to have a pee. Having finished his ablutions, Ralph called gently to the loon, and the loon replied, swimming into distant view around a little offshore island. Ralph called again, and again the loon replied, swimming closer.

In the magic of the moment, Ralph heard footsteps behind him, and the voice of Carpenter saying, "Oh, Ralphie, what a beautiful moment. Call him again."

Ralph called, and the loon swam closer, calling back.

"Again, Ralphie," cooed Carpenter.

Ralph gave his purest call, and the loon, consumed with pleasure, propelled itself into close range, when — BLAM! Over Allen's shoulder, Carpenter fired a 12-gauge shotgun, both barrels, and blew the loon to smithereens.

His ears ringing, Allen blurted, "Christ, Chief, why did you have to do that?"

"Sons of bitches eat too damn many fish," snorted Carpenter. "Fifteen pounds a day they eat, did you know that?"

Allen did not deign to reply. He stomped back to the camp and maintained a hurt and surly silence for the rest of the trip. And in all his remaining days, he never called a loon again, nor heard one call, without cursing Carpenter.

Carpenter was given to saying that he would like to donate a trophy to his fishing companions of the Canadian War Correspondents Association, and finally it was decided to have a Toby jug made in Carpenter's rotund image, into which his ashes could be inserted after he died. Carpenter undertook to underwrite the work, provided the annual winner of the trophy would keep the urn on the mantelpiece at home and agree to throw a pinch of Chief's ashes into whatever waters we were fishing the next year.

Greg Clark's older brother Joe was commissioned to make the urn, since he was studying pottery as therapy following a stroke. But how big should the urn be? We asked an undertaker at the funeral of one of our departed brethren — the esteemed Lionel Shapiro — and after carefully eyeing Carpenter's great bulk, the undertaker whispered, "About a quart and a half." The word was passed to Joe Clark and he set to work.

The project was well advanced (despite the opposition of various wives who expressed distaste at the prospect of having Carpenter's ashes on their mantelpieces) when an unexpected thing happened.

Carpenter fell deathly ill and lost weight dramatically. But he didn't die. He got better but a lot smaller. Now we had the problem of a quart-and-a-half urn for a man whose ashes, we assumed, would only occupy half that space. (We didn't learn until years later, from the physician to Her Majesty the Queen during the patriation of the constitution, that the flesh has little to do with the volume of the ashes and that "it mainly depends on the size of the bones.") Word went out to Joe Clark to halve the size of the trophy, but he said it was too far along for that — he would have to break it and start again. As fate would have it, Joe died first. Carpenter hung on for years and there never was another urn. So Chief remains uncommemorated, though not forgotten by his comrades.

A recurring subject on our fishing trips was the matter of guides and how their presence complicates matters more often than it helps. My worst experience with a guide came after a speech I made in Halifax, in the course of which I berated the Nova Scotia government for luring tourists into the province on the promise of trout fishing in lakes and streams, which, so far as my own researches could establish, were barren of fish. (The fact, I have since ascertained, is that Nova Scotian trout are for Nova Scotian anglers and nobody else. Only the natives know where the fish are, and only the natives are in the province during the single week when the fish are biting, right after the ice goes out. The rest is silence.) Better, I said, to offer light-tackle angling in salt-water inlets and coves, where the tinker mackerel and small pollock would take wet flies or small spinning lures and put up a good fight, besides being good to eat.

This so inflamed the Nova Scotia tourism department that they challenged me to a day's trout fishing back of Liverpool, on waters near New Germany, and they referred me to the man they called the "best damn guide in the province." Guide, hell. I had not been in his company more than half an hour before realizing that, like so many rustic residents of the hinterland, he was at heart a poacher. Indeed, the word "poacher" is a city word that does not occur in the rural vocabulary. Whatever the method, the locals just call it "fishing," and they go about it with much the same irreverence they bring to bear on the business of "drinking," and with the same regard for the laws pertaining thereto.

We had tried fly fishing for less than an hour when my "best guide" suggested we forget the fine points and get out the hardware, consisting of windmill spinners and flashing lights and cowbells, which we dragged through the water with worms attached, to no avail. At lunchtime, his wife fed us a big, juicy raspberry pie (which the son of the house compared unfavourably to "the restaurant raisin pie down in Bridgewater") and then my companion suggested we head to the nearby LaHave River to try for some salmon, which were running at the time.

I said I had no proper salmon gear, and he smiled and said none of that crap would be needed. He equipped himself with a series of fearsome weapons that he called jigs — lead lumps with big cod hooks protruding from them, all fastened to heavy monofilament line. My wonderment at how this scoundrel ever got the government's good-guiding seal of approval increased when an RCMP car got on our tail the minute we turned off at the first salmon pool, and my companion referred to the Mountie as "a skunk who's out to get me."

The officer stayed right behind us for the balance of the afternoon; and my guide, mercifully, never did get to unlimber his dreadful assortment of hooks, lines, and spears, though the pools contained a good number of salmon and the guide kept chain-smoking cigarettes which, he explained, were an essential part of salmon-fishing, backwoods style. The trick, which he did not get to demonstrate, was to throw a jig over the back of a salmon and give it a pluck. That, he explained, would embed one of the gang hooks in the fish. You would then heave away on the line, hauling the fish ashore and hoping all the leaping and splashing would not attract a game warden. If an officer of the law burst on the scene, you touched your lighted cigarette to the heavy nylon line and it would melt in an instant, whereupon the fish would swim away with the evidence and you would be free and clear. I returned home empty handed, but considerably wiser about poaching and vastly wiser about guides.

A guide also led me astray when I was fishing with Gillis Purcell. I had not intended to mention Gillis Purcell, the former general manager of the Canadian Press, because he tends to dominate any book he gets into. But on one fishing trip he and I had a falling out, he having suggested that some of my recent writings had been short on facts and long on conjecture and supposition. The thought struck me that I had not come fishing to listen to such things, so I stifled the urge to respond, gave Purcell a look of silent hatred over the remains of my bacon and eggs, and hurled myself down to the dock where the guide was waiting in the canoe.

"Take me," I snarled, "as far from Purcell as you possibly can, with all speed!"

Away we went, lake after lake, portage after portage, pausing only briefly for the occasional cast, and it wasn't until after lunch that we got down to some serious fishing. There was not a trout to be had, though I quested assiduously with everything in the flybox. Ah, but it was quiet and peaceful, and I was quite composed by the time we reached the outermost lake on the club limits and waited for the truck that was to pick us up at day's end. To while away the time, the guide asked me if I *really* would like to catch a trout, and I said I would; and from under the gunwale of the canoe he brought out his secret weapon, the willowtree of spinners and flashers and reflectors and noisemakers usually reserved for fish-hungry publishers from the States.

I eyed this vast apparatus with appropriate horror and he tied it on, instructing me to troll while he paddled. Within ten seconds there was an enormous tug on the line that signalled contact with a trout of some consequence. The fish gave one swirl to reveal its enormous length and girth, the size of the dorsal fin suggesting something from *Jaws*. Then it headed for the bottom for a sulk.

Just then, at the landing, the truck arrived to pick us up and out stepped Purcell, the very man I sought most to avoid. My sorrow at seeing Purcell was heightened by the realization that he had caught me in the act, and I had a terrible premonition of what was to come. But when Purcell saw my rod bent with the strain of the giant fish, his sporting instincts got the better of his abusive side, and he shouted with enthusiasm, "Oh, good man! Oh, bloody fine show, old boy!" (Purcell had a knack of talking like that without sounding Limey at all.)

Just then, the monster fish chose to break water right in front of where Purcell was standing, revealing the whole of its gleaming length, hooked onto that terrible train of hardware. There was a clatter when all that metal re-entered the water, and the din was still echoing when, his face contorted with contempt, Purcell shouted, "Son of a bitch! Bastard!"

There was nothing to be said, but I mumbled something about it having been a long empty day on the water, and how it was the guide's idea that it would be nice to see a fish, and how the dreadful lures certainly weren't mine. Purcell kept pointing his cane at me and calling me the most dreadful names for defiling the natural wilderness and betraying the sporting bond between the gentlemen and the trout. Mercifully, that trout shook himself off before he could be netted. Or maybe the guide, fearing retribution back at the lodge, shook the fish off, though I suspect he had landed plenty of them under similar dire circumstances for Yankee publishers. At any rate, I avoided the ultimate shame of exposure at Purcell's hands, and though he told the story with embellishments at dinner that night, he didn't have the evidence.

The lost fish, like the poets who die young, are the ones that grow into legends, as witness the trip to Laurentides Park when we were fishing the Pikauba River. Two days went by without a single fish being landed, though we had enjoyed fabulous catches on a previous visit to those fabled waters, including thirty-eight trout from one dark hole on a single muddler fly that I and a companion took turns casting until there were just two tiny hairs left on the shank of the hook, and still they were biting.

I was sharing a canoe on this later trip with Ralph Allen, and finally he lost patience with what he called the whole tedious business of fly fishing and announced that he was going to tie on a weapon known as the Norwegian wobbler. (In answer to the riddle of why Canadian fish go for flies and imported hardware resembling nothing native to their habitat, Alberta author Mervyn Huston has noted that a trout has a brain the size of a BB shot, and there are five million species of insects in the world, and a trout can't be expected to remember them all.) Three flicks of the wobbler and Ralph had a good one on. He played it with delicate care, slowly bringing it in and instructing me to be ready with the net from my place amidships in the canoe.

The fish swirled several times and Allen, frostily at first but with mounting fury, invited me to "net the bastard." What happened next became an epic poem, the operative verse of which went:

The fish and Lynch were nose to nose,
The fish at Lynch he frown,
The fish he stare, and Lynch he stare,
And the fish he stare Lynch down!

With a shake of his head, the fish was gone, and there was a silence in the boat that continued for weeks afterwards, Allen having declared me *persona non grata*. But his description of the incident in the fishless camp that night was so vivid that he was awarded the prize mug for the best catch, with an asterisk engraved after his name to denote that the fish in question was still at large.

I don't know why it is that while we remember all the funny things about an awful thing like war, we remember all the mishaps of a lovely thing like fishing. Take the time I fished the ponds of the Avalon Peninsula in Newfoundland during the 1957 election, when our CBC TV crew, brave pioneers all, got marooned in St. Jonn's by fog. We were offered a day of trouting "on virgin ponds" by the local CBC people, and so it was that four of us set out one chilly June morning, with the wind whipping in off the ice floes and the big bergs offshore.

We brought along an outsized bottle of overproof rum against the chill, and when we reached the appointed spot on the barren rocks we split up, each of us going to his designated pond, and agreeing to meet every hour for the consolation of a stimulating snort. As I waded into my pond, I found myself up to my ankles in old sardine cans, ketchup bottles, and empties of liquor and beer. So much, I groaned, for the fishing, so I resigned myself to vigorous casting to keep warm until the first rum rendezvous.

Less than half an hour had passed when I beheld the expedition leader, Ted Brophy, heading my way over the rocks. I gave a prayer of thanks that he was early, for it was perishing cold. But as he drew near, I could see that he was walking strangely, sort of crotchbound, and that his clothes were darker in colour than when he had set out. As he drew nearer, I perceived that he was dripping wet, from his silver hair to his slippery feet.

"What's up?" I called, for lack of better words, though I had a terrible premonition.

"Fell in!" came the reply, through chattering teeth.

"God," I said, "you must be cold!"

"That's not the worst of it, me son." And when he came alongside he opened his wicker creel, in which he had placed the precious bottle only thirty minutes before. Nothing remained but a pitiful pile of broken glass.

"Oh, my God," I sobbed. "You lost it all?"

"Well," said Brophy, "not exactly. Quite a bit of it seemed to go down into my rubber boots."

"Glory," said I with a surge of hope. "How old are they?"

"I'm not sure," Brophy shuddered, "I got them from my dear father thirty years ago and I never knew how long he had them before that."

I gulped but invited him to sit down on a rock while I pulled the hip waders off him. When the first boot came free there was lots of liquid sloshing around inside it, and I stuck my nose down the top, took one deep sniff, and reeled back in shock. The effluvium that emerged from the dark recesses of that boot was comprised, in equal measure, of the smells of feet, old canvas, old rubber, old socks, decades of fish scales, musty cupboards, car trunks — and, only faintly discernible in the background, rum.

I poured some of the goo out onto the ground, reflecting that in colour and texture it resembled the crankcase oil of a Jeep that has gone across the Sahara without a pit stop. We ruled it to be undrinkable, despite the desperation of our circumstances, having determined that the contents of the second boot were of no higher quality than the first.

We built a fire to dry Brophy out, and when our two companions joined us we commiserated with one another and contemplated our next move. Just then, a speck appeared on the rocky horizon and we could make out the figure of a man, headed in our direction. As he came close, it became clear that it was our crew chief, Morley Safer, who, not being an outdoorsman, had remained behind in the safety of the city while we sported ourselves on the ponds.

Morley reached us, explaining that he had grown lonely in town and decided to join the party and watch the action. Each of us had only one question: Had he brought any? Smiling, Safer produced a mickey of rum.

A mickey to do for the four of us, excluding the owner, to whom we gave no thought. We grabbed the bottle, and each of the four took a great swig, and it was gone, and the sun came out, and the day was saved. Since then, I've forgiven Safer everything in his glamorous television career.

I have fished the waters of the Hugetuk River in the Northwest

Territories, where in the fast rapids the plump lake trout and char come swirling to the fly. On one occasion I was there with Governor General Ed Schreyer, who had no equipment of his own and borrowed mine, the greatest sacrifice I have ever made for my country, considering that we had only an hour allotted to the sacred spot. His Ex caught a fish on every cast, and then, when we were descended upon by a pack of barrenland wolves, the Gov. repelled them by hurling stones in their direction, having handed my rod to the chairman of the Metric Commission, Sandy McArthur, who had also come unequipped to the best fishing hole in the world. I played the supreme sport but suffered pangs that have bothered me to this day about the vice-regal office and the whole business of metric. I didn't get to make a single cast.

Then there was Viscount Hardinge of Lahore, the most unlikely companion ever to set out with on the wilderness trail, at least in this century. He owned Greenshields and the Ritz Carlton in Montreal and heaven knows what else, including a string of race horses, and always believed in going first class. He would arrive at our fishing club in western Quebec with his "man" in tow and a wagonload of gear, including a case of Dom Perignon champagne, a big wheel of Stilton cheese, and what we called his IGA meat loaf — a great hunk of the finest paté from the Ritz. The cheese and the paté were for the camp cocktail hour, but the champagne was for the trail, along with a freezer full of sirloins and a charcoal grill, all of which the "man" would lug on his back, together with the fishing gear. For Hardinge's fellow fishermen, the trick was to be somewhere in his vicinity at lunch time, when the steaks would be sizzling on the grill and the champagne corks would be popping like firecrackers. The only distraction would be Hardinge himself, trying to crank up his portable radio in quest of race results involving his nags.

His career as a fisherman very nearly ended prematurely when, at a formal dinner held to mark the opening of the trout season, Hardinge of Lahore took exception to a remark by a fellow club member that indicated a lack of reverence for the Queen. The remark so incensed His Lordship that he leapt to his feet, and though still at the soup course, proposed the Loyal Toast. Whereupon thirty fishermen rose to drink the health of Her Majesty. Hardinge, having drained his glass, hurled it in the direction of the huge stone fireplace, a monumental structure that occupied an entire wall of the club dining room.

218

But he was so overcome by emotion that he hooked his shot and his glass went flying off at right angles, embedding itself in the bald pate of an unoffending fisherman from Toronto, whose life's blood proceeded to spurt from the gaping wound.

There were two doctors present, and their ministrations saved the life of the innocent victim, while Hardinge retired to his upstairs room in disgrace and sent down word via his "man" that he was, of course, resigning from the club forthwith. This produced protestations from all present, including the wounded one, who had recovered consciousness and rejoined the dinner party wearing a turban. Hardinge was summoned to return too, and he called for champagne all round.

We enjoyed his company to the day he died with his waders on, angling for salmon on his favourite Quebec water. But we never really trusted him within range of a fireplace.

3/The Joy of Friendship

Dan McArthur was my idea of the all-round Canadian, at home in town or country, at ease with ruffians or scholars, generous and kind, yet given to fits of rage and stubborn as a mule when convinced he was right, which he most often was. His name is perpetuated in the broadcast industry through an award for excellence in news.

Like so many Canadians of his generation and my own, he was born in the United States. His father was poet and author Peter McArthur, and Dan grew up in a world of letters and independent thought. As the founding father of the CBC news service, he overcame all the phobias about the corporation indulging in its own news gathering, the fear being that it would develop into a government-controlled propaganda agency. Dan not only put that one to rest, he insisted that the shallow pitfalls and temptations of electronic journalism could and should be avoided. And while he had anything to say in the matter, they were.

As an amateur naturalist, he knew the name of everything that grew in field and forest. He was a fearless wild mushroom gatherer, though he used to roll his eyes in horror while talking of the fatal mushroom known as the Angel of Death, and he was misled only by the funguslike wads of Kleenex in the distance that caused him many a fruitless clamber over a barbed-wire fence.

In spring, he combed the Gatineau Hills for the wild leek, a delicacy he made so popular that the picking of it has since been forbidden in the name of saving the species. He was the discoverer of the leaping armadillo, whose tracks are found through the Gatineau in winter, beside the ski trails — circular imprints in the snow, with tail marks dangling behind. Nobody has ever seen one of these creatures, and there is a theory that the prints are those of ski poles, an idea that McArthur refused to entertain. He was an ecologist before his time, cursing DDT and all chemical weed killers, growing marvellous flowers and vegetables without the use of artificial aids or store-bought seed. He was a poet and a philosopher who mostly kept his dark side to himself, and he had wonderful music in his soul that he poured out through his concertina.

McArthur was not a great fisherman, but he enlivened many a trip with his music. On one outing, an ice fishing expedition organized by Purcell, McArthur took along his concertina while the anglers paid a visit to the cabin of the local mad trapper. Following an hour of revelry, they all repaired back to Purcell's cottage, only to find that McArthur was missing. A search party retraced their steps through the snow, but could find no trace of the lost minstrel until finally somebody noticed what looked like a pile of rags atop a steaming pile of cow manure. Upon being prodded, the pile turned out to be McArthur asleep, with his concertina curled up in his arms, a scene to rival any Madonna and Child ever chiselled in stone.

One of our great fishing revels took place at Westport, on the Rideau Lakes, and we wound up with fifty people cavorting on the lawns of Tweedsmuir Lodge, with McArthur on the squeezebox and me on the mouth organ, playing up a storm by the light of the full moon. I became so possessed that I hurled my best Hohner chromatic into the lake, and McArthur, in a fit of musical frenzy, dervished himself amid the dancers and collided violently with a tree, fracturing his arm. It was as honourable an injury as any musician could sustain, and our cheers drowned out his cries of pain.

Another time, when his arm had mended, McArthur, in sombre mood, was riding in the club car of the train from Toronto to Montreal. The car was filled with young Quebeckers, who in the course of the journey, indulged in revelry and song. Finally, things got so noisy that one of the youths approached the glowering McArthur to apologize for the disturbance.

"Disturbance, hell!" quoth McArthur, breaking into a satanic grin. He snapped his briefcase open and pulled out his concertina, striking up a tune from his extensive repertoire of Québécois melodies. There were loud cheers from the revellers, and the rest of the trip was a riot, with the train crew joining in the choruses.

Dan McArthur and I once played for thirteen hours on a train from Toronto to Winnipeg, and at the end of it he said the sawing motion of the harmonica had scarred my face like a Heidelberg duelling wound, adding that my eyes "looked like two mad assholes."

He could not abide canned music, being obsessed with the idea that the sounds were made by musicians long dead and buried. Portable radios drove him to distraction, so much so that when a group of Imperial Oil executives insisted on listening to a "Hockey Night in Canada" game in the dining room of the Nova Scotian Hotel in Halifax — and refused McArthur's plea for silence — he asked the waiter to bring him a pair of scissors and, approaching the table of the oil men, cut his Esso credit card into confetti and showered them with the pieces.

Next to McArthur in my scale of esteem came Jack Sanderson of the Canadian Bankers Association, who always said he would rather fish with newspaper people than with bankers, because newspaper people were a lot more fun. I have always found this a comforting notion, particularly when I have been dealing with bankers. Sanderson was a man of aristocratic mien, and he would have made a marvellous eighteenth-century duke. He was the most knowledgeable fisherman I have ever known, and it was marvellous to spend a day on the water with him, sometimes in total silence.

It was under Sandy's tutelage that I assembled, ever so slowly over a period of years, my fishing tackle from Hardy's Angling in Pall Mall — an establishment where, in earlier times, the attendants wore frock coats and striped trousers. It was well, in those times, to have an introduction to the firm before attempting to do business, though today Hardy's is part of a conglomerate and they will sell you any fish killer from a sledge hammer to an exploding harpoon.

Sandy had Hardy's figured out to a T, having first ventured into the sacred precincts two years before the war, when he was the Canadian Press chief correspondent in London, and hence an intimate of the great and soon-to-be-great, including Lester B. Pearson, who was Sanderson's card-playing buddy and news tipster. Having come into a small windfall, Sandy had decided to fulfil his life's ambition by buying a Hardy fly rod, so he ventured into the Pall Mall emporium, full of anticipation. When one of the fishy-eyed gents in the claw-hammer coats deigned to recognize his presence, Sandy said he would like to buy a fly rod, and when he was asked where he proposed to use it and in quest of what fish, he said, "Canada, on large-mouth bass."

A shocked silence came over the establishment and the attendant's expression indicated that he would like to wash Sandy's mouth out with soap. "Not one of our fly rods, sir," he clucked. "Not for coarse fishing, you understand."

"I understand," said Sandy, "no such thing. Do your rods have prices on them?"

"Why yes, in fact they do."

"And do I or do I not have money here in my hand?"

"Why yes, it appears so."

"And is it any of your god-damned business what I do with the rod when I have bought it?"

"I suppose not, sir."

"And can I not use it to prop up a clothes line if I want to?"

"Certainly sir, if you are so disposed. Yes sir, you could."

Having thus established his standing, Sandy bought the rod, and a good deal more gear from Hardy's through the years, and he took a lot of bass on the fly, arguing that they were better sport, for their size, than the trout. Like most anglers, he was full of praise for Hardy's gear until the plastic revolution overtook the realm of split bamboo, and the Americans, led by the Orvis firm in Vermont, took away the play.

It was part of Sanderson's job for the Bankers Association to suborn the press, and particularly the weekly newspapers, but he operated in such a gentlemanly way that nobody ever felt pressure, and I venture to say that no man in the news field is more warmly remembered by those who knew him. Among these is Joe Clark, the son of the publisher of the *High River Times*, our sometime youngest prime minister, who remembers Sanderson as a frequent and treasured guest in his father's house.

Sanderson's career as a fisherman ended abruptly, by his own decision, when after a liquid day on the waters of a Quebec lake he stepped ashore and fell backwards into a bush, with just his protruding feet visible to his companions, who roared with laughter at the sight. When we pulled him out of the bush, he brushed off his clothing with great care and said, "Fellows, that's it for me." He explained that while he enjoyed a good spectacle, he had no interest in becoming one himself, and that when he started to fall down on the shore it was time to quit.

So he did.

By Way of Conclusion

1/The Incurable Pundit

Having travelled the equivalent of a hundred and sixty trips around the world, I find that my favourite city anywhere is Ottawa. Stop laughing. Set on one of the world's great rivers at a point where two smaller historic streams teem into it, the capital city of Canada is a marvellous place in which to live and work. And play. It has urban playpens, and rural ones amid the most varied hinterland of any capital city in the world. And if these things pall during any of the vividly varied four seasons, Montreal is just down the way in one direction and Toronto in another, and there's always New York. Ottawa is filled with people-places for young and old. The man-made ones draw on the national treasure for their splendour — taxpayers throughout the country contribute to the building and upkeep of the driveways and parks and canals and culture domes and palaces of power that make the city what it is.

Residents glory in it, for the most part. For the least part, there are people who keep saying that on the whole they would rather live in Montreal, or Winnipeg, or Vancouver, or Halifax. Often, they join the stream of transients and go back whence they came, or they go to Toronto for the money. Most of them look back wistfully on their time in Ottawa as the time of their lives, and they keep talking about it the way we used to talk about the adventures of the war. Visitors marvel at it, whether they come in summer, autumn, winter, or for the tulip festival in the spring. Pleasures that mean major effort in bigger cities, and are not to be found at all in smaller ones, are readily to hand in Ottawa at small expense.

Yet to most Canadians, Ottawa is a dirty word — the place where the bad news comes from, the pit into which taxes are poured. To Quebeckers, it is a symbol of Anglo tyranny; and to Anglos, it is a place where too damn much French is spoken. To Westerners, Ottawa is East. To Maritimers, it is Up. To the people of western (darkest) Ontario, it is nowhere, and to French Canadians it spoils Hull.

It's often described as a bush-league town, but compared to what? A remarkable number of world-class athletes, entertainers, and academicians have come from Ottawa. Young people revel in the place, and old fogeys live fuller lives than they could anyplace else, if the ice doesn't bring them down. Eccentrics abound, not all of them in Parliament.

Above all, there is the yeast of politics in what Lester Pearson called the most difficult country in the world to govern. It may be make-believe — like the practice of diplomacy, carried out by an army of ambassadors from foreign lands and their counterparts in our diplomatic service, signifying nothing — but it animates our national life. It puts faces on our TV screens, and the backdrop of Parliament Hill has become our biggest TV cliché — Presbyterian gothic, Disneyland North, athrob with life almost four hundred years after Samuel de Champlain first passed this way and lost his astrolabe in the bushes.

After Niagara Falls, Parliament Hill is the biggest tourist attraction in the country. And after Parliament Hill, the biggest tourist attraction in Ottawa, for the last fifteen years, has been Pierre Elliott Trudeau, Canada's first and only global celebrity, our counterpart to John F. Kennedy, or is it Frank Sinatra, or Rudolf Nureyev? With maybe a touch of Mahatma Gandhi and Idi Amin!

In fact, he is unique — one of a kind. We have had others in our public life who were as rare. John Diefenbaker. Joey Smallwood. Wacky Bennett. René Lévesque. But Trudeau is rare on a broader canvas, for the combination of qualities he possesses. Intellect, jock, outdoorsman, actor, playboy, sexpot, fast-car buff, politician, and, finally, statesman. At the peak of his popularity he drove crowds to frenzy, people who wouldn't know a politician from a lollipop. At the lowest of his many dips in public esteem, he drew the crowds just to see him getting in and out of his armour-plated limousine. And they still applauded and he still waved, and sometimes he moved among them, clutching hands, eyes agleam at the sight and touch of them. People who claim to have known him best say that he has always loved being the centre of crowd scenes because these are the only times he can be alone.

He came to power in a prosperous, comfortable, well-run nation where, it was said, little of interest ever happened. His has been the longest prime ministership since Mackenzie King's, and after fifteen years the country is broke and the people uncomfortable and nobody says Canada is well run, or even remembers when it was. While all this was happening, he enlivened our lives as no previous prime minister had done and hoarded his own money while squandering ours. His public deficits surpassed anything previously seen in a developed country. His personal fortune, frozen away from his touch, grew in other hands from the $4 million he got from his father Charlie to $20 million, and counting.

Having hated Ottawa, the way most Montrealers do, he came to revel in it — in the big house on Sussex Drive, in affairs of state, in his three boys, and above all the vast estate in the Gatineau Hills that is bestowed on our prime ministers as a perk beyond anything lavished on the Indian princes of old. And after all these years, we still don't know where the man came from or where he is going, or what manner of person he is. We don't even know whether he has been the saviour of the nation, as he believed himself to be, or its destroyer, as many have come to believe. It may be that we are blessed to have had him enter politics when he did and dominate our affairs (if not his own) for all those years. Or it may be that the principal lesson is Canada's survivability — having survived Trudeau, the nation can survive anything and is indeed more than the sum of its parts. No other nation has ever been put to such a test, since no other nation has produced a Pierre Elliott Trudeau, at least as far back as the pharaohs of ancient Egypt.

When Trudeau started his run for the leadership, he described himself as a joke played on the Liberal party by the press. Some joke! And, he might add today, some party! Some press! He has a funny bone, but it isn't like other people's. The sense of mischief is a leftover from his formative years as a spoiled brat, fuelled by an overactive mind and his father's overstuffed bankroll. The Jesuits did the rest, and out of it emerged an argumentative, bloody-minded, occasionally fun-loving rebel who set out to change the world and who, in a lesser country, would have been either a jetset playboy or a self-centred tyrant, mixing fascism, communism, socialism, and capitalism into a doctrinal pot and calling it pragmatism.

Just as he found no word or action too outrageous, there is nothing too outrageous you can say about him. Call him randy, and he calls me crummy. Call him lazy, and he fires back that we are lags.

Call him old, and he turns handsprings. Call him bright, and he acts stupid. Retire him, and he bounces back. He was once described as the least amusing man with whom one could be marooned on a desert island, because he would spend all the time on boat-building, having first written a treatise on the subject. Yet he always enjoys a good laugh, at someone else's expense. How to understand him? Voters kept re-electing him without bothering to try, and the whole country went into a mania over him without having any clear idea of where he came from or what he believed.

To this day, we still don't know. But oh! what juice he has given us to write about and talk about, to marvel at and despair!

I remember a shadowy figure when I first interviewed him in 1957 at the copper-mining strike at Murdochville in the Gaspé. The miners were taking up the torch that had been lighted years earlier by the asbestos miners, and the fight wasn't just against the bosses. The main protagonist of the workers was Premier Maurice Duplessis, Le Chef, the nearest thing Canada has ever seen to a dictator, with the possible exception of Joey Smallwood in Newfoundland. Duplessis took tribute from the capitalists who developed Quebec's natural riches, and in return he gave protection, Mafia-style. But instead of hired guns, he used his provincial police. It was the asbestos strike that set in motion the events that led Quebec out of the eighteenth century and into the twentieth. The copper strike at Murdochville speeded the transition. And the two events hastened the politicization of Pierre Trudeau, just as the subsequent strike of Radio Canada producers in Montreal drove René Lévesque to lay down his microphone and pick up his sword.

Murdochville is a copper mountain in the middle of the Gaspé Peninsula. It is remote from the coastline, indeed it is remote from anywhere. Duplessis may have believed he could strong-arm the strikers back to work without the population at large knowing, or caring. But reporters poured in, and the cameras came too, making Murdochville the first televised strike in the nation's experience. The film clips we did endure to this day, enlivening historical documentaries: the police swinging their batons and erecting their barricades, the strikers marching, and me, as the CBC's man on the scene, interviewing the man in the trenchcoat who came out of the shadows to say things that the strike leaders themselves dared not say — about the bosses, about Duplessis, about police tyranny.

The strikers had told me to talk to Trudeau, and they said in hushed tones that he was a lawyer from Montreal who was advising them without a fee and that he never charged labour unions for his services. He was, one gathered, a sort of Scarlet Pimpernel of socialism in Quebec, helping to build unions up and give courage to the workers, and helping to wear Duplessis down towards the day when the church-state tyranny in Quebec would be broken and Quebeckers would live and work in freedom, and see their children educated to be more than lawyers, priests, or nuns.

Trudeau's credential for penetrating police barricades was his part-time editorship of a periodical named *Cité Libre*, of which few people outside Quebec had ever heard, and not many inside. *Cité Libre* has become much more famous since it died than it ever was when it was alive, because of Trudeau's role in it. For its size and its irregular publication schedule and the uneven quality of its contents, it could rank as the paper with the most overblown reputation in the world. Contained in its pages, though, we can find the roots and some of the branches of Trudeau's socialism — and not very dilettante socialism, either.

His wealth gave him his lifestyle — that was an expensive trenchcoat he was wearing at Murdochville — but some stirring of conscience gave him his beliefs, just as it had given him his opposition to the war effort and impelled him to leave the country rather than serve what he held to be an alien cause. He was becoming a rare Canadian example of that phenomenon well known in England, the wealthy socialist — distant cousin to the patrician socialist Franklin Roosevelt in the United States and descendant of that power-hungry, pragmatic socialist of depression and wartime Canada, Mackenzie King.

Pierre Trudeau was in sympathy with the CCF in its radical days, and then with its successor the New Democratic Party. To his critics in high and low places, he was a Commie. Certainly, he was an opportunist, as his spectacular career in politics proved, once he had abandoned the socialist party, come out of the shadows, and joined the Liberals, without turning a hair on his balding head. It was a switch based on cynicism and crass reckoning of self-advantage, and it was totally successful. Three years after signing on with the Liberals and being allotted a safe seat, Trudeau was prime minister. Like so many of his Quebec Liberal colleagues, he never had to fight for a seat in the House of Commons — he had it handed to him on a platter. To that extent, as Commons Speaker Jeanne Sauvé once remarked to me, most Quebec Liberals have been successful without ever being involved in competitive politics, and they regard the levers of federal power as theirs by right.

Trudeau shared this impression, but he differed from his Quebec colleagues in the flair and style with which he went about the business of governing. Even when he wasn't paying attention, which was much of the time, he was the star attraction, giving a more vivid portrayal of the cult of personality than even Diefenbaker had done; and amid his flamboyant carryings-on, he proceeded quietly with the building up of big government, moving the state into the board-rooms, if not the bedrooms, of the nation. What he accomplished was in line with the welfare statism and strong central government founded by Mackenzie King and carried forward by Louis St. Laurent, C. D. Howe, and Lester Pearson. Pushed by the osmotic osculation between the Trudeau Liberals and the New Democrats of Tommy Douglas, David Lewis, and Ed Broadbent, Canada became the most highly socialized country in the Western developed world, without violence, without any high-flown rhetoric, almost without anybody noticing at all.

Privately, I have had only a few conversations with Trudeau in all the years of watching him, and none of those talks was about politics. On one early occasion, I went to 24 Sussex for lunch at his invitation, in company with about twenty press colleagues, and he sat us around in a circle and asked our ideas on the questions of the day. In each case, he methodically dissected our observations and proved each of us deficient in knowledge, intelligence, motivation and/or good sense, as well as slothful, overweight, and full of shit. We left wondering what the exercise had been about and resolving never to return. We were never invited, apart from the occasional garden party where Trudeau could home in on the prettiest face and bod on the premises, and the rest of us could sop up the people's booze.

Since nobody in the press corps is close to Trudeau, what we get of the man are snapshots and slapshots in both directions. Picture the annual Press Gallery dinner in the beautifully domed and pillared parliamentary restaurant, high above the House of Commons. For the occasion, this subsidized bistro is all candlelight and fine linen and sterling silver, the men in dinner jackets and the women in marvellously coloured, low-cut gowns. The occasion is Ottawa's version of the running of the bulls at Pamplona, but early in the evening all is formality, and the head table is piped in — the prime minister, the leader of the opposition, the speakers of the Senate and the House of Commons, and the Governor General.

As soon as Governor General Jules Léger has reached his place, I strike up the vice-regal salute on the harmonica, and there is a stir in the room as people recognize the bars of "God Save the Queen." The Governor General stands stiffly at attention, the trace of a smile on his lips, and I am squeezing every last high note out of my little Marine Band. Then I swing into the closing bars of "O Canada" to complete the salute.

Trudeau, at head table, is only a short way from where I am standing, and our eyes meet. Mine are bulging. His have that look they get when he's going to do something outrageous. Right in the middle of the "O Canada" passage he shrugs, turns away, and I hear him say, "Surely we don't have to listen to this crap!" And he sits down. I still have half the salute to play, but it's hard to carry on when the prime minister has sat down and sent you to hell. The natural reaction is to gasp, but it's hard to gasp and play the mouth organ at the same time. Somehow I finish the thing, whereupon the Governor General proposes the Loyal Toast and everybody stands and drinks, except Trudeau, who sits and smirks.

Was he making a statement or just kidding around? I once wrote that he was a radical, and this prompted the only serious question the man ever put to me. Why had I called him that when he was anything but? My answer did not satisfy him, based as it was on his early socialist writings, his admiration for radical leaders around the world, his irreverence for established values, and his determination to impose change by official decree — language change, tax change, energy change, marketplace change — more changes than had been brought about in many countries through bloody revolution.

In the nature of things, most of the essays I have written about Trudeau have been critically inclined, since columnists — and all journalists — are most at ease when knocking and they find it embarrassing to praise public figures or government policies. It's also easier to sound wise when you're kicking somebody's head in (which may, come to think of it, be why Trudeau does so much kicking himself, especially of media people).

Most of the national press corps joined in the mania for Trudeau in 1968. But I did not, and I spent most of the campaign in a fruitless

232

attempt to document Trudeau's background. His aides at the time regarded any and all questions about his past as part of a smear attempt. My most favourable impressions of him in that campaign came from the day he pulled the cheap wine off his plane and substituted Pommard. And then there was his triumphant return to Ottawa at the windup of the campaign.

A huge crowd greeted him at the airport, and the Grits had built a raised platform outside the terminal so that he could address the multitude. Carried in triumph to the microphone, he launched into a few words about his impending victory. It was heady stuff, and the crowd was transported. So, it seemed, was Trudeau — until, in mid-sentence, he looked at his wrist and broke the flow of oratory to snap, "Who the hell stole my watch?"

The crowd was stunned into silence, and Trudeau just stood there, casting accusing glances at the faces below. His principal adviser on that tour was William Lee, a master manipulator who had helped Paul Hellyer unify the armed forces. Lee remembered that Trudeau had slipped his gold watch off before plunging into the crowd, "so nobody would break it." Fumbling in his pocket, Lee found the watch and raised it on high, shouting to Trudeau that it was in safe keeping. Thus reassured, Trudeau resumed his bombast about the quality of life and the quest for excellence. But he always put first things first, including his personal possessions.

Unlike previous prime ministers, he has not played any favourites, nor has he used press cronies to further his own ends. All writers have been treated with equal contempt, an attitude towards the mass media that Trudeau brought with him from academe, and one that he has never moderated. Although he recognized that he had to have media dealings, he never concealed the fact that he would far rather not. The annual Press Gallery dinner was for him an ordeal and a bore, touching neither his funny bone nor his sense of the ridiculous. The only time he stayed late was the year that Margaret, who was a guest of one of the gallery members, kept disappearing into the darker corridors of Parliament to smoke pot and wouldn't go home. She outstayed him and eventually got home at dawn. Trudeau missed a subsequent Press Gallery dinner because it was being held on the weekend of his final marriage break-up. And he passed up the 1983 bloodletting, saying that on the whole he would rather be in Toronto.

I tried to be supportive of various Trudeau policies, notably his assertion of the French Fact through the Official Languages Act. But I insisted on reflecting and explaining some of the viewpoints of English-speaking Canada, in response to demands for open dialogue from some of the Quebec voices. This, and my unswerving support for the monarchy in Canada, branded me as hostile among my Quebec media colleagues and caused a complete split between me and Trudeau's principal lieutenant of the time, Gérard Pelletier, the former editor of Montreal's *La Presse*.

When Trudeau assigned Pelletier, as secretary of state, to tour western Canada to explain the new language policies, I protested that this was bound to backfire and that Trudeau himself should be the one to carry the message. My fears were borne out when Pelletier made speeches about Quebec now having her fair chance after two hundred years of Anglo perfidy — an approach that few Westerners could appreciate, much less shoulder the burden of guilt that Pelletier was laying on them.

On the question of patriating the constitution and incorporating into it a Charter of Rights, I had much less difficulty and had written in support of unilateral action by the federal government long before the idea was accepted by Trudeau, with the support of Premier William Davis of Ontario and Premier Richard Hatfield of New Brunswick. The decisive argument, to me, was that a series of federal-provincial conferences had failed, and there seemed no chance of ever getting agreement on how to get the constitution home from Westminster, and where to put it when it got here, and what to include in its amendment provisions.

Not wishing to spend the rest of my life covering failed federal-provincial conferences, and weary of absorbing each new federal or provincial initiative, and trying to explain it to readers only to have it scrubbed, I concluded that Trudeau, in his fourth term, was the man to grasp the nettle and do the thing himself. Great was my delight when he signalled his intention of doing just that, so I fell in behind and, for the first time in my life, supported a political initiative whole-heartedly. The scorn of my colleagues was immediate — I had sold out in hopes of a Senate appointment. Tory politicians were equally critical — at last, my true political colours were showing.

At no time did I waver, and in speeches across the country I voiced support for what Trudeau was doing. I got a standing raspberry from members of the Calgary Chamber of Commerce at their annual banquet, when men and women in full evening dress climbed upon the tables to shake their fists and boo my advocacy of the Trudeau constitutional package. Two weeks later, the same thing happened when I addressed the Women's Canadian Club in Winnipeg, and even the elders shook their blue-rinse coiffures and howled that Trudeau must never have his way. I supported Trudeau's threat to teach the British a lesson if their Parliament tried to block his ploy to have them imbed the Charter of Rights, in the knowledge that the provinces would never agree to it once the constitution was home. I supported him when the Supreme Court sounded its warning — to hell with the judges, said I, full speed ahead.

By this time, Trudeau was getting little or no support from any other media quarter, and with public opinion setting in against him he started to moderate his position and wound up with a compromise constitution that was weaker than his original draft. So much weaker, in fact, that he lamented having to leave such a flawed document as a guide to future generations. But he signed it, and it became the most outstanding, and doubtless the most lasting, of his slim list of achievements as prime minister.

To this day, people think I am a Liberal because of the constitutional episode. But from Trudeau or any of his courtiers there was never so much as a nod of acknowledgement, much less a word of appreciation. In a subsequent press conference, indeed, Trudeau handled a question of mine by turning to his press secretary and asking, "Who is this guy? Who does he work for?"

He may have been kidding. I think perhaps he was. Because on a full-hued fall day in 1982, when I was out tramping the trails of the Gatineau Hills with the companion of my later life, Claudy Mailly, two cyclists went by on their ten-speed bikes and I caught the eye of one of them, who turned out to be Trudeau. He was out for a woodland spin with a young woman who, I learned subsequently, was a page in the Senate. I bade him good day and he stopped his bike, and amid the autumn foliage we stood talking about bicycling and wines and personal relationships and garb — it was the most rounded conversation I ever had with him. He asked Claudy if she trusted me, and she said she did; and he asked her why, and she said because though in her career she was privy to many political secrets, I had never betrayed her. Trudeau expressed surprise at this and seemed to have trouble seeing how anybody could trust a newsman, in love or in life.

Unlike a previous encounter I had with him in the vicinity of Harrington Lake, there were no bodyguards or outriders of any kind. That earlier time he had been with Margaret and he had one of the baby boys strapped to his back, and they made a picture in toques and buckskins, but the bodyguards sort of spoiled it.

Claudy and I agreed that Trudeau looked fatigued on his cycling tour and that his face was pallid and the bags under his eyes more pronounced, as they seem to become when he is weary — the way Robert Stanfield's back used to bend into a stoop when he was pooped. I thought with a shudder that the man *looked* sixty-three — and he was only three months my senior. But next morning the prime minister was up bright and early, and he hustled himself out to Uplands Airport, where he climbed into a flying suit and went zooming off for a demonstration flight in the F-18, the most sophisticated and controversial jet fighter in the world. In the pictures that appeared everywhere, he looked very dashing indeed. Not bad for an old geezer.

If Trudeau would be a poor companion on a desert island, he's even worse on a trip. I don't mean a canoe trip, never having been on one with him (and while those who have shared his company in the wilds say he doesn't talk much and fusses over the arrangements, they agree that he does his share of the chores and the paddling). Nor am I talking about his pre-prime ministerial travels when he was bumming around either on his own or on junkets to the Soviet Union and the People's Republic of China, all expenses paid by his hosts. To judge by Trudeau's companion in China, Jacques Hébert, they made a merry company, to the point where the Chinese comrades concluded they were entertaining a bunch of lunatics. You can check it out in the book *Two Innocents in Red China*, the only book of humour to bear Trudeau's name, though it is widely suspected that Hébert wrote all the funny parts.

What I'm talking about are travels with Trudeau when he's on the job — or at least when a trip is supposed to be official. It's always tough to tell when Trudeau is on the job and when he isn't, partly because he himself doesn't draw a fine line between the two, while at the same time insisting that his private life be kept private. We've never been able to get it straight, and neither has he. But there isn't a place on earth I wouldn't rather visit without Trudeau than with him, and I'm sure he feels the same about me. One of my reasons is that he loves publicity but resents the presence of reporters, commentators, photographers, and cameramen.

Most government leaders have a death watch kept over them so that the press won't be caught short by assassinations. With Trudeau abroad, it has always been a case of a death watch and a life watch at the same time. By all odds, he has been the most assassinable Canadian prime minister in history, and hence the most closely guarded. The same things that aroused women to fits of ecstasy at the sight of him made him a potential target for people who wanted to kill him. Put it down to charisma — the same sort of vibrations sent out by John F. Kennedy.

At the same time, he was the most antic man imaginable, and his actions were totally unpredictable, both in terms of what he would decide to do on the spur of the moment and with whom he would decide to do it. The result was that there could be no rest periods for the press corps on a Trudeau trip, though he chided the press about treating travels as holidays. You never knew when you were going to miss Trudeau on the tiles, and the photographers had it worse than the reporters, because the local paparazzi always seemed to catch him.

It wasn't always that way, and one trip that was enjoyed equally by Trudeau and his press entourage was his tour of the Soviet Union in 1971, the journey on which he embraced the northern neighbour and told his hosts they were needed by the Canadians as a counterbalance to the cultural, economic, and military pressures exerted on us by our neighbours to the south. That was one trip on which Trudeau might have welcomed no media coverage. Not that he minded our reporting his gospels and epistles and mash notes to the Russians. In any event, nobody at home seemed to get the message or even care what their head of government was saying on their behalf. Rather, it was because this was the first trip abroad for the newlyweds Pierre and Margaret — in effect, it was their expenses-paid honeymoon — and Trudeau was deeply in love with his beautiful bride.

In retrospect, it would be more correct to say he was as deeply in love as an ageing, self-centred bachelor could be. As deeply smitten, certainly, as he had ever been by any woman, or ever would be. He had things he very much wanted to see in the Soviet Union, and he wanted to share them with Margaret — especially the exotic places like Tashkent and Samarkand, and the remote reaches of Siberia, so reminiscent of our own northland where Trudeau always seemed to be most at home and at peace with the environment.

Trudeau's old friend and admirer Roger Lemelin was along on that trip, ostensibly as a correspondent for the Montreal newspaper *La Presse*, of which he subsequently became the editor at the behest of his and Trudeau's benefactor, Paul Desmarais. I don't remember Lemelin ever filing any dispatches to his paper from that trip, but he acted as a benign bridge between Trudeau and the press corps, and he added enormously to the air of camaraderie that prevailed.

A highlight came one night when Lemelin and I went forth into the moonlit streets of Kiev, beneath the blossoming chestnut trees, and Roger burst into song, while I played the mouth organ, and hundreds of young men and women emerged from the shrubbery and strolled along with us. They were hungry for western music and for news of their secret passions, Jimi Hendrix and Janis Joplin, whose records were forbidden but whose music they had heard on their radios. We led the throng back to our hotel and asked if anybody would like a Coke, and everybody said yes, so we went in and got a carton from Trudeau's chief press officer Victor Chapman. There was a small riot when we passed out the cans of Coke, and they all drank our health, and we went to bed at dawn, feeling good.

Chapman got hell from the KGB that day and Lemelin and I were called on the carpet and made to promise we wouldn't do the strolling-player bit again, and above all, that we wouldn't dispense any more Coca Cola. Trudeau was amused, and the incident didn't hurt Chapman's career in the slightest. (Having started as the man who taught Trudeau how to kick off a football for the Grey Cup game, he went on to a series of commissions that included press arrangements for royal visits to Canada and wound up with him being appointed a press officer at Buckingham Palace, in charge of the Charles and Diana show.)

It was on the Russian trip that I found myself designated the dean of the Canadian press corps, in which capacity I had to respond to toasts from the host journalists in various Soviet cities. The main toast was to the eternal friendship of Soviet and Canadian journalists, and I dutifully emptied my glass of vodka on each occasion, until I noticed that our hosts were merely sipping theirs. Finally, in Kiev, I expressed surprise, having heard that the Russians always drank toasts bottoms up. The local press club president shrugged and smiled: "Oh, yes, but we only do that on *important* toasts!"

That put things into perspective, and the message was hammered home on the last night of the tour, when we had a big party in Leningrad with the Intourist guides who had been with us throughout the trip and with whom we thought we had established a warm rapport. Unbeknownst to the rest of us, the photographers and cameramen in our group had decided to make a presentation to their Soviet counterparts, and in the midst of the farewell party they called for silence and the head of the Intourist team was called to the middle of the room, where speeches were made and a brown package presented with due solemnity.

When the unfortunate Russian opened the wrapping, what was revealed was a copy of the latest issue of *Playboy* magazine. The recipient dropped the thing to the floor as though it had been red hot, which in terms of his countrymen, and his job, it was. He flushed with anger and stomped on the *Playboy* as though to crush the life out of it. Then he launched into a tirade, in which he was joined by his Intourist colleagues, who expressed sorrow that they had ever encountered us and that the trick confirmed their worst suspicions of us, of the West, and of journalism as practised by the likes of us. No amount of explaining would heal the breach, and it was on that note that we said farewell to the Soviet Union. Our camera colleagues were true to their creed of never saying they were sorry and were unreceptive to suggestions from the reporting side that they might have consulted saner heads.

Trudeau didn't mention the incident during the long flight home. He invited us, in twos and threes, up into the VIP cabin on the Boeing jet and lectured us on another subject, namely our relationship with Margaret. We were not, he said, to involve her in his official life in any way, nor were we to seek her opinion on anything. Whatever opinions there were, were to be his and his alone, and so far as we were concerned, she did not exist as a public figure. He was displeased at the attention Margaret had received during the trip.

One correspondent who refused to visit Trudeau's compartment on the plane was Christina McCall-Newman, who had come on the trip to do a job on Trudeau and went about her task with the fury that only a disillusioned former Trudeaumaniac would bring to bear.

Everywhere we went, Newman was like a glowering harbinger of doom — she was dressed like a circus ringmaster, and you could hear the whips cracking as she contemplated the flaying she would give the former darling of her set. During the tour, she had refused even to speak to Trudeau, concentrating instead on filling her notebooks. When she sent word on the plane that she wouldn't see him, Trudeau came back to where she was sitting and tried to jolly her out of her shitfit, which had lasted for three weeks. He cajoled and asked her to tell him how he had offended her, but nothing worked and she wouldn't budge.

When her account of the Soviet trip appeared in *Maclean's*, it was the worst savaging Trudeau had ever received in print, accompanied by art work that bordered on the obscene. Thus Christina accomplished what she had set out to do, but her victim survived, and years later she would write a book about him, disguised as "an intimate portrait of the Liberal party," and it would be one of the most sympathetic of the long shelf of books about Trudeau.

The lesson of the Newman episode seemed to be that Trudeau could survive whatever scurrilous things were written or said about him. He had the presence to put down his persecutors, or at least to win their respect, if not affection. This was one of the many ways he differed from Joe Clark, a much nicer guy who had a job done on him by correspondents Allan Fotheringham and Don Sellar on his world tour in 1978. They were no harder on Clark than Newman had been on Trudeau, but in Clark's case the poison took. Out of the Clark tour came the legend of the lost luggage, the falling on the bayonet and the wimp figure, from which Clark never recovered. And even though he became prime minister, there were hardly any books written about him at all.

From the outset, Trudeau's travels were basic to his prime ministership. Not that globetrotting was anything new in leadership — Mackenzie King had been a great wanderer and was more at home in the United States than any prime minister before or since, except for Mike Pearson, who treated the world as his oyster and was a baseball buff long before Canada made it to the major leagues. Louis St. Laurent toured the world and so did John Diefenbaker. Elizabeth II took the Crown on tour as no monarch had ever done, and Eisenhower did the same with the American presidency, an example followed by John Kennedy, Lyndon Johnson, and Richard Nixon.

Yet Trudeau's travels differed from those of other leaders. He was a celebrity in his own right, and the people he visited had difficulty reconciling his personality with that of the country he was representing. Whatever image, if any, the world had of Canada, it was not reflected in this man any more than it was in the woman he chose as his mate. The manner of his marriage, and the subsequent mishaps leading to the break-up, made headlines everywhere, but the notoriety smacked more of Hollywood than of humdrum old Canada, whose only contributions to world ferment were Marshall McLuhan and the Quebec separatist movement.

The other thing about Trudeau has been his durability. He survived in office to the point where he became the senior statesman of the Western world. But here again, it was hard to make the connection with Canada. The reputation he assembled, together with whatever prestige went with it, belonged more to him than to his country. In a sense, he came to stand taller in world councils than Canada did. And he came to be more highly regarded outside his own country than inside it. His global reputation, like his earlier reputation with Canadians, was based more on style than substance. In an international scene devoid of evocative leadership, perhaps it was enough that Trudeau enlivened a world that was as dull as it was uneasy.

But however much he enlivened the Canadian scene, it was not enough. Clearly, he would leave his country poorer than he found it. Just as clearly, he inflated the costs of government to the bursting point, saddling the nation with a staggering load of debt. To run the burgeoning apparatus of government, he assembled a cabinet whose pitiful weaknesses became apparent to all. And his quarrelsome nature poisoned the stream of political affairs to the point where no subject could be usefully debated, whether in the House of Commons or provincial legislatures, or in federal-provincial conferences.

The kindest thing that can be said about Trudeau as we head into the mid-1980s is that he stayed too long for his own good or that of the country. The only possible good that emerged from his comeback from retirement in 1979 was that he patriated the constitution. Perhaps that was achievement enough, a sufficient legacy to his successors to go with the debt load he would leave them.

Whatever the stresses and strains of office, they made remarkably little mark on the man. He did not age in office as visibly as St. Laurent, Diefenbaker, and Pearson did, even granting that they were much older than him when they achieved power. Trudeau's keenness of mind did not lose its edge, and his step kept its spring and the lines of his face held firm. Physically, the man seemed indestructible, an inspiration to those of his generation who felt themselves sagging at the seams.

But would he never go? What was left for him to do? His party was in the pits in the public opinion polls and without any strength in the West. Provincially, the Liberal party had never plumbed such depths, being out of office, if not out of existence, everywhere except in Ottawa. Trudeau's name, like that of Ottawa's, became a dirty word almost everywhere, including in the very Quebec whose place as an equal partner he had made his life's ambition, and to an extent his life's achievement.

We sang a parody of a song from *Camelot* that brought cheers from Anglo audiences everywhere. It went:

If ever he should leave us,
It wouldn't be a bummer.
What would be a bummer
Is if he should STAAAAY!
Not for an hour,
Not for a day,
Maybe next year, he'll just go away.
We've had him fifteen years now,
And how could we be glummer?
Winter, fall, and summer.
Well, maybe next MAAAAAY
He'll send us a wire
And say, "I retire!"
Please hold your applause, or he'll stay!

Can there be life after Trudeau? Yes, there can be. He no more fractured the country than René Lévesque did, or John Diefenbaker, or provincial satraps like Smallwood, Duplessis, and Wacky Bennett, or Social Credit in Alberta or the New Democrats in three of the western provinces.

The real survivor, it appears, has not been Trudeau, nor any individual. It has been Canada. An artificial creation in the beginning, one of the few countries in the world whose boundaries were drawn by quill pens rather than swords, the country took root and thrived.

It became one of the few lands in history where the poor were a minority. And one of the few places that risked choking on good fortune — luck in location, luck in resources, luck in history and in the sinewy people who came and settled here in the early years. They brought with them the richness of the two dominant European cultures, English and French, together with one of the bloodiest and most historic enmities.

If French and English could be induced to get along with one another in toleration, Canada could achieve something that has not been accomplished anyplace else on earth. Partly, that is what Trudeau was all about, and the extent to which he helped imbed the French fact in the national consciousness is a measure either of his total failure or his partial success. But we now know that the very existence of the country was not at stake — not when a royal commission proclaimed it so, not during Quebec's Quiet Revolution or the FLQ crisis or the haggling over the constitution; not when there was independence talk in the West, and not when the Native peoples asserted their sweeping claims to recover control of the northern land mass.

2/Song-and-Dance Man

In this nation of political illiterates, it behooves the political commentator to use every trick in the book in the hope of getting across some information, or at least some honest bias (there being no such things as accepted facts in politics). The two best communications bridges, in my experience, are music and humour — crossing the chasms between generations and social levels, and between the political cognoscenti and ignorami. Canadians tend to be at their most receptive when you can get them laughing, and if you can get them humming too, or at least tapping their feet, you can slip them a mickey of information and they hardly feel it.

By using music and humour, hopefully both at the same time, I have risked losing the respect of the students of politics and the scholars, but even they have funny bones if you probe deeply enough. I stand accused of "the cop-out of the absurd," and I sympathize with the serious practitioners of politics and power, who lack a serious periodical press and must rely on mass media for the flow of information, background, and comment.

The quality of mass media reporting has improved, but the quantity and variety has diminished, and the dictates of the marketplace have given "performers" the edge in catching the public's fancy, and occasionally its attention. Bruce Hutchison once said that the first duty of a political columnist was to be read, and in an antic world I have broadened that out to listenability — in terms of singing and playing — and visibility, including the dance.

Political satire is one of the more highly developed antic arts in Canada, and it has always seemed remarkable to me that our songs about our politicians have been more penetrating and prescient than anything we pundits wrote or said by way of serious political commentary. In our 1947 ditty, we accurately predicted the retirement of Mackenzie King and his replacement by an impatient Louis St. Laurent. We heralded the election of John Diefenbaker in a 1956 number and saw it happen a year later. We sang about the 1958 crash of Lester Pearson before it happened, and then about Pearson's 1963 resurrection when he smote Diefenbaker.

We crucified Robert Stanfield in a series of songs, and then we did the same thing to his replacement, Joe Clark. We rhymed portraits of Pierre Trudeau that were more accurate each year than anything we wrote about him in the public prints. We did the same for Joey Smallwood, Richard Hatfield, Allan Blakeney, and Peter Lougheed, and we hymned the shortcomings of Ed Schreyer and the glories of his consort, Lily the Pink. We discovered that these ditties, put together originally for our annual Press Gallery revels in the presence of the victims, were appreciated even more when we took them outside Ottawa.

Usually, we played benefits for symphony orchestras and theatres, dubbing ourselves "the poor man's Canada Council." In good causes, we raised close to half a million dollars, and we entertained our armed forces in Europe without causing them to wonder (any more than they were doing anyway) whether the country was worth defending. My principal weapon was the mouth organ, and it has sounded over the radio and TV networks of the land and from a hundred podiums, vulgarizing the august air of hallowed halls. Peter Gzowski once told me to bring all my harmonicas for a late-night TV engagement, and I dumped a hundred and fifty of them on the studio floor, to the general disbelief. I did play one of them on the show, which may have accounted for the brevity of Gzowski's career as Canada's answer to Johnny Carson.

With our National Press and Allied Workers Jazz Band, I have played in the Grand Ballroom of the Waldorf Astoria Hotel in New York City — and in lower joints, including a lodge hall in Kelowna, in support of the Okanagan Symphony Orchestra. It was there that the three-legged milking stool of our drummer, Don Laver, collapsed under him during a spirited rendition of "Alexander's Ragtime Band," pitching him backwards off the platform. His head hit the emergency latch of a door behind the bandstand, which swung open and deposited him outside the building into the parking lot.

Years of this sort of thing have caused serious-minded people to say that what I was doing had nothing to do with journalism or politics, but I cling to the belief that we have communicated some tidings in the process of entertaining people. Certainly, I know there is no sweeter sound than a hallful of people laughing, even if they are usually well lubricated by the time we get on. We once had a thousand sorority sisters on convention tear our clothes off and autograph us on intimate portions of our anatomies, which caused some of us to refrain from bathing for weeks afterwards.

In the course of hundreds of after-dinner speeches (in the process, setting a course record for the Association of Canadian Clubs, the cheapest speech in town), I have found that nothing so rivets an audience's attention as the sudden realization that the speaker has broken into ribald song or has undertaken to play the mouth organ. On occasion, I have saved time and treasure for my hosts by piping the head table into the room as a prelude to providing the feature speech of the evening. This knack for double duty once led me, in my militant feminist mode, to join the female protesters marching outside the scene of the last great Canadian stag party, Winnipeg's Beer & Skits, following which I laid down my placard and went inside and performed.

These ventures into the higher realms of artistry all come naturally, without a prepared plan of attack and in the case of speeches, without a text. This has won me no friends among my colleagues at the press table, a singular number of whom are on their first assignments and who like nothing better than a printed copy from which they can prepare their reports in absentia, going on to more profitable pursuits than listening to speeches. Lacking the accustomed text, they either stay away or prepare reports that bear no resemblance to what I thought I had come to say. This, in turn, serves to keep me humble about my own profession and enables me to sympathize with politicians who complain they can't get their ideas across because the reporters either can't, or won't, communicate them.

One can never be the judge of the validity of one's own ideas or the impact thereof. The late great historian Dr. Frank Underhill once heard me say on a public platform that working conditions in the Parliamentary Press Gallery were so sordid and distracting that I estimated I was working at about fifty per cent of my potential. "Sir," he hastened to tell me, "the fact that your work is so mediocre has nothing to do with your working environment. It is that your mind itself is mediocre. You are doing the very best you can with what you have."

Gordon Fairweather, a serious-minded fellow New Brunswicker and Red Tory, who became commissioner of human rights, once expressed public doubts about my ability as a reporter and commentator, but said no man could be all bad who would dare to appear as soloist with a symphony orchestra. From the scholarly set, that's as close to praise as I have ever received, and I don't think Fairweather even heard me play.

During one of our national downers, near the end of Trudeau's third mandate, I concluded we were short of rallying cries so I wrote one out and recited it at a concert with the Central Band of the Armed Forces. It took the form of a prose poem with musical accompaniment, the air being the haunting "Un Canadien Errant," a cliché now but still the most beautiful passage of music to come from a Canadian heart. The words may seem a bit extreme in the relative political calm of today, with its assurance that the union is secure, but here is how it goes, with a nod to our men of war and to the man of peace, Lester Pearson, who once agreed with me that the way to see Canada whole was to live away from her awhile:

A land so vast is best seen from far off
To catch the wholeness of it, and to see
How it compares with all the other lands
That people who live in them love.
At times, it seems they love our land the most
Who have been most away;
Including those who've served her colours far
In war as well as peace,
Ensuring that our hallowed battle places
Exist in other lands, on other continents,
Where we have fought our wars, and dreamed of home,
And stood on guard, O Canada, for thee.

Our songs have rung through Europe through two wars,
We've sung them in Korea and Hong Kong,
Amid the guns.
And then, to keep the peace,
And in the name of order and good government,
We've sung and served from Suez to Kashmir,
From Congo up to Cyprus,
From Vietnam to Sinai's dusty plain,
And in the smoky skies and lush terrain of Germany,
While ships of ours have sailed the seven seas,
That we might share our peace and unity with all.

How stands our home and native land?
Terre de nos aïeux?
Is her brow girded with garlands glorious
And does she command true patriot love in all her sons and
    daughters?
Or is she troubled sore, as lands in which we've sought to save
    the peace?
It's said that to describe our love of land
A minute is too long, a lifetime not enough,
That if we love in happy, joyful way
We'll keep our heritage intact, though time be short
And we are wracked by doubts about our worth.
What good is done if we have served mankind
And failed ourselves?

Recitation of these words could, and did, bring audiences to their feet from Newfoundland to Victoria, and people flocked to the podium to ask what they could do to check the rot. But it wasn't as bad as it seemed, though it might be as well to keep the poem handy for the next convulsion.

Canada can, it seems, withstand any degree of incompetence in her governors. She can live beside the American giant and pocket the gains without carrying any of the responsibilities. Her people can plead detachment from their own national affairs and drift into a state of political ignorance unmatched by people in any other developed country. Our entrepreneurs can let us down and sell out to foreign owners. Our risk-takers can invest their capital elsewhere, and our factories can close because our buyers prefer imported cars, imported clothes, imported appliances, and imported amusements. Given more recreation than our fathers ever dreamed of, we import our boats and our fishing gear and our sporting equipment, even our hockey sticks.

Finding our faults has become our biggest domestic industry, but we can't seem to bring ourselves to brood about it. In politics, there is always the prospect of another mania down the road to match the ones we threw for Diefenbaker and Trudeau. And in the things that matter most to us, our individual prosperity and well-being, God ordained that the people who settled Canada, with the possible exception of the aborigines, should be the fortunate ones on earth.

Didn't she?

Index

Picture Credits

p.103 upper: R. Norwood
p.118: Ottawa *Citizen*
p.119 upper: Hamilton *Spectator*